Harry S. Truman Versus the Medical Lobby

Harry S. Truman
Versus the Medical Lobby

THE GENESIS OF MEDICARE

MONTE M. POEN

UNIVERSITY OF MISSOURI PRESS
COLUMBIA & LONDON, 1979

Library of Congress Cataloging in Publication Data
Poen, Monte M   , 1930–
    Harry Truman versus the medical lobby.

    Bibliography: p.
    Includes index.
    1.   Insurance, Health—United States—History.
2.   Medicare—History.   3.   Truman, Harry S., Pres. U.S.,
1884–1972. I.   Title.   [DNLM: 1.   Health insurance for
ages, Title 18—History.   2.   National health insurance,
United States—History.   3.   Politics—United States.
W275 AA1 P8h]
HD7102.U4P62   368.4′26′00973   78–59724
ISBN 0–8262–0257–8

To my sons,
John, Gregory, and Mark

Contents

Preface, ix

vii

Preface

"I have had some bitter disappointments as President," reflected Harry Truman after leaving office, "but the one that has troubled me most, in a personal way, has been the failure to defeat organized opposition to a national compulsory health-insurance program."[1] Truman had promoted enactment of such a program throughout nearly two full terms as president only to find bills incorporating the scheme bottled up in congressional committees and his advocacy of health security labeled socialistic and un-American by forces led by the country's richest and most influential post–World War II lobby, the American Medical Association. But, although nearly sixty-nine years old when he retired from public life in 1953, Harry Truman lived to see inauguration of medicare twelve years later, during the Johnson administration. True, medicare, a government health insurance program for the aged, fell far below the universal, comprehensive coverage Truman had sought initially, but it represented a significant benchmark in a movement for health security that, only now—three decades, six presidencies, and thirty-two congressional sessions after Truman first gave it his presidential endorsement in 1945—has reemerged as a serious proposal vieing for congressional approval and national implementation.

Hence, this volume is not a study of failure, at least not from the long-term perspective of those who, like Harry Truman, identified themselves with the branch of American liberalism that promoted national acceptance of social-justice programs designed to provide minimal economic security for all—a reform tradition dating back to the rural Populist agitation of the 1880s and 1890s, redefined and applied to the urban setting during the Pro-

1. Harry S. Truman, *Memoirs: Years of Trial and Hope,* p. 23.

gressive movement of this century's first decades, and extended further during the depression thirties by Franklin Roosevelt's New Deal. Rather, this is a study of one aspect of Harry Truman's domestic leadership and the political conflict it produced, which was due to the fact that America has another tradition than Truman's, one that emphasizes the virtues of an individualistic, libertarian society placing a premium upon self-help and favoring, when absolutely necessary, private and local philanthropy rather than federal governmental assistance. Throughout most of our history this latter tradition has dominated; to most it is the "American Way," a condition of "normalcy," in the truncated lexicon of Warren G. Harding. And it was Harry Truman's fate to be president during a time when the forces of conservatism, assisted greatly by a fragmented and competitive American legislative system (which by its very nature resists quick acceptance to change), had regained their strength following more than a decade of centralized governmental, especially presidential, direction of national affairs.

What political influences and personal motivation brought Harry Truman to champion national health insurance? How did the thirty-third president of the United States conduct himself as a policymaker and advocate of legislative reform? Why did promotion of the health security idea arouse such an impassioned (and expensive) organized reaction by medical practitioners and their allies? What factors contributed to organized medicine's immediate, if not ultimate, victory over health reformers during the Truman presidency? When I first broached these questions in my doctoral dissertation written a decade ago at the University of Missouri, I concluded that Harry Truman's advocacy of national health insurance, while sincere, was woefully inadequate. I have changed my mind. Additional research and reflection have convinced me that no matter how sincere and skillful, no president, given the restraints placed upon him during this postwar era, could have surmounted the intellectual and institutional obstacles barring enactment of a com-

prehensive health security program. While still acknowledging Truman's ineffective performance as a legislative
salesman before the public, I have become more appreciative of what skill he did demonstrate in his dealings with
Capitol Hill over the health issue. As to the role played
by organized medicine, I have become more impressed
by the medical community's ability to influence public
opinion and by the power enjoyed by lobbies in general
to block consideration of domestic reform legislation
even when public opinion favors its passage. More than
anything, I have become more aware of the complexities
of human personality and motivation, certainly of the
inharmonious, even abrasive character of executive-
legislative interaction in our national government, not
only during Truman's presidency, but throughout most
of our recent political history.

Because their manuscript collections and private records have been opened to researchers, those individuals
and groups who fought in behalf of medical reform have
granted me the clearest view of their motives, methods,
and aspirations. Conversely, with few exceptions, unpub-
lished materials held by those who led the opposition to
Truman's health program were not made available. Nevertheless, I have tried to present a balanced and objective
analysis of their position and legislative strategy by using
the *Journal of the American Medical Association* along
with other published accounts of organized medicine's
activities during the half-century contest over medical
reform.

Acknowledgments must begin with a special thanks to
Franklin D. Mitchell of the University of Southern California, a longtime friend and counselor, for reading the
entire manuscript and proffering many valuable and chal-
lenging suggestions concerning clarity of expression and
scholarly precision. Richard S. Kirkendall of Indiana
University, under whose direction I originally explored
this subject in dissertation form, and Alonzo L. Hamby
of Ohio University also rendered valuable critiques on
the manuscript. Two grants-in-aid from the Harry S.
Truman Library Institute and a grant from the Northern

Arizona University Institutional Research Committee made possible the bulk of my research. Among the many people who helped facilitate my investigation, I am appreciative especially of assistance given by former Truman Library Director, the late Philip C. Brooks, and his staff; Elizabeth B. Drewry, Director of the Franklin D. Roosevelt Library, and staff; John E. Wickman, Director of the Dwight D. Eisenhower Library, and staff; Josephine L. Harper, Manuscripts Curator of the State Historical Society of Wisconsin; and by the many competent people at the National Archives and the Library of Congress. J. Joseph Huthmacher of the University of Delaware and Donald P. Chvatal of the University of Montana helped me find my way through the Robert F. Wagner Papers and the James E. Murray Papers respectively. U.S. Rep. John D. Dingell and Mr. Oscar R. Ewing were most cooperative, allowing me access to private papers in their possession, as was Mary W. Lasker, who permitted me to draw upon her Columbia University Oral History reminiscences. I also want to acknowledge the generous assistance given me by President Harry S. Truman, Michael M. Davis, and Isidore S. Falk, all of whom granted me personal interviews, and by Samuel I. Rosenman, Arthur J. Altmeyer, Mary W. Lasker, and Wilbur J. Cohen, who after reading various sections of the manuscript wrote me expressing their views concerning the history's validity. Richard Dalfiume of the State University of New York at Binghamton, also deserves a thank you for sharing knowledgeable insights gained through his own investigation of the health insurance subject for his master's thesis. Finally, my very special friend, Jan Scott, helped immeasurably by proofreading and retyping some of the text and by suggesting sharper prose where too often confusion lurked. Any errors of fact, omission, or interpretation contained herein remain, of course, my sole responsibility.

M.M.P.
Flagstaff, Ariz.
1977

1

The Early Conflicts Over Health Security, 1915–1941

For Independence, Missouri, it was a typically hot and humid midsummer afternoon as the VIP-laden limousines paused at the door of the Truman Library. But for those who had come to gather in the air-conditioned comfort within, 30 July 1965 was a momentous day, a day that signaled the signing of the medicare bill into law, the most significant addition to the nation's old-age-insurance system since passage of the Social Security Act thirty years before.

No one relished that fact more than did the host of honor, former President Harry S. Truman, eighty-one years old and a bit unsteady afoot but still able to recall the prolonged and heated debate that had been generated over his national health insurance proposals back in the forties and early fifties. He had been, after all, the first president to endorse publicly the government health insurance idea; he had repeatedly asked Congress to enact it into law and had boldly carried the issue to the American people in the presidential election campaign of 1948. When organized opposition led by the American Medical Association had proved too strong and his comprehensive insurance program suffered defeat in Congress, it had been Harry Truman who shifted in early 1951 to a hospital insurance plan for the aged under social security, the precursor to medicare.

Now, fourteen years later, the former president was a "very, very happy man." Equally elated was his guest, President Lyndon Johnson, who had come to Missouri to pay tribute to Harry Truman and to sign into law America's first national system of governmental health insurance. It had "all started really with the man from Independence," President Johnson told the jubilant gathering; it had been Harry Truman who "planted the seeds

1

of compassion and duty which have today flowered into care for the sick, and serenity for the fearful."[1]

In the longer perspective of history, the Truman presidency in fact marked the midway point in a half-century of political maneuver and agitation that culminated in the passage of the Medicare Act. For it had been in the summer of 1915, three decades before Truman first asked Congress to legislate a health insurance program, that a small group of social workers and reform-minded economists launched the initial American health security campaign, adopting the slogan "Health Insurance—the next step." These socially attuned pioneers did not get very far with their ventures, it is true; and their movement was largely restricted to lobbying for industrial-sickness-insurance schemes on the state level. But the ideas they developed, the people they inspired, and the organizational methods they used all became part of a second and even more ambitious legislative drive during Franklin Roosevelt's presidency in the depression thirties and of the post–World War II movement.

This early effort to secure governmental insurance against sickness arose from the buoyant optimism and crusading spirit that characterized the Progressive movement, a mighty reform impulse unleashed at the turn of the century by societal stress born of the nation's recent industrialization and urbanization. It was a time when social workers, journalists, educators, ministers, and some labor and business leaders discovered inequities and poverty in America and set out to do something about it. As pioneer medical social worker Ida Cannon recalled, the century's first decade saw "great personalities loudly calling for social justice and for more attention to the conditions of living in our cities and of work in our factories."[2] Poverty and social injustice had to be eliminated, and to people like Ida Cannon and the other mem-

1. Remarks with President Truman at the Signing in Independence of the Medicare Bill, 30 July 1965, in Lyndon B. Johnson, *The Public Papers of the Presidents of the United States, 1965*, pp. 812–14.
2. Ida Cannon, *On the Social Frontier of Medicine*, p. 39.

bers of her emerging social-work profession, there was a close link between the ills of society and the impaired health of the individual.

The example of successful movements abroad for governmental insurance schemes provided additional inspiration for American reformers. First in Germany in 1883 (one year before Harry Truman's birth), and then in other European industrial nations, programs had been established to protect workers against the economic calamities that accompany sickness and industrial accidents. By 1911 nearly every major European nation, including England, had legislated some kind of tax-supported health insurance program.[3]

In the United States, social workers in alliance with political activists called attention to the need for similar protection for the American laborer. Working through charity societies and philanthropic enterprises like the Russell Sage Foundation and the Milbank Memorial Fund, they gathered fat volumes of social statistics on accident and disease; by the end of the century's first decade, the social reformers were deeply involved in legislative campaigns to provide better housing, to control tuberculosis and venereal disease, and to eliminate industrial health hazards.[4] The next step was to convince the public that government-sponsored insurance programs were essential.

The educational effort proceeded on many fronts. The Sage Foundation sponsored a two-year study of European social insurance programs and in 1910 published a laudatory report, *Workingmen's Insurance in Europe*. The same year, Henry Seager, a noted political economist, delivered the first American lectures on social insurance at the New York School of Philanthropy; shortly afterward the school sponsored another series of talks on the subject by physician, economist, and social worker Isaac Rubinow. Both Seager and Rubinow stressed that an indus-

3. George F. McCleary, *National Health Insurance*, p. 39; Isaac M. Rubinow, *Social Insurance*, pp. 13–27.

4. Robert H. Bremner, *From the Depths*, pp. 16–85, 123–39, 201–3.

trial society needed a state-supported insurance system to protect against sickness and poverty. A similar message appeared in the influential social-work magazine, *Survey*. Starting in 1911, readers of *Survey* were exposed to articles that praised the recently enacted British insurance system and demanded that similar protection be provided American workingmen.[5]

Gradually a social-work group, the National Conference of Charities and Correction, began to serve as an organizational catalyst, transforming individual inquiry and uncoordinated promotion into a cohesive reform movement. The NCCC had shown sporadic interest in devising an American insurance plan since 1902, appointing commissions and holding discussions on the topic; and the group had become quite serious about the issue by 1911, the year Louis Brandeis gave an electrifying address to its annual meeting. Brandeis was already famous for his precedent-shattering sociological brief at the time that the Supreme Court upheld Oregon's law limiting women to a ten-hour workday. Now, he urged his listeners to work for the adoption of social insurance to cover "sickness, accident, invalidity, premature death or premature old age." The NCCC responded to Brandeis's challenge the following year by unveiling its "Platform of Industrial Minimums," a comprehensive reform program to guarantee the worker basic protection against economic ruin.[6]

Since 1912 was a presidential election year and the Republicans were convening their national convention as the NCCC meeting drew to a close, a few of the NCCC

5. John M. Glen, Lilian Brandt, and F. Emerson Andrews, *Russell Sage Foundation*, 1:213; Lee K. Frankel and Miles Dawson, *Workingmen's Insurance in Europe*; Henry R. Seager, *Social Insurance*; Rubinow, *Social Insurance*; "The Next Step in Workingmen's Compensation"; "Social Forces"; and "Free Health."

6. "Report of Special Committee," *Proceedings of the National Conference of Charities and Corrections* 33 (1906):452–57; "Workingmen's Insurance—The Road to Social Efficiency," *Proceedings of the National Conference of Charities and Correction* 38 (1911):162; "Platform of Industrial Minimums."

delegates attempted to have their reform platform adopted by the GOP. When the conservative-dominated Republican platform committee rejected their proposals and the contested delegation pledged to former President Theodore Roosevelt bolted the convention, the social workers followed Roosevelt to the new Progressive party. Even though health reformers distrusted Roosevelt, doubting his sincerity as a true champion of domestic reform, they recognized that the former president might endorse their ideas and thus further their cause. Consequently, when Roosevelt did accept the NCCC program as an important part of his Progressive party's platform, the social workers enthusiastically joined him at Armageddon, backing the Roughrider in his campaign to recapture the presidency.[7]

Woodrow Wilson's defeat of Roosevelt in 1912 disappointed health reformers, but it was not totally unexpected. Besides, there was heartening news concerning the results of investigations conducted by numerous state commissions on the need for, and the feasibility of, workman's accident-compensation programs. The previous year, ten states had established such systems, and more important, the courts (which had declared earlier attempts unconstitutional) had begun to validate state-sponsored insurance schemes.[8]

The organization most responsible for this development was the American Association for Labor Legislation. Founded in 1906 by reform economist Richard Ely and his associates, the AALL, in alliance with the social workers, investigated industrial working conditions, drafted model legislative proposals to eliminate major occupational hazards, and lobbied for their enactment. The AALL's first legislative campaign had resulted in the elimination of phosphorus, a very toxic and crippling substance, from use in the manufacture of matches. With this accomplished, the association began lobbying for

7. Allen F. Davis, "The Social Workers and the Progressive Party," pp. 671–83.
8. Ibid.; Forrest A. Walker, "Compulsory Health Insurance: 'The Next Great Step in Social Legislation,' " p. 293.

state systems of accident compensation, an effort that achieved its greatest momentum in 1911.[9]

Still, accident insurance did not protect the worker against disability incurred from sickness, so Miles Dawson, insurance expert and coauthor of the Sage Foundation-sponsored *Workingmen's Insurance in Europe*, took the floor at the 1912 AALL meeting to urge that the association back a governmental health insurance scheme like that in Germany.[10] Soon the AALL Committee on Social Insurance, with Edward Devine, founder of *Survey*, serving as chairman, had arranged for a conference on social insurance to meet the following year. Held in Chicago, the conference concentrated mainly upon the need for health insurance, and when the AALL gathered for its own meeting later that year, sickness compensation dominated the discussion.[11]

By June 1914, the accelerating health security campaign had reached the point where Edward Devine thought that America stood on the verge of "The New Health." "We are now at a point in our economic development," announced Devine, "wherein we can devote the fruits of abundance to the health of all. The prime characteristic of the New Health is that it is social, not self-centered; to be won by all together by corporate effort."[12]

The following year the AALL began to agitate for state systems of health insurance. Meeting with association secretary John Andrews, social workers Jane Addams, Paul Kellogg, Edward Devine, and Isaac Rubinow launched the legislative campaign, adopting the slogan "Health Insurance—the next step."[13] In July 1915, the AALL's Social Insurance Committee issued its nine "standards" for a health insurance law, and by November the first tentative

9. John R. Commons, *Myself*, pp. 138–39; Cannon, *Social Frontier of Medicine*, pp. 179–80, 182–84.

10. "General Discussion."

11. Pierce Williams, *The Purchase of Medical Care Through Fixed Periodic Payment*, pp. 36, 40; "Sickness Insurance."

12. Edward T. Devine, "The New Health."

13. Bremner, *From the Depths*, pp. 258–59.

draft of its standard bill was published. If enacted, workers who earned less than twelve hundred dollars annually would receive a cash benefit equal to two-thirds of their weekly pay as well as contracted medical care in case of sickness. The standard bill also contained a funeral payment. To distribute the burden of its costs, financing would be divided equally between the employee and his employer, with the state providing 20 percent. Local insurance societies, supervised by the state's social-insurance commission, would administer the program.[14]

At first the standard bill appeared to be following the same path to legislative success as did the workmen's accident compensation for industrial workers. By the time Isaac Rubinow undertook a cross-country examination of the spreading health insurance movement in 1917, thirty-one states had already passed compensation laws, and health insurance bills had been introduced in twelve of them. Laboring men would soon be protected from sickness as well as from injury, Rubinow reported optimistically; every stage of legislative evolution was under way, all, that is, except the final stage of enactment.[15]

The biggest effort came in New York and California. The first in a series of health insurance bills was introduced in the New York legislature in 1916, and two years later California health reformers, bolstered by a favorable report from the state's Social Insurance Commission, sought an amendment to the state constitution to assure the legality of their plan. Although California voters defeated the amendment in 1918, another insurance commission soon formed and it, too, recommended adoption of a state-supported program. At the same time, Gov. Alfred E. Smith assisted the movement in New York by sending a special message to the legislature endorsing a health insurance bill. The state senate held public hearings on the legislation in the spring of 1919, and after a

14. Walker, "Compulsory Health Insurance," pp. 294–95.
15. Algie M. Simons and Nathan Sinai, *The Way of Health Insurance*, p. 180; Isaac Rubinow, "20,000 Miles over the Land: A Survey of the Spreading Health Insurance Movement."

few weeks the senate passed the measure; things looked so favorable in Albany that the *Rochester* (New York) *Democrat* predicted its passage into law.[16]

The elation was premature, however. Because of the obstructionist tactics of the conservative speaker of the house, the New York assembly version of the bill never reached the floor for consideration.[17] In California and elsewhere similar health measures failed to get beyond the committee stage. For more than a decade thereafter the government health insurance movement lay dormant. As one observer noted, "Society's feet, taking 'the next great step' in social progress, remained in mid-air."[18]

It was not easy to overcome the intellectual and institutional barriers and gain quick acceptance of such a system. Indeed, many of the problems then confronting American health reformers would continue to frustrate health security advocates over the next four and a half decades. While attitudes concerning the government's societal responsibility had begun to change at the turn of the century, many Americans still believed that sickness and impoverishment were private affairs, the sole concern of one's family, or, at most, of private charity, the local poorhouse, or the church. Also, being required by the government to help pay for a system to protect the sick and the poor ran counter to traditional beliefs in restricted government and individual liberty, against frontier-bred tenets that consider centralized authority and its tax-collecting agents to be somehow un-American.[19]

Moreover, the nation's political institutions acted, then as now, like brakes, slowing up the process of social and economic reform. It is no accident that medicare, the first system of national health insurance (and a limited one at

16. Walker, "Compulsory Health Insurance," pp. 298; Roy Lubove, *The Struggle for Social Security*, pp. 82–84; "Strong Editorial Support for the Health Insurance Bill," p. 261.

17. "Opposition to Welfare Bills Called 'Political Folly.'"

18. Wade Wright, "Insure for Health."

19. Harold L. Wilensky and Charles N. Lebeaux, *Industrial Society and Social Welfare*, p. 42; Abraham Kaplan, "American Ethics and Public Policy," in *The American Style*, p. 6.

that) was enacted in 1965, more than a half-century after Great Britain and the other major European countries had legislated programs of much broader scope. As James Bryce noted long ago in his *The American Commonwealth,* "There is an excessive friction in the American [political] system. . . . Power is so much subdivided that it is hard at a given moment to concentrate it for prompt and effective action."[20] Because this power is not only diffused through a federated system of semisovereign states but is also divided within the state and national governments between the executive, legislative, and judiciary branches, any one of the constituent parts, if out of step with the others, serves as a barrier to social change.

This is the major reason that the initial drive to secure social-insurance legislation in this country originated and remained confined largely at the state level; a federally sponsored compensation program was considered to be unconstitutional. After President Franklin Pierce's 1854 veto of Dorothea Dix's national mental health bill (on the grounds that the government had no business getting involved in its citizens' health problems), private groups and local government authorities increasingly assumed primary responsibility for sick and elderly indigents. By 1900 a vast network of county poorhouses dotted the countryside, while in the crowded city, political machines, settlement houses, and soup kitchens tended in sporadic and inadequate fashion to the minimal needs of the industrial poor.[21]

Even when progressive reformers did begin to win some legislative victories in their fight to make accidents, sickness, and impoverishment a state responsibility, the courts at first struck down as unconstitutional many of their public-sponsored programs. By interpreting the Fifth and Fourteenth amendments to the Constitution in a way that sanctified the power of private contract, the judiciary, from the 1880s until 1937, curtailed the police power of government, blunting many state and especially

20. James Bryce, *The American Commonwealth,* 1:302.
21. Ralph E. Pumphrey and Muriel W. Pumphrey, eds., *The Heritage of Social Work,* pp. 124–46, 432–33.

national attempts to regulate the conditions of labor.[22]

Compounding the divisive and uncomplementary instruments of American government were the loosely organized, coalition-type political parties. Their inability to legislate quickly in the absence of a national crisis such as war, the threat of war, or economic depression, or, as in the case of the Kennedy assassination, in the wake of a national crisis, served as another obstacle to enactment of major reform. Most important, this lack of party cohesion and ideological commitment granted, then as now, powerful special-interest groups—the ubiquitous lobbies—inordinate influence in the legislative process. Unprotected and little assisted by their national political party affiliation, whether it be Democratic or Republican, congressmen and state legislators must look beyond the party organization for publicity, finances, and votes to get elected; they also need information and drafting assistance on complex legislative proposals. For a price, lobbies have gladly filled their needs.[23]

In great measure, then, the history of the American social-insurance movement for health protection, both in the formative period and later, during and after the Truman years, must be viewed as an evolving struggle between the conflicting branches of government and the competing lobbies, the former constructed to forestall action and the latter organized either to promote or to defeat the program. It may be true that the American political system enables majority will to triumph eventually, but in the short run divisiveness between the agencies of government and the powerful special-interest groups influence and decide the fate of major legislation.[24]

22. Merle Fainsod and Lincoln Gordon, *Government and the American Economy*, pp. 58–59. For an excellent study of the development of judicial conservatism, see Arnold M. Paul, *Conservative Crisis and the Rule of Law*.

23. Elmer E. Schattschneider, *Party Government*, pp. 66–128, 187–204; David B. Truman, *The Governmental Process*, pp. 262–87, 321–94; Grant McConnell, *Private Power and American Democracy*, pp. 191–92.

24. Some argue, of course, that legislative delay has served a positive function, forcing compromise and studied conclu-

Whether the American people generally favored the government health insurance idea in 1919 is open to question, for there were no public opinion polls taken on the issue at the time. But the major interests that counted most in the political power structure were against it. Employer groups and commercial insurance companies were especially hostile to a system that would not only hurt them financially but would also further the extension of governmental power.[25] Most outspoken in opposition to sickness compensation schemes was Dr. Frederick L. Hoffman, statistician for the Prudential Insurance Company. Lecturing widely and writing extensively on the matter, Hoffman attacked the AALL's standard bill, using arguments that future opposition leaders would echo in their half-century battle against recurring proposals for government health insurance. Hoffman claimed that the standard bill was an alien, un-American product; that it was a state-imposed program that was not needed nor wanted by the public; and that if enacted it would result in the deterioration of the nation's medical practice.[26]

However, the special-interest opposition that most disappointed and frustrated exponents of health reform before 1920 came not from insurance and business spokesmen but from the largest national labor union, the American Federation of Labor. Despite endorsement of the idea by a number of state labor affiliates, the president of the AFL, Samuel Gompers, remained an outspoken critic of the movement. To Gompers, government compulsion, even when it was intended to help the workingman, threatened individuals' and organized labor's freedom. As Gompers saw it, voluntary health insurance coverage provided by his trade union, and not social insurance, was best for the laboring man. "Is it wise," he asked in 1916, "to open up opportunities for government agents to interfere lawfully with the privacy of the lives of wage-

---

sions. For such a view see E. Pendleton Herring, *The Politics of Democracy.*

25. Williams, *Purchase of Medical Care,* pp. 51–52.

26. Frederick L. Hoffman, *More Facts and Fallacies of Compulsory Health Insurance,* pp. 86–97.

earners?"[27] and following their president's lead, the AFL Executive Council denounced compulsory health insurance in a report adopted without dissent at the federation's 1916 convention. Then Gompers and other labor leaders joined with Frederick Hoffman and representatives of business to launch publicly "an alliance between the unions and the employer to fight their common foe—the social workers," prompting *Survey* to conclude bitterly, "The lion and the lamb have lain down together."[28] Not until 1935, after Samuel Gompers had died and the Great Depression had set in, would the AFL reverse its stand and become a leading promoter of national health insurance.

The loss of support from organized medicine also came as a heavy blow to the early movement. At first the influential American Medical Association, which represented most of the nation's physicians, had shown friendly interest in compulsory health insurance; accident-compensation laws were sweeping the states, and the growing agitation for the inclusion of health insurance seemed irresistible. Starting in 1916, medical reformers like Dr. Alexander Lambert (Theodore Roosevelt's personal physician) and Isaac Rubinow found themselves directing the newly organized AMA Committee on Social Insurance and working hand in hand with the Association for Labor Legislation in redrafting the latter's standard bill. Soon the AMA's enthusiasm cooled, however, largely because America's involvement in the world war against Germany gave critics within the association an opportunity to attack the German-born social-insurance idea as un-American. Had the legislative effort begun a few years earlier, it might have ridden the tide of progressivism to fruition; but stamped with the label "Made in Germany," health insurance did not have a chance. Lambert and Rubinow were quietly removed from their influential AMA positions, and in 1920 their committee

27. Samuel Gompers, *Labor and the Common Welfare*, p. 119. See also Philip Taft, *The AFL in the Time of Gompers*, pp. 364–65.
28. "Capital and Labor on Each Other's Necks," p. 495.

was disbanded. From that time forward, the American Medical Association stiffened its resistance to any alleged incursion upon the sanctity of the private practitioner.[29]

Actually, the AMA's momentary flirtation with the health compensation idea had been a historical aberration, an eddy resisting currents of thought and action that had long before been set into motion within the nation's medical profession. From the earliest days of their profession, physicians had organized their practices in the individualistic, fee-for-service, free-enterprise pattern; they had always been businessmen as well as public servants, and most wanted to keep it that way. And why not? The private practitioner lives in the best of two worlds, enjoying financial rewards and professional independence denied government employees while at the same time performing an essential, prestigious, and humanistic function.[30]

Even if the nation's medical rank and file had not been so imbued with individualistic precepts, those who have traditionally directed AMA policy have been among the more conservative and business-oriented members of their profession. It has been largely the well-to-do big-city specialists who have had the time and money to participate in medical politics and to become long-tenured AMA officers. Lording over the association's reference committees, holding important posts like that of AMA secretary, speaker of the AMA House of Delegates, or editor of the association's journal, such men have long used their influence to pose as guardians of the physician's economic and professional well-being, going so far in the twenties and early thirties as to foster an AMA stance against the growth even of group medical practice and private, voluntary hospital prepayment plans.[31]

29. James G. Burrow, *AMA, Voice of American Medicine,* pp. 139–51.

30. Talcott Parsons, "Social Change and Medical Organization in the United States: A Sociological Perspective," pp. 23–25.

31. Oliver Garceau, *The Political Life of the American Medical Association,* pp. 13–129; Burrow, *AMA,* pp. 171–84, 230–51.

For a few years after the Great War, however, the AMA
had little to fear from the health reformers. Taking note
of the prevailing political climate during the country's
hedonistic plunge into the Jazz Age and its love affair
with Warren G. Harding's presidential stewardship, the
American Association for Labor Legislation abandoned
its sickness compensation scheme "to await a more favorable time."[32] Likewise, most social workers lost enthusiasm for the political agitation. As their work fell under
the influence of Freudian psychology and became more
specialized in the twenties, the aura of sedate profession-
alism set in and replaced the evangelical reforming zeal
of the prewar era. Now they quietly worked in numerous
private and public agencies. In the health field, social
workers found opportunities to serve in hospital social-
service departments and on the staffs of various philanthropic foundations like the Milbank Fund, the Russell
Sage Foundation, and the Julius Rosenwald Fund.[33]

Toward the end of the decade these foundations joined
with several other foundations to finance an intensive
five-year study of the nation's health needs, thus compil-
ing information upon which they could base a new drive
for health insurance. Conducted between 1928 and 1932
by a group called the Committee on the Costs of Medical
Care, the investigation uncovered data regarding the incidence of diseases, the number and adequacy of medical
facilities, and the costs of medical care both in terms of
patient's expenses and the physician's financial return.
In the committee's final report, a majority of its members
endorsed the idea of voluntary health insurance, group
medical practice, and greater coordination of health services at the local level.[34]

The onset of the Great Depression and the coming of
Franklin Roosevelt's New Deal seemed an opportune time

32. "Report of Work."
33. Paul Kellogg, "New Beacons in Boston," p. 341; Clarke
A. Chambers, *Seedtime of Reform*, p. 264.
34. Committee on the Costs of Medical Care, *Medical Care
for the American People, The Final Report*, pp. 104–43.

to press for a renewed campaign for governmental health insurance. Statistics regarding national health needs were now adequately documented; middle-class Americans as well as those of the working class were feeling the sting of economic dislocation; and the Congress was legislating a broad range of innovative programs to alleviate social and economic distress. Also, a number of health reformers were now in important positions within the federal government. When in 1934 President Roosevelt appointed the Committee on Economic Security to study the need for social insurance, he named his new secretary of labor, Frances Perkins—a woman trained in social work—to serve as the committee's chairman. One of Perkins's colleagues in the undertaking was Harry Hopkins, another social worker who had become Roosevelt's relief administrator. Others on the committee were either participants in the earlier health security fight or, as in the case of Arthur J. Altmeyer and Executive Director Edwin Witte, students of the Wisconsin school of progressive economics.[35] Two others associated with the committee were destined to be of monumental importance during the Truman administration's health insurance campaign. They were Michael M. Davis and Isidore S. Falk.

Davis and Falk probably best personify what one writer calls the "internal [ideological] polarization of the medical profession," the split between the private practitioner, as represented by the American Medical Association, and the institutionalists, that is, the academic practitioners, researchers, and teachers.[36] Davis and Falk, as medical economists concerned with the organization and distribution of medical services, reflected the attitudes of most of the institutional group. Recognizing that hospital, research, and teaching services require vast sums of public money, the institutionalists were, and remain to this day, less fearful of an encroaching governmental bureaucracy.

35. Robert Sherwood, *Roosevelt and Hopkins*, pp. 21–28; Arthur J. Altmeyer, "The Wisconsin Idea and Social Security."
36. Parsons, "Social Change and Medical Organization," p. 32.

Also, because they worked for fixed, predetermined salaries, they had less incentive than did the private practitioner to be business oriented. A growing faction within the profession, they were, and still are, more intimately involved in the scientific and technological advance of medicine, therefore their demands have carried some weight.[37] In the formative period, as well as later, Davis and Falk were among the most vocal of the institutionalists.

The two had first met while working for the Committee on Medical Costs in 1929, and they became close friends. Although each traveled a different route to medical economics (Davis got his doctorate in sociology, while Falk took his in public health) they agreed on the essential requirements for adequate medical care. To both, increasing specialization within the profession plus the costs of new, intricate, and expensive equipment signaled the need for medical reform. The days of the family doctor who took care of just about everything, and sometimes received in return a chicken or a hog, were gone for most Americans. New techniques and higher costs demanded that the dispensers and consumers of medical services organize.[38] As Davis expressed it, "without organization you have no guarantee of cooperation or the advantages of efficiency."[39]

There were also humanitarian considerations. Davis and Falk had worked on research staffs of philanthropic foundations; and, earlier, Michael Davis had been a close associate of Dr. Richard Cabot, Ida Cannon, and other pioneer medical social workers in Boston. In 1913 he had organized a pay clinic for people of modest means in Boston and later had established a similar clinic in New York City. In the judgment of Davis and his colleague Falk, modern medical care was simply beyond the reach of the

37. Ibid.
38. Interview with Michael M. Davis. For an expression of their early views on this matter, see Davis, "Organization of Medical Service"; Isidore Falk, *Security Against Sickness*, pp. 4–6.
39. Interview with Davis.

masses. Social insurance seemed the best way to bring it to them.[40]

Davis's influential friend Harry Hopkins agreed. At a March 1934 meeting of the Milbank Fund, Isidore Falk outlined a plan for national health insurance, and Harry Hopkins told the gathering, "You aren't going to get health insurance if you expect people to do it voluntarily. I am convinced that by one bold stroke we could carry the American people along not only for health insurance but also for unemployment insurance. I think it could be done in the next eighteen months."[41]

Hopkins was proved wrong. Despite his presence and that of so many other health insurance enthusiasts on the President's Committee on Economic Security, health insurance was omitted from their executive version of what became the Social Security Act of 1935. When rumors that it had been included brought forth opposition from the American Medical Association and others, Roosevelt told the committee to dampen its zeal and to present its report in favor of national health insurance without publicity. They complied, and then Roosevelt and the congressional sponsors of social security allowed the issue to languish, lest it endanger passage of the entire social security proposal.[42]

Later, leaders on both sides of the question claimed that the omission of health insurance in 1935 was due partially to influence exerted upon FDR by Dr. Harvey Cushing, a prominent Harvard physician whose daughter had married Roosevelt's son James.[43] This is highly questionable in light of the president's typical approach to legislative strategy and his later endorsement of national health insurance in 1944. No doctrinaire, Roosevelt

40. Cannon, *Social Frontier of Medicine*, p. 28; Michael M. Davis, *Medical Care for Tomorrow*, pp. 1–2; interview with Davis; interview with Isidore Falk.

41. Quoted in "Compulsory Health Insurance."

42. Daniel S. Hirshfield, *The Lost Reform*, pp. 44–49; Thomas R. Byrne, "The Social Thought of Robert F. Wagner," (Ph.D. diss.), pp. 193–245.

43. Interview with Falk; Hirshfield, *The Lost Reform*, pp. 49–50, 53.

sought compromise not only within the executive branch but also in legislative matters.[44] Frances Perkins observed, "He recognized that to assert leadership and to develop a plan for legislation required tact, and that it had to be done slowly."[45] John Kingsbury, formerly with the Milbank Fund and a leading health security advocate, was closer to the truth when he asked a group of colleagues in early 1937: "How can social workers expect the President and the Congress to act on a controversial issue, in the face of such vociferous and politically powerful opposition to health insurance, if there is no organized expression of public opinion in favor of it?"[46] Kingsbury further noted that those pressure groups who would normally back the measure were either too busy fighting the depression or were more concerned with other aspects of the social security program.[47]

Still, the Roosevelt administration kept the health reform issue alive. Various cooperative prepayment medical plans were initiated through the auspices of the Farm Security Administration while another of the New Deal agencies, the Works Progress Administration, not only provided limited health care for thousands of the nation's workers but also conducted a national health survey. Moreover, after passage of the Social Security Act, the president appointed the Interdepartmental Committee to Coordinate Health and Welfare Activities. A subcommittee of this group, which included Isidore Falk, his longtime friend Edgar Sydenstricker of the Milbank Fund, and other liberal-minded medical economists, investigated the health needs of the nation and found them

44. Arthur Altmeyer and Samuel Rosenman (who served as FDR's speech writer and adviser) disclaimed such influence by Cushing or by any other one individual, with Rosenman calling the notion "extremely ridiculous." Arthur J. Altmeyer to author, 4 May 1967; Samuel I. Rosenman to author, 7 April 1967.

45. Frances Perkins, *The Roosevelt I Knew*, p. 172.

46. John A. Kingsbury, "Health Insurance in a National Health Program," *Proceedings of the National Conference of Social Work* 64 (1937):485.

47. Ibid.

wanting. Acting upon the suggestion of the president that they call a conference to discuss the problem, the committee laid plans for a health conference in Washington, D.C., to be held on the 141st birthday of the U.S. Public Health Service in July 1938.[48]

The National Health Conference marks an important turning point in the history of medical reform agitation in the United States. It was not only the first meeting of its kind, airing as it did a wide range of group opinion on health matters, but it also gave promise of the organized public support that the Roosevelt administration needed to pursue the insurance issue. On the first day, the interdepartmental committee's findings and proposals were laid before the two hundred delegates for consideration, and although its recommendations did not specifically call for compulsory health insurance and were rather vague in most respects, its five-point program became the basis for much of the Truman health program seven years later. The recommendations were:

I.   Expansion of existing federal public health, maternal and child health services.

II. Expansion of national hospital facilities through federal grants.

III. Federal assistance to state medical care systems for the medically needy.

IV. A general program of medical care, paid for either through general taxation or social insurance contributions.

V.   Establishment of federally-assisted disability insurance to provide cash payments for temporary loss of wages.[49]

Evidence of organized support had also come by 1938 in the form of the American Federation of Labor's reversal of its earlier opposition to governmental health insurance. The AFL president, William Green, in contrast to

48. Hirshfield, *The Lost Reform*, pp. 84–86, 108; Isidore Falk to author, 15 May 1967.

49. United States Interdepartmental Committee to Coordinate Health and Welfare Activities, *Proceedings of the National Health Conference*, pp. 29–32.

his predecessor, Samuel Gompers, had favored such legislation even before World War I; and Green's attitude,
coupled with a growing awareness that government need
not be a promanagement, antilabor force, had led the
AFL Executive Council to recommend a study of health
insurance in 1934; the next year the AFL gave a general
endorsement to the sickness compensation concept. Publicly reiterating this stance at the National Health Conference in 1938, Green pledged an AFL campaign to
amend the states' accident compensation systems to include sickness insurance.[50]

A sense of euphoria swept over the health reformers as
the national conference drew to a close. The only dis-
sonant note sounded at the conference had come from
the representatives of the American Medical Association,
and they were in a minority. When the delegates adjourned, a majority of them had endorsed an ambitious
governmental health program, going beyond the conference chairman's statement that the meeting's purpose was
simply to give the interdepartmental committee's five-
point recommendation public attention and constructive
criticism. Soon Arthur Altmeyer, who had become chairman of the Social Security Board, was conferring with the
president to chart a legislative drive to implement the
proposals; by December he had even obtained the unani-
mous support of the Social Security Board in favor of the
five-point program.[51] "For the first time," Michael Davis
reflected later, "a political base had been established for
a broad legislative health program."[52]

Another observer reported at the end of 1938, "No one
knows where the country is going with health insurance,
but many [with] hope, and some with fear, believe we are

50. "Previous Policy of the American Federation of Labor
on Health and Disability Insurance," and "Statement by President Green," Director of Research Files, box 3, American Federation of Labor Papers.
51. *New York Times*, 21 July 1938; U.S., Interdepartmental
Committee to Coordinate Health and Welfare Activities,
Health Security, pp. 74; Arthur J. Altmeyer, *The Formative
Years of Social Security*, pp. 96–98.
52. Davis, *Medical Care for Tomorrow*, p. 278.

on our way." [53] Outside the government a new organization called the American Association for Social Security (AASS), led by insurance expert Abraham Epstein, had begun to agitate for sickness compensation. Like the American Association for Labor Legislation before it, the Epstein group drafted a model health bill (much like the AALL's proposal), held discussion sessions on the measure, and then lobbied for its enactment. Various versions of the bill were introduced in several states and one, sponsored by Sen. Arthur Capper of Kansas, was introduced in Congress. Then, fittingly, the AASS labeled its 1937 discussion section on medical care "Health Insurance— The Next Step." [54] Once again there would be an effort to reach that elusive prominence.

While the Epstein group sought action in Congress on its Capper bill, others were backing another health insurance proposal introduced by Sen. Robert F. Wagner of New York, sponsor of the Social Security Act. First from Albany and later from the nation's capitol, this immigrant's son from New York's east side had observed and investigated the working conditions of the laborer. His prolabor social philosophy had become crystallized in 1911 as a result of New York City's tragic Triangle Shirtwaist Company fire, and it had been strengthened further in the late twenties when he had investigated deplorable coal-mine conditions while serving on a Senate subcommittee. [55]

With the coming of the New Deal, Wagner played a

53. Glen Leet, "Amendment Season for Social Security."
54. The Capper bill provided for state programs of medical insurance for low-income workers and did not receive much congressional attention. Herman A. Grey, "Practical Problems Underlying Health Insurance," in The Ninth National Conference on Social Security, *Social Security in the United States, 1936*, pp. 91–97; "Health Insurance—The Next Step," in The Tenth National Conference on Social Security, *Social Security in the United States, 1937*, pp. 149–77. Capper bills S. 3252, 74th Cong., 1st sess.; S. 855, 75th Cong., 1st sess.; and S. 658, 76th Cong., 1st sess.
55. J. Joseph Huthmacher, *Senator Robert F. Wagner*, pp. 4–11, 33–35, 63–64.

major role in advancing its relief measures, and he also
sought to further the concept of economic security by
sponsoring a monumental reform measure to guarantee
organized labor recognition and bargaining rights, as well
as by sponsoring social-insurance legislation for railroad
employees, the unemployed, and the aged. In addition,
Wagner wanted protection against the debilitating effects
of sickness. Shortly after the passage of the Social Security
Act he revived the health insurance issue by telling a
group of social workers that more attention should be
paid to protection against disease and industrial accidents. After the Supreme Court upheld his Social Security
Act as constitutional in 1937, Wagner told a national
radio audience that methods must soon be devised "for
removing the risks which the wage earner faces through
ill health."[56]

When the National Health Conference drew to a close,
Wagner saw his chance and embodied its five-point program into an omnibus health bill. Introduced into Congress on 28 February 1939, Wagner's proposal amended
the Social Security Act to provide additional federal funds
for maternal and child-care services, more public health
work in the states, hospital and health-center construction, temporary disability compensation, and a general
program of medical care. Under the last item, states were
to be given grants to encourage development of health
insurance plans, medical services for the needy, or comprehensive systems of public health care.[57]

Because Robert Wagner had earned the reputation of
being a successful reform leader in the Senate, his health
proposal commanded a great deal of public attention.
But President Roosevelt remained uncommitted in 1939,
even though he had enthusiastically told the chairman of
the Social Security Board, Arthur Altmeyer, the previous
summer that he was considering making the national conference's five-point plan part of his 1940 campaign for
reelection. Roosevelt, excelling in the Machiavellian

56. Byrne, "Social Thought of Robert F. Wagner," pp. 246,
254–55.
57. S. 1620, 76th Cong., 1st sess.

game, also disappointed Josephine Roche, chairman of the National Health Conference. When Roche submitted the interdepartmental committee's final report on health security to FDR in December 1938, she suggested that the president recommend legislation to implement the program in his upcoming state of the Union message and follow this with a special message on health. She even included a fifteen-page message draft for the president's use. The draft was never used. Instead, FDR submitted the committee's report to Congress in January 1939 with a very short presidential statement recommending it for careful study.[58]

Franklin Roosevelt had other domestic problems on his mind following the congressional elections of 1938. His attempt in 1937 to expand Supreme Court membership in an effort to reverse the Court's judicial negation of major New Deal agencies, a growing rural and southern disenchantment with his urban-oriented welfare and labor programs, the economic recession that had befallen his recovery program in the winter of 1937–1938, and his largely unsuccessful intervention in the 1938 campaign to purge the Senate of its antiadministration Democrats had all resulted in a weakening of public support and with it loss of the pro-Roosevelt, reform-minded majority in Congress. Ironically, while the Court had moved into Roosevelt's ideological corner by 1939 (due to the retirement of anti-New Deal justices and their replacement by liberals), the Congress had shifted to take its place as a barrier to reform; now a coalition of conservative Democrats and Republicans controlled both the House and the Senate, and it quickly pulled the brake on further New Deal adventures.[59] More importantly, this conservative

58. Altmeyer, *Formative Years of Social Security*, p. 96; Josephine Roche to Franklin D. Roosevelt, 14 December 1938, and unused special message draft, Press Secretary's File, Health Message folder, 1938, Franklin D. Roosevelt Papers; Franklin D. Roosevelt, *The Public Papers and Addresses of Franklin D. Roosevelt*, 8 (1939):97–98.

59. The development of the conservative coalition is ably chronicled in James T. Patterson, *Congressional Conservatism and the New Deal*.

alliance, while changing in membership through the years, would exert a controlling restraint upon domestic matters for a quarter of a century. Not until 1965, after Lyndon Johnson had so overwhelmingly defeated Barry Goldwater at the polls—pulling a host of liberal legislators into Congress on his proverbial coattails—would another major reform impulse spring forth.

In early 1940, however, Franklin Roosevelt's problems with Congress notwithstanding, health reformers screamed in anger after the president announced at a press conference that he had instructed the interdepartmental committee to propose a more modest health program, while at the same time giving his endorsement to a limited federal hospital construction proposal. To the health insurance advocates this signaled an ill-advised retreat.[60]

But reformers could do little other than protest, for they were too divided and uncertain about the proper approach to medical security. For its part, organized labor's attention had been diverted by the internal split within the AFL over the question of industrial versus craft unionism, as well as by the battle for recognition of labor's bargaining rights as defined by the recently passed Wagner Labor Relations Act. Consequently, health insurance had to take a secondary place on labor's list of priorities. Nor were the other proinsurance groups unified. Abraham Epstein, for instance, bitterly criticized the old-age-pension provisions of the Social Security Act as enacted in 1935; and when it came to health insurance, Epstein and his American Association for Social Security opposed features in the Wagner bill that would have denied beneficiaries cash payments while ill, preferring instead the compensatory system envisaged in the Capper bill.[61]

60. Roosevelt, *Public Papers and Addresses* 8 (1939):598–603, 9 (1940):65–68; John B. Andrews, "While Millions Suffer"; Edith Abbott, "Hospitals are not a Health Program."

61. Edwin Witte, *Social Security Perspectives, Essays*, p. 333; Abraham Epstein, "The Turning Point in Social Security," in The Ninth National Conference on Social Security, *Social Security in the United States, 1936*, pp. 2–7; Hirshfield, *The Lost Reform*, pp. 75–76.

As for the social workers, those outside the government were now a diverse group, working in many different specialties with little coordination. By the 1930s America's free-enterprise system had nurtured a vast network of voluntary, private welfare agencies dominated by the businessmen who controlled their governing boards, hence social workers found themselves captives of interest groups who opposed the expansion of governmental power. It was not possible for the social workers to attain a united, militant stance in the realm of political action either then or during the post–World War II period.[62]

Complicating matters further for the health reformers, interagency jealousy and suspicion within Roosevelt's Interdepartmental Committee had caused executive disunity over the insurance question. While Isidore Falk, who represented the Social Security Board, favored giving health insurance high legislative priority in the administration's national health program, others, especially Martha Eliot of the Children's Bureau and those who represented the Public Health Service, did not. The latter were not only fearful that the controversial insurance issue would harm chances for their own less-inflammatory proposals in Congress, but they also feared that if it were enacted the Social Security Board's administration of the health insurance program would further erode their own time-honored positions of administrative preeminence in governmental health and welfare matters. Unable to develop a united posture on the question, the committee members turned to compromise. Assigned a lesser priority in the scheme of things, health insurance received only halfhearted public support from the Children's Bureau and the Public Health Service.[63]

At the same time, the forces arrayed against national health insurance were united, with the American Medi-

62. Wilensky and Lebeaux, *Industrial Society and Social Welfare*, pp. 148–68, 269–82; John A. Fitch, "The Nature of Social Action," *Proceedings of the National Conference of Social Work* 67 (1940):487–97; Alan D. Wade, "Social Work and Political Action."

63. Hirshfield, *The Lost Reform*, pp. 104–7, 118–19, 136–44.

cal Association giving them cohesion and direction. The opposition included the American Hospital Association, the American Public Health Association, and the conservative American Farm Bureau Federation. When it looked as though health insurance would be part of the Social Security Act, the AMA held an emergency session in February 1935 to roundly condemn its inclusion. From that point on, the association shifted its opposition away from private health insurance and began to encourage its development under the supervision of its local medical societies. When danger loomed again after the National Health Conference, the AMA held another emergency session, this time in September 1938; it also accelerated all three aspects of its strategy to defeat any system of compulsory health insurance: direct attacks in the pages of its *Journal* and other AMA publications, the encouragement of plans by its constituent medical societies to help the needy and thus remove fuel from the health security campaign, and resistance to further federal control of state health activities. Association spokesmen also attempted to strike a bargain with the Roosevelt administration. Drop the health insurance proposal from the five-point program as outlined in the Wagner bill (S. 1620), they said, and the AMA would endorse what remained. But the negotiations came to an impasse when a majority of the interdepartmental committee members refused and the president would not force a compromise. When the AMA House of Delegates convened again in May 1939 they went on record opposing the entire Wagner bill, and when AMA representatives appeared at the Senate hearings on S. 1620 a week later they presented a united front against the proposal.[64]

Increasing world tensions also helped the opposition. After Hitler's Germany marched into Poland in September 1939, Franklin Roosevelt's attention as well as the nation's was focused upon foreign affairs. Roosevelt knew by 1940 that to antagonize an already recalcitrant Congress by urging passage of S. 1620 and other domestic re-

64. Ibid., pp. 126–27; Burrow, *AMA*, pp. 195–97, 205–6, 221–24, 228–51.

form legislation would only harm his efforts to obtain its support for his foreign policy.[65] He would not have been successful even had he tried, for the modest hospital construction bill (also sponsored by Robert Wagner) was killed in a House committee after it passed the Senate.[66] When the president, in a speech on 31 October 1940, announced that "the Nation today, I am certain, is better prepared to meet the public health problems of our emergency than at any previous time in the history of this country,"[67] it was evident that for the time being Roosevelt considered medical reform a dead issue. A year later an advocate of such reform reported sadly that the national health program now smoldered "beneath the avalanche of defense legislation."[68] The second great campaign for governmental health insurance had come to an end.

As Civilian Conservation Corps camps took on the air of army posts and their unemployed conservationists traded their hoes for rifles, as the Joads stopped their wandering among the grapes of wrath and went to work in a California defense plant, the United States stood nearly alone among the world's industrial nations as one that had not established some system of governmental health insurance. Twice health reformers had battled for health security and twice they had met defeat. Enjoined by the dictates of a fragmented political system, the reformers found themselves fighting on too many fronts, against conservative-dominated state legislatures, against judicial precedent, and above all, against powerfully entrenched lobbies that possessed the muscle—even during the nation's worst economic crisis—to make a president

65. Walter Johnson, *1600 Pennsylvania Avenue*, pp. 126–37, 99–100.

66. This measure had active support from the American Hospital Association, but the AMA was cool to the bill. After it passed the Senate in amended form to satisfy the AMA, the association requested many new changes. This contributed to its defeat in the House. See Burrow, *AMA*, pp. 226–27.

67. Roosevelt, *Public Papers and Addresses* 9 (1940):526.

68. Kathleen Rivet, "Lost: A National Health Program," p. 120.

procrastinate and a Congress balk. Divided in their own councils, unable to obtain dynamic and popular leadership from President Roosevelt, and cursed by the coming of a second war with Germany—the progenitor of social insurance—health reformers were forced to postpone, once again, that final assault upon what they considered to be the next great step in social and economic fulfillment.

2

A Presidential Health Program: From FDR to HST

America's mobilization for defense, beginning in 1940, diverted attention from domestic reform; but the war effort that followed provided the basis for a renewed campaign for health security. Whereas Franklin Roosevelt had spurned the national health insurance question before the war, by the end of his third term in office health reform leaders had won private assurances of the president's support. Before Roosevelt could publicly espouse the cause, however, death intervened; and it remained for his successor, Harry Truman, to grant presidential sanction to what became the postwar era's most controversial domestic reform issue. Truman not only accepted that responsibility, he did so in a quick and decisive manner.

Following the attack on Pearl Harbor, government involvement in the health field expanded rapidly. Federal funds trained and equipped medical personnel for the armed forces; the military constructed hospital facilities; millions were spent on government-sponsored medical research projects; and thousands of servicemen's wives became accustomed to free maternity health care, while their GI husbands received treatment for everything from scalp infections to fallen arches.[1]

To a generation that had become accustomed to the proliferation of national programs during the Great Depression, an extension of public health services in wartime seemed only natural, so natural that many wondered why the services should not continue after the war. Had it not taken the massive infusion of federal-defense spending to bring the country out of the depression? Would

1. Thomas Parron, "The United States Public Health Service in the War," pp. 249–73; Charles M. Griffith, "The Veterans Administration," pp. 321–35; Michael M. Davis, "Government Participation in Medical Care."

not peacetime bring a return to the hard times endured in the thirties? If that horrible specter were to prove certain, then, many believed, the government should provide low-cost health protection for its people. In a poll taken by *Fortune* in 1942, an impressive 74.3 percent favored national health insurance. The following year a Gallup poll indicated that 59 percent wanted the program.[2]

Disconcerting news that the nation's youth was not as robust and hardy as once believed added to public concern over health matters. Of the first 1 million men called up for the draft in 1941, over 40 percent were found to be physically or mentally unfit for military service. When the president received this information, he thought that there had been a mistake and asked for a recheck. But the figures proved accurate, and Roosevelt told reporters that something had to be done. He was sure, he said, that the subject of physical fitness would arouse much attention and would "cause people to talk about it."[3] When the rejection rate remained at this high level, people did talk about it, so much so that a Senate subcommittee scheduled an investigation into the health and educational fitness of the civilian population.[4]

Events abroad further stimulated interest in health. The International Labour Organization was hard at work promoting worldwide expansion of social security legislation. In a December 1940 meeting in Lima, Peru, the ILO had created an international agency to expand social security in the Western Hemisphere, and President Roosevelt's chief social-insurance administrator, Arthur Altmeyer, became an active member. Two years later, Sir William Beveridge created a stir in England with the release of a government-sponsored report tagged immediately as the "Beveridge plan." Published in November

2. "The Fortune Survey"; Hadley Cantril, ed., *Public Opinion, 1935–1946*, p. 441.

3. Franklin D. Roosevelt, *The Public Papers and Addresses of Franklin D. Roosevelt* 10 (1941):196.

4. *New York Times*, 9 July 1944.

1942 under its official title, *Social Insurance and Allied Services,* and quickly reprinted and read by thousands in the United States, the Beveridge plan prescribed a British postwar battle against poverty. Included in that mighty effort, said Beveridge, should be the extension of comprehensive public health services to encompass the entire population. Workers had been protected by government health insurance since 1912; now it was time to expand that protection to their dependents. By early 1943, the British government had endorsed the report and began agitating for parliamentary action.[5]

Encouraged by these developments, the American health security movement gained renewed momentum. Government health insurance advocates submitted eighty-two bills in thirteen states during the period from 1941 to 1944, and in Rhode Island they met with success. Seven months before the Beveridge plan hit the headlines, the Rhode Island legislature established an insurance system —the first of its kind in the United States—to pay cash benefits to workers unemployed due to sickness. Moreover, the clamor for state health insurance schemes caught the attention of New York City's spirited reform mayor, Fiorello La Guardia. In early 1943, La Guardia appointed a committee to formulate a medical insurance program for his city's middle-income employees; a year later, the Health Insurance Plan of Greater New York was incorporated. While this went forward, La Guardia's fellow New Yorker Sen. Robert Wagner, along with Sen. James Murray and Rep. John Dingell, revived the campaign on the national level by introducing in June 1943 the first of what became a long and controversial series of Wagner-Murray-Dingell bills.[6]

5. "Social Insurance and Assistance"; International Labour Organization, *Provisional Bulletin,* no. 6, pp. 4–5; Sir William Beveridge, *Social Insurance and Allied Services;* George Rosen, *A History of Public Health,* pp. 449–50.

6. Elizabeth W. Wilson, *Compulsory Health Insurance,* pp. 7–10; U.S., Public Health Service, *Notes on Compulsory Sickness Insurance Legislation in the States, 1939–44,* Public Health

The national measure was an omnibus bill, a far-ranging and ambitious proposal to expand existing federal social security programs and to create new ones; it was an American answer to the Beveridge plan. Included were provisions for the payment of unemployment compensation to returning veterans while they looked for jobs; for the nationalization of both the United States Employment Service and the country's unemployment insurance system; for increased old-age social security payments; for the addition of millions of temporary and permanently disabled workers to the benefit rolls; for liberalization of federal aid in support of state welfare systems; and, most important, for the creation of a comprehensive, government-directed prepaid medical-care program. When sickness struck, the family doctor (if he participated in the system) would care for an individual's needs with his fee paid—subject to a rate limitation imposed by the government—through a fund established and maintained by payroll taxes. If hospital services became necessary, national health insurance would underwrite a patient's expenses for up to sixty days confinement per year.[7]

Significantly, the Wagner-Murray-Dingell bill centralized postwar responsibility for economic welfare. Whereas Wagner's 1939 proposal had envisaged state-operated health and welfare services, his 1943 manifesto called for federal sponsorship and direction. There were a number of reasons for the shift: Labor supporters favored centralization, Supreme Court decisions since 1937 sanc-

Reports, reprint no. 2685, pp. 3–5; Franz Goldmann, *Voluntary Medical Care Insurance in the United States*, pp. 178–80; *New York Times*, 23 April 1943; S. 1161 and H.R. 2861, 78th Cong., 1st sess.

7. S. 1161 was not the first congressional health insurance proposal introduced during the war. Rep. Thomas Eliot of Massachusetts introduced one in 1942, and Sen. Theodore Green of Rhode Island submitted another in 1943. They had two things in common: both restricted health insurance to hospital care and both received little publicity. H.R. 7534, 77th Cong., 2d sess.; S. 281, 78th Cong., 1st sess.

tioned it, and wartime experience demonstrated its value.[8]
"We could not win this war with forty-eight state com-
manders," said Wagner in 1944, "we cannot win the peace
with forty-eight separate economic programs."[9] With its
focus upon national supervision of welfare services, the
Wagner-Murray-Dingell bill embodied the spirit of that
proposition.

Woodrow Wilson once observed that the preparation
of a legislative proposal "is an aggregate, not a simple
production. It is impossible to tell how many persons,
opinions, and influences have entered into its composi-
tion."[10] But in the case of the W-M-D bill of 1943, enough
is recorded to piece together a composite, if imperfect,
picture of its development. The genesis of the measure's
preparation can be traced back to early 1942 when, after
reading an article on national health insurance, Arthur
Altmeyer asked his technical adviser and assistant, Wilbur Cohen, to write a memo on the subject. It went to
Isidore Falk, by now director of the Social Security
Board's Bureau of Research and Statistics, and instructed
Falk to gather information on mortality rates, selective
service rejections, the incidence of sickness among various
income groups, and on voluntary health-and-accident insurance. Armed with this material, and aroused further
by release of the Beveridge plan, Cohen and Falk approached Senator Wagner in December.[11] As Cohen recalled years later, "Senator Wagner heard us out and,
after five minutes' discussion, gave us the O.K. He didn't

8. J. Joseph Huthmacher, *Senator Robert F. Wagner*, p.
293; "Notes on Labor's Position," National Health Program,
1938–1940 folder, box 211, Edwin E. Witte Papers.

9. Quoted in Huthmacher, *Senator Robert F. Wagner*, pp.
293–94.

10. Woodrow Wilson, *Congressional Government*, p. 320.

11. Arthur J. Altmeyer to author, 10 April 1967; Wilbur
Cohen to I. S. Falk, 26 March 1942, Records of the Social Security Board Chairman, Social Security Administration, Central Files, file 011.1, box 60, Record Group 47, National Archives. Hereafter cited as Social Security Board Chairman's
Records.

have to know what was in the bill, word for word, because he knew that it would never be passed in anything
like its original form. . . . But he also knew that something
of the sort would go through ultimately, and he wanted
to start things moving." [12]

Things did indeed start moving within Arthur Altmeyer's social security offices. According to a former member of Isidore Falk's staff (one who defected to the opposition in later years), the sickness-insurance provisions
of the W-M-D bill were drafted by Falk and designated
within his bureau as the "AFL bill." According to Falk,
the label served as a convenient intraoffice designation to
distinguish the health insurance section, which had
strong labor support, from the bill's other titles.[13] The
designation was appropriate: Organized labor considered health insurance must legislation for the postwar
period and became its most powerful advocate.[14]

After Congress had failed to include health insurance
in amendments to the Social Security Act in 1939, labor
had increasingly turned to collective bargaining to secure
hospital and medical benefits for workers and their dependents.[15] But collective bargaining alone would never
give workers the low-cost protection afforded by a national program; compulsory health insurance would cost
less by spreading the risks among millions. Consequently,
as the W-M-D bill took shape in the winter months of
early 1943, Wilbur Cohen worked in close alliance with
AFL president William Green's assistant, Florence
Thorne, to assure that the measure included labor's objectives and to win labor's wholehearted support.[16]

When Senator Wagner introduced this bill to the Seventy-eighth Congress in June 1943, he sent a copy to President Roosevelt, pointing out that it had the strong

12. Quoted in Richard Harris, "Annals of Legislation:
Medicare," *New Yorker*, 2 July 1966, pp. 40–41.
13. Marjorie Shearon, *Blueprint for the Nationalization of
Medicine*, p. 21; Isidore Falk to author, 13 May 1967.
14. Harry Becker, "Organized Labor and the Problem of
Medical Care."
15. Ibid.
16. Wilbur Cohen to author, 11 July 1967.

endorsement of both the AFL and the CIO. FDR replied that he was delighted to have a copy, and he wished the senator luck with it; the president did not, however, offer his open support.[17] The dictates of political prudence continued foremost in Roosevelt's mind, despite a sincere desire to associate himself with—indeed to lead—the growing movement for expanded social security services. In May, a few weeks before, Sir William Beveridge, strutting around in a white Palm Beach suit loaned him by Arthur Altmeyer because his tweeds proved too hot for comfort,[18] had conducted a U.S. lecture tour. Roosevelt winced at the Englishman's looming notoriety as Mister Social Security. "Frances, what does this mean?" FDR asked Secretary of Labor Perkins when he first read the Beveridge plan reports. "Why does Beveridge get his name on this? Why does he get credit for this? You know that I have been talking about cradle to grave insurance ever since we first thought of it. It is my idea. It is not the Beveridge plan. It is the Roosevelt Plan."[19]

Yet, except for scattered, titillating allusions to the subject buried deep in official communiqués, the president had refused to proclaim a Roosevelt plan, nor would he do so in 1943. When Arthur Altmeyer visited FDR in December 1942 concerning preparation of the social security recommendations for inclusion in the president's forthcoming state of the Union message, Roosevelt told Altmeyer to construct a general statement, "to paint goals rather than cross t's and dot i's."[20] And when, at about the same time, Secretary of the Treasury Henry Morgenthau, Jr., searching for a scheme to expand wartime revenues and to allay inflationary pressures, pressed for

17. Robert Wagner to Franklin Roosevelt, 13 June 1943, Robert F. Wagner Papers; Roosevelt to Wagner, 16 June 1943, Franklin D. Roosevelt Papers, President's Personal File (hereafter cited as PPF) 1710.

18. Arthur Altmeyer, *The Formative Years of Social Security*, p. 144.

19. Frances Perkins, *The Roosevelt I Knew*, p. 283.

20. Arthur Altmeyer to the president, 29 December 1942, FDR Correspondence, 1941–1945 folder, box 3, Arther J. Altmeyer Papers.

presidential endorsement of an American-style Beveridge plan, he, too, met with Rooseveltian circumspection. As Morgenthau saw the situation in late 1942, "Every single person in England is going to be insured. They are going to get unemployment insurance; they are going to get sickness insurance, and the whole business."[21] Why not, then, extend social security in this country, deducting payroll taxes during the war (as a hedge against inflation), with delivery of increased benefits postponed until peacetime?[22]

The idea seemed reasonable to Morgenthau, but to Roosevelt it was political dynamite. Republicans had just bolstered their congressional strength in the November 1942 elections, and old-line, stand-pat Democrats like Walter George, powerful chairman of the Senate Finance Committee, remained as surly as ever. When Morgenthau persisted with his scheme in 1943, enlisting the aid of Harry Hopkins and others close to the president, Roosevelt demurred, "The only person who can explain this medical thing is myself. The people are unprepared."[23] So, too, was Franklin Roosevelt. Reassuring Senator George in September, FDR told him, "You don't want, I am sure, to have anybody come up and present a Social Security program at this time. . . . I know you don't want it. . . . We can't go up against the State Medical Societies; we just can't do it."[24] Whereupon Morgenthau concluded that the president and his aides were "only interested in what they [could] get through Congress."[25]

Actually, for Roosevelt in 1943, it was not so much a question of getting proadministration measures through Congress as of preserving some semblance of executive leadership in domestic matters. With his own party divided and Republican congressional strength greater than at any time since the 1920s, FDR stood on the defensive

21. John Blum, *From the Morgenthau Diaries: Years of War, 1941–1945*, p. 53.
22. Ibid.
23. Ibid., p. 72.
24. Ibid.
25. Ibid.

and often lost in legislative contests over tax policy, price stabilization, and labor relations. Some symbolic slaps at lingering New Dealism, like the cancellation of those largely defunct, depression-born relief agencies, the Civilian Conservation Corps and the Works Progress Administration, were expected. But Congress's liquidation in 1943 of Roosevelt's chief long-range domestic planning organization, the National Resources Planning Board, loomed as a warning to the president that any schemes to construct a postwar New Deal would receive a hostile reception on Capitol Hill, at least until a new Congress convened in 1945.[26]

The president initially responded to the congressional action with characteristic sarcasm. "I saw the other day that they voted to abolish the National Resources Planning Board," FDR told reporters in early 1943. Well, Congress had the right to do that, he intoned, but somebody had to develop a program for peace, even though " 'planning' . . . [was no longer] a popular term."[27] In March, supplementing rhetoric with restrained action, Roosevelt sent Congress the NRPB's last two reports on postwar planning, of which one, called *Security, Work, and Relief Policies*, seemed to be an American-style Beveridge plan.[28] Heralding a "New Bill of Rights," the board's voluminous swan song contained nine basic guarantees, including the right to adequate food, clothing, shelter, and medical care.[29] In his transmittal statement, the president wrote that all citizens should be given security "against fear of economic distress in old age, in poverty, sickness, involuntary unemployment, and accidental injuries."[30]

Congress's retort came in June. Following through with its earlier committee decision, funds for the National

26. Roland Young, *Congressional Politics in the Second World War*; James MacGregor Burns, *Roosevelt: The Soldier of Freedom*, pp. 305–7, 331–43, 361–64, 421–22.

27. Roosevelt, *Public Papers and Addresses* 12 (1943):98–99.

28. Edwin Witte, *Social Security Perspectives*, p. 341.

29. An analysis of this report and its development is contained in Stephen Bailey, *Congress Makes a Law*, pp. 26–27.

30. Roosevelt, *Public Papers and Addresses* 12 (1943):122.

Resources Planning Board were struck from an appropriations bill, and the NRPB ceased to function after midyear 1943.[31] As the president had said, planning was no longer a popular subject.

But Roosevelt knew that things could change. Military victories over the Axis in Africa, Russia, and the Pacific had made the first half of 1943 a transitional period in the war; reconversion problems and domestic reform opportunities might be close at hand. Thus, while Sir William Beveridge conducted his tour of the United States in May, stimulating discussion on postwar needs, the president asked members of the soon-to-be-defunct NRPB to confer with Basil O'Connor, head of the American Red Cross. Following Roosevelt's instructions, the meeting dealt with the feasibility of organizing a national health program, and the group advised FDR afterward that "nothing less than a committee set up with the prestige of the President's office behind it would be effective in drawing the various lines together."[32]

The president obviously considered such action premature, because the committee was not established. Instead, Roosevelt bided his time and kept his options open. He would not discourage further talk about postwar social security, but neither would he lead it. Concerning health reform, FDR did allow Arthur Altmeyer to include a provocative statement in a presidential message commemorating the joint anniversary of the Atlantic Charter and the Social Security Act on 13 August 1943. In it, the president recommended, "We should extend social security to provide protection against the serious economic hazard of ill health."[33] In October, FDR also assured both William Green of the AFL and Philip Murray of the CIO that he wholly sympathized with their desire to extend social security, and he sent word to Senator

31. Bailey, *Congress Makes a Law*, p. 27.
32. Frederick A. Delano to the President, 22 May 1943, Roosevelt Papers, Official File (hereafter cited as OF) 103.
33. Altmeyer, *Formative Years of Social Security*, p. 145. The quotation is from Roosevelt, *Public Papers and Addresses* 12 (1943):351.

Wagner that as far as he was concerned Wagner could "handle all the social legislation relating to the veterans, as well as any other he thinks he should do."[34]

The man who conveyed this presidential note to the senator was Roosevelt's special counsel, Samuel Rosenman. Rosenman had long acted as liaison between Wagner and the White House; and, as the president's close adviser and speech writer, he was in a strategic position to help shape administration policy.[35] According to Grace Tully, the president's private secretary, "The imprint of Sam Rosenman [is] probably to be found on more of Roosevelt's utterances than that of any other individual besides FDR himself."[36]

That imprint was decidedly liberal when it came to social security matters. After Rosenman graduated from the Columbia University Law School in 1920 he set up practice with Susan Brandeis, daughter of the progressive-minded Supreme Court justice Louis Brandeis. Later, as a New York assemblyman, Rosenman sponsored housing and rent laws to aid the poor and also fought to improve the state workman's compensation program.[37]

By 1928 Sam Rosenman had worked into Gov. Al Smith's inner circle of advisers, and when he first met Franklin Roosevelt he feared that the Hyde Park aristocrat was not progressive enough for Smith followers like himself. He soon discovered otherwise, and during the 1928 New York gubernatorial campaign Rosenman joined FDR as a speech writer, a position he continued after Roosevelt won the election. During the depression, as his boss directed his New Deal from the White House, Rosenman served as a New York Supreme Court justice,

---

34. Roosevelt to William Green, 6 October 1943, Roosevelt to Philip Murray, 19 October 1943, Misc. 1943–1945 folder, Roosevelt Papers, PPF 1710. Quote is from Roosevelt to Samuel Rosenman, 29 October 1943, in Elliott Roosevelt, ed., *FDR: His Personal Letters*, p. 1462.

35. Samuel B. Hand, "Samuel I. Rosenman: His Public Career" (Ph.D. diss.), p. 204; Samuel Rosenman, *Working with Roosevelt*, p. 8.

36. Grace Tully, *FDR, My Boss*, p. 94.

37. Hand, "Samuel I. Rosenman," pp. 6–19.

but he still wrote speeches for FDR; and when the war broke out the judge began dividing his time between Albany and Washington. Finally, Rosenman resigned his court post in September 1943 to become the president's special counsel, and one of his first White House duties was to draft a presidential message to Congress entitled "The American Plan," recommending enactment of national health insurance.[38]

Rosenman had begun collecting material on health insurance in December 1942, just after announcement of the Beveridge plan, apparently expecting that FDR would soon ask for a speech on the subject.[39] Nine months later the president's position became clear, and by early October 1943 Rosenman had completed the first draft of the American plan. Stretching across fourteen legal-size pages, and reviewing presidential statements issued in the aftermath of the National Health Conference held five years earlier, the American plan proposed that medical services be made available to everyone through national health insurance, that participating doctors and hospitals be guaranteed a fair payment for their services, that physicians remain free to choose their own patients, and that federal funds be provided for medical education and research. Leaving the specific details for Congress to work out, but suggesting that it might consider voluntary rather than compulsory enrollment to counter charges that national health insurance would result in federal regimentation, the message concluded: "Until the hazards of ill health are covered by social insurance, we will not enjoy freedom from want nor will we have the health and vigor that a great people must possess to meet the challenge of their opportunities and responsibilities."[40]

Again, however, the president hesitated; Congress did not receive the American plan. For the British Parlia-

38. Rosenman, *Working with Roosevelt*, p. 15; Hand, "Samuel I. Rosenman," pp. 25–67.

39. Arthur Altmeyer to Rosenman, 21 December 1942, Central Files, box 60, Social Security Board Chairman's Records.

40. "The American Plan," 4 October 1943, Health Message folder, no. 3, box 1, Samuel I. Rosenman Papers.

ment to consider an executive-inspired Beveridge plan, constitutionally wed as the plan was to its administrative sponsors, was one thing; it was a far different matter to confront the U.S. Congress, a separate and now quarrelsome branch of government, with an American plan for postwar health services. Rather, the president waited until his January 1944 state of the Union message, wherein, upon the suggestion of Rosenman and the director of the OPA, Chester Bowles, he included a visionary statement on his postwar domestic policy.[41] Cautioning the nation against "the whining demands of selfish pressure groups" and rightest appeals for a return to "normalcy" as in the days of Harding, the president asked Congress to affirm an economic bill of rights, to supplement the original Bill of Rights with guarantees against postwar economic insecurity. Among those guarantees was the right to adequate medical care.[42]

If health reformers hoped that this message would turn Congress around in 1944, they were quickly disappointed. As Roosevelt engaged in one bitter contest after another with the legislators, Sam Rosenman could see that FDR now had little influence with the Democratic leadership on Capitol Hill.[43] For example, after the president vetoed what he considered an inept tax measure in February, calling it "a tax relief bill providing relief not for the needy but for the greedy,"[44] the Senate Democratic majority leader, Alben Barkley, denounced FDR's action from the Senate floor and resigned the leadership. Congress meanwhile determinedly overrode the veto. The rift between Roosevelt and Barkley soon healed, with the senator resuming his leadership duties, but an everwidening philosophical gulf separated the White House from the Seventy-eighth Congress. Conservative Demo-

41. Rosenman, *Working With Roosevelt*, pp. 425–26.
42. Roosevelt, *Public Papers and Addresses* 13 (1944):41–42. The-economic-bill-of-rights idea originated in a National Resources Planning Board report sent to the president early in the war. See Rosenman, *Working with Roosevelt*, p. 43.
43. Rosenman, *Working with Roosevelt*, p. 427.
44. Roosevelt, *Public Papers and Addresses* 13 (1944):80.

crats working in coalition with Republicans effectively barred legislative reform during the session, and the economic bill of rights had to wait better times.[45]

Nevertheless, national health insurance advocates began organizing a legislative campaign to secure eventual passage of the Wagner-Murray-Dingell bill. They had to begin from scratch because by 1944 both the American Association for Social Security and the American Association for Labor Legislation had passed from the scene after the deaths of their respective executive secretaries and guiding lights, Abraham Epstein and John Andrews.[46] To coordinate the renewed effort, Senator Wagner held a social security conference in his office on 5 February 1944. Present were representatives of organized labor, a small group of liberal doctors called the Physician's Forum, and the reform-oriented National Farmers' Union. Also present were Michael M. Davis and the congressional sponsors of the health bill.[47]

The discussion revealed overwhelming support for a new organization to promote the idea of expanded social security, and a subcommittee was appointed to consider the various problems involved as well as to guide the group's work until a governing board could be established. Adopting the name "Social Security Charter Committee," the delegates moved that Michael Davis, director of the philanthropic-foundation-supported Committee on Research in Medical Economics, serve as acting chairman during the initial period.[48] Thus was born the organizational nucleus of what later became known as the

45. For examples of their effectiveness see Young, *Congressional Politics in the Second World War*, pp. 84–89, 138–43.
46. There was an attempt to revive the Epstein group in early 1944, but organized labor effectively blocked its reorganization on the grounds that its acting executive director was inept and his supporters too radical. Florence Thorne to William Green, 1 February 1944, Thorne to Matthew Woll, 7 February 1944, General Files, Commission on Social Security, series 8A, box 35, American Federation of Labor Papers.
47. The conference is described in Robert Wagner to William Green, 3 March 1944, Wagner Papers.
48. Ibid.

Committee for the Nation's Health, which would function under Davis's direction as the chief lobby in behalf of Truman's national health program.

By May, Davis had begun requesting contributions for the Charter Committee and could outline its immediate work. Although its supporters recognized that the W-M-D bill would remain dormant in Congress during that session, the new organization aimed to educate the public to the need for expanded social security and to coordinate strategy among constituent groups like the AFL, the CIO, and the other liberal bodies.[49]

While Davis attended to organizational aspects in the summer of 1944, others working from within the office of cosponsor Sen. James Murray were already trying to gain favorable publicity for the health bill. Murray, one of the richest men in the Senate, was also one of its most reform minded. Coming to Congress in 1934, he began a few years later to champion a wide range of social and economic legislation. To Murray, whose wealth had come from many and diverse investments, the average businessman and wage earner required protection from powerful special interests. He also deserved better health care. As a young man Murray had been appalled by the ravages of the lung disease silicosis while working in a Butte, Montana, copper mine; and it had further troubled him that it took so long before adequate treatment could be developed for the ailment.[50] "All through my life I have seen examples of the effect of lack of medical care in the early stages of illness," the Montana Democrat told one of his legislative assistants. "Working men with families are prone to neglect their own health because of the fear of the costs involved in medical advice and care. The consequences are that they put off health protection sometimes until it is too late."[51]

49. Michael M. Davis to William Green, 22 May 1944, Early History folder, Records of the Committee for the Nation's Health, Michael M. Davis Papers. Hereafter cited as CNH Records, Davis Papers.

50. Senator Murray to Bert Gross, 8 May 1946, James E. Murray Papers.

51. Ibid.

An influential friend of Senator Murray's, Mrs. Albert D. Lasker of New York City, held similar views and joined the senator in his promotion of the W-M-D bill, contributing money, time, and talent to the enterprise. Mary Lasker had decided while still in her teens that health insurance and funds for medical research (which was practically nonexistent at the time) were necessary. She had been a sickly child; had been angered by what cancer, arthritis, stroke, and other diseases could do to people; and had vowed that if she ever gained the means she would do something about it. That opportunity arose when Mary became successful in a dress-pattern business in the late thirties, and it became even more of a reality after her marriage to Albert Lasker in 1940. Lasker had made a fortune in pioneering modern advertising techniques, and shortly after meeting his future wife he asked her, "What do you want to get done in life? What are you most interested in accomplishing?" Mary said, "I'm really most interested in trying to push for national health insurance. I'm interested in health insurance and research in cancer, arteriosclerosis, and tuberculosis." "Well," Albert replied, "for that you don't need my kind of money. *You need federal money,*" and he pledged to help her obtain the necessary government programs. "Money is frozen energy," Albert Lasker maintained. If one assigned a certain amount of money to a project, the chances were that with intelligence and good direction something worthwhile could be accomplished.[52] After their marriage (in a simple ceremony arranged by their good friend Sam Rosenman), the Laskers devoted more and more of their time and money to health causes.

During the summer months of 1944, Mary Lasker worked closely with Senator Murray's legislative secretary, J. Anthony Marcus, to secure favorable publicity for the health bill.[53] However, with few exceptions, most of the nation's press opposed expansion of social security

52. Mary Woodard Lasker Memoir, Columbia University Oral History Project.

53. Correspondence between J. Anthony Marcus and Mary Lasker, July, August 1944, Murray Papers.

to include health care. In 1944 the exceptions included liberal magazines like the *New Republic*, the publications of organized labor, and a few newspapers such as the *New York Post* and the two Marshall Field publications, *PM* and the *Chicago Sun*.[54] On rare occasions health reformers were able to obtain favorable articles in publications of wider circulation and appeal, such as the December 1944 issue of *Fortune*.

As the *Fortune* article took shape the summer before, the magazine's editor checked with Senator Wagner to see if the information on medical economics was correct. Wagner sent the inquiry to Isidore Falk for verification and also for a statement in behalf of the health bill. At first, the magazine had planned to conclude the story with a judgment adverse to the W-M-D bill, but thanks to Wagner's tactful protest and the information supplied by Falk, the finished article portrayed a picture decidedly favorable to the proposed health program.[55]

At the same time, the opposition, led by the American Medical Association, prepared an intensive lobbying effort of its own. From the beginning of America's defense effort, the AMA had watched the growth of federal involvement in the health field with a fearful eye, and association spokesmen had gone to great lengths to deflate claims that the high percentage of draft rejections proved that the nation suffered serious health problems.[56] After the introduction of the W-M-D bill to the Seventy-eighth Congress in 1943, the AMA quickly reorganized its committee structure to do battle, urged its state medical societies to establish local organizations to handle com-

54. Senator Wagner expressed appreciation for the support of the *New York Post*, *PM*, and the *Chicago Sun* in Robert F. Wagner to Marshall Field, 30 December 1943, and Wagner to Mrs. T. O. Thackrey, 21 January 1944, Wagner Papers.

55. Wagner to A. W. Jones, 24 July 1944, Jones to Wagner, 24 October 1944, Wagner Papers; "U.S. Medicine in Transition."

56. Olin West to Paul McNutt, 27 June 1941, Central Files, box 60, Social Security Board Chairman's Records; James G. Burrow, *AMA, Voice of American Medicine*, pp. 292–93; *New York Times*, 21 April 1941.

munications on compulsory health insurance, and laid
plans to conduct regional seminars on the question. In
order to keep its membership better informed about political developments and to exert additional influence
upon Congress, the AMA also opened a Washington office
in September 1944.[57] All the while, physicians were constantly alerted by the conservative *Journal of the American Medical Association* to the need for continued
vigilance against the critics of American medicine.

Chief responsibility for the AMA's propaganda campaign fell to Morris Fishbein, who as editor of the *Journal* since 1924 had wielded so much power in shaping
AMA policy that he had become known as the "czar of
the industry."[58] An articulate and dedicated foe of what
he perceived as the menacing dangers of regimented
health care, Fishbein traveled from city to city, speaking
on radio forums and before medical societies and other
health groups. After the W-M-D bill was introduced in
Congress, Fishbein in one editorial after another informed his *Journal* readers about the imposing threat
from Washington. Denying that there were serious health
needs, the editor claimed that if the Wagner bill was enacted, "it is doubtful if even Nazidom confers on its
'gaulieter' Conti the powers which the measure would
confer on the Surgeon General of the U.S. Public Health
Service." It would, he concluded a few months later,
"abolish the volunteer control and inspiration that have
brought medical education, hospital management, drug
purity, research and medical service to their present
eminence."[59]

Even more militant and denunciatory was the National
Physician's Committee for the Extension of Medical Ser-
vice, which was founded in 1939 and directed by John
M. Pratt, who had been employed earlier by the violently

57. Burrow, *AMA*, pp. 297, 335.
58. Oliver Garceau, *The Political Life of the American
Medical Association*, p. 86.
59. Editorials, *Journal of the American Medical Association*
(hereafter cited as *JAMA*) 122 (26 June 1943):601; 123 (16 October 1943):418.

anti–New Deal National Committee to Uphold Constitutional Government. Although NPC officials claimed no connection with the AMA, most of them were active association members, and the AMA House of Delegates endorsed the organization in 1942.[60] When Senator Murray embarked upon an investigation of the group in early 1944 (hoping at the suggestion of Michael Davis to find evidence with which to deprive the NPC of its tax-exempt status), Murray wrote Pratt asking about its origin, organization, and finances.[61] The director's reply revealed that the NPC had been organized as an "agency that could function in fields beyond the scope of the charter limitations of the American Medical Association."[62]

These functions embraced an intensive pamphleteering and advertising campaign to defeat what the National Physician's Committee called state medicine or socialized medicine. Between 1 November 1942 and 31 October 1943, the NPC spent $129,000, of which nearly $97,000 went into printing, letter processing, mailing costs, research, and editorial writing. During the same period it reported an income of over $154,000. Of this amount about 60 percent had come from pharmaceutical and drug manufacturers and related industries. Remaining contributions had come from physicians.[63] With an annual budget of this magnitude, the NPC could afford to place full-page illustrated ads accompanied by editorials in newspapers of wide circulation. For instance, on 22 April 1945, *Washington Times-Herald* and *New York Sunday News* subscribers viewed a stern Uncle Sam draped in judicial robes, clutching a folder labeled "Socialized Medicine," and taking "Testimony of an Expert." The expert witness was a distinguished-looking

60. American Medical Association, *Digest of Official Actions, 1846–1958*, p. 324.

61. Michael Davis to Isidore Falk, 6 January 1944, Social Security–General Correspondence File, box 2, Wilbur J. Cohen Papers; James Murray to John M. Pratt, 6 March 1944, Health Message folder, box 1, Rosenman Papers.

62. John M. Pratt to James Murray, 15 March 1944, Health Message folder, box 1, Rosenman Papers.

63. Ibid.

gentleman attired in white and identified as the "Family Doctor."[64]

The National Physician's Committee also sought to influence the outcome of political campaigns. Just before the 1940 Democratic National Convention, the NPC ran a double-page advertisement in the *Saturday Evening Post,* obviously directed against Franklin Roosevelt, urging the convention delegates to preserve America's priceless heritage, "our system of Free Enterprise," for it had made us the healthiest nation in the world.[65] During the presidential campaign between Roosevelt and Willkie that followed, the NPC helped organize the National Committee of Physicians for Wendell L. Willkie and mailed 125,000 letters and booklets to doctors all over the nation urging FDR's defeat in order to prevent "eventual" political control of medicine.[66]

Despite Willkie's defeat that November, administration forces well appreciated and were greatly angered by the political power wielded by the National Physician's Committee. Had Roosevelt sent the American plan message as originally drafted by Rosenman to Congress in 1943, history would record that the president of the United States had labeled a private pressure group called the National Physician's Committee as a propaganda agency "notable for the complete absence of reasoned statement; [for] it appeals only to unthinking emotion."[67]

Congress, of course, never received the American plan. But the president proved more receptive to prodding by Judge Rosenman and others that he outline forthrightly his support for national health insurance after he won an unprecedented fourth term in his victory over Thomas

64. *Washington Times-Herald* and *New York Sunday News,* 22 April 1945.

65. *Saturday Evening Post,* 13 July 1940, pp. 46–47.

66. Letter from "a friendly doctor" to Franklin Roosevelt, 23 October 1940, Socialized Medicine folder, Roosevelt Papers, OF 511-A.

67. "The American Plan," 4 October 1943, Rosenman Papers.

E. Dewey in November 1944.[68] The war was about won, and old New Deal stalwarts reelected to Congress were joined by a few progressive-minded newcomers like Helen Gahagan Douglas from California. This had not made a great chink in the conservative citadel, but it was encouraging.[69] "The Chief is ready to go ahead on health insurance," Harry Hopkins telephoned Michael Davis in December. "Can you come down?"[70] Arriving at Hopkins's office a few days later, Davis learned that a presidential health program including health insurance would be presented in the spring, and he was asked to help Judge Rosenman in his drafting chores.[71]

The winter months following the elections were filled with activity in anticipation of the upcoming congressional contest over health. Shortly before his trip to Washington, Michael Davis and selected representatives of the medical profession and organized labor held the well-publicized Health Program Conference in New York City, wherein they drafted and announced a proposal similar to the Wagner bill. By now other groups had also lined up behind the effort. The American Public Health Association had come out for the first time for the concept, and Arthur Altmeyer's Social Security Board had again endorsed the health insurance principle. In January 1945, the special Senate subcommittee (popularly called the Pepper committee after its chairman, Sen. Claude Pepper, liberal Democrat from Florida) also released an interim report on its investigation into wartime health and education matters, which was conducted in the wake of the draft-rejection controversy. Stating that it had found many Americans victim to preventable ailments due to poor sanitation, a maldistribution of doctors, and inadequate medical facilities, the Pepper committee recommended federal construction of hospitals

68. Mary W. Lasker to author, 14 August 1967.

69. Burns, *Roosevelt: The Soldier of Freedom*, pp. 532–34.

70. Quoted in Michael M. Davis, *Medical Care for Tomorrow*, p. 280.

71. Ibid.

and health clinics as well as the establishment of some form of group financing of medical costs.[72]

The nation's news media carried a flood of articles on the subject; health insurance was debated as never before. On 27 January, Amy Porter of *Collier's* posed a question, "Do we want National Health Insurance?" and answered, "yes." In early February the *New York Times* held a forum on the topic and Michael Davis began a weekly series in the *Survey Graphic*. In April, *United States News* ran a critical article entitled "State Medicine Ahead," and in May the *Saturday Evening Post*, noting the many health insurance proposals then under consideration in numerous states, editorialized that "The States are Feeling the Heat." By July, the *Journal of the American Medical Association* could complain, "No other year has seen such a demand for compulsory health insurance."[73]

Meanwhile, Rosenman and Davis had continued their labors on the promised presidential health message. Earlier, in December, Senator Wagner had contacted Roosevelt concerning the introduction of a revised Wagner-Murray-Dingell bill and, in accord with the president's wishes, delayed its submission so that its appearance might coincide with release of Roosevelt's health pronouncement.[74] "An expanded social security program, and adequate health and education programs" are essential, FDR stated in his January 1945 state of the Union message, and he pledged to "communicate further with the

72. *New York Times*, 5 December 1944, 23 January 1945; "Medical Care for All"; "Medical Care in a National Health Program"; U.S., Social Security Board, *Fifth Annual Report, 1944*, pp. 16–44; U.S., Congress, Senate, Committee on Education and Labor, *Interim Report from the Subcommittee on Wartime Health and Education: Subcommittee Report No. 3 Pursuant to S. Res. 74.*

73. Amy Porter, "Do We Want National Health Insurance?"; *New York Times*, 8 February 1945; Michael M. Davis, "Health—Today and Tomorrow"; "State Medicine Ahead"; "The States are Feeling the Heat"; "Health Insurance," *JAMA* 128 (21 July 1945):870–78.

74. Robert Wagner to Franklin D. Roosevelt, 21 December 1944, Roosevelt Papers, PPF 1710.

Congress on these subjects at a later date."[75] Then trag-
edy intervened that spring. The health movement and
the nation lost their leader; Franklin Roosevelt died on
12 April 1945.

To many, the man who succeeded Roosevelt seemed
anything but a forceful champion of liberalism. Even
years later, astute observers concluded that Harry Truman, during the early months of his administration, per-
formed as a moderate conservative who had inherited a
liberal mandate, liberal advisers, and a liberal political
coalition. He was pictured as a bewildered little man with
thick glasses who was swept along by political exigency.[76]

Truman did face monumental and complex problems
in 1945. As the war came to an end first in Europe and
then in the Pacific, the untested president had to grapple
with a myriad of challenges in diplomacy, demobiliza-
tion, and reconversion; and he leaned heavily upon the
advice of seasoned administrators while doing so. Sam
Rosenman, for one, was asked to stay on for a year; and
the judge served as an important link between the domestic aspirations of the Roosevelt administration and
those of the Truman presidency. However, in the case of
the health program, White House staffers soon learned
that the man from Missouri quickly and sincerely embraced their ideas about postwar health security.

Harry Truman's active interest in health care dated
back to the 1920s when he presided as judge of Jackson
County, Missouri. Among his activities (because a county
judgeship in Missouri is an administrative rather than a
judicial position) Truman visited the local poorhouse
and found that many of the elderly lacked adequate medical attention.[77] "A hospital at the home of the aged is

75. Roosevelt, *Public Papers and Addresses* 13 (1944–1945):
505.

76. Eric F. Goldman, *The Crucial Decade—And After*, p. 21;
Tris Coffin, *Missouri Compromise*, p. 27; Robert S. Allen and
William V. Shannon, *The Truman Merry-Go-Round*, pp. 22–
23; Cabell Phillips, *The Truman Presidency*, p. 144; Barton J.
Bernstein, "America in War and Peace: The Test of Liberal-
ism."

77. Interview with Harry S. Truman.

absolutely necessary," Judge Truman told Kansas City
civic leaders in 1927. "If you gentlemen will just make it
your business to pay a visit to your county home for the
aged you will come back and decide that a hospital is
necessary."[78] The following year Truman obtained a
county bond issue to construct the hospital as well as a
home for feebleminded children.[79]

When the county judge became a United States Senator in 1935, interstate transportation became his major
concern; later, during the world war, he championed efficient defense production. But as one who believed strongly in party loyalty and who had been supported in
Missouri by organized labor, Truman's New Deal voting
record followed Roosevelt's leadership right down the
line.[80] Moreover, although the senator from Missouri
made few speeches, concentrating instead on committee
work, he did address himself on several instances to the
subject of health care. In the summer of 1938, about the
time plans were being made to hold the National Health
Conference, the Senate deliberated on an emergency-
relief-appropriation bill. The debate centered on an
amendment that would provide federal money for eleven
nonprofit hospitals on which construction had begun
earlier but which, through a technicality, had been deprived of government funds after partial completion.
During the debate Truman unsuccessfully sought approval of an amendment to expand government assistance to all nonprofit hospitals.[81] On a different occasion,
a few years later, a friend of the Missouri senator became
ill and could not present a scheduled talk before a health
group. Truman took his place and forcefully told the
gathering about his own interest in health matters.[82]

78. *Independence Examiner*, 8 December 1927.
79. *Kansas City Star*, 16 October 1928.
80. Eugene F. Schmidtlein, "Truman The Senator" (Ph.D.
diss.), pp. 20, 97, 130–31, 134, 218–20.
81. *Congressional Record*, 75th Cong., 3d sess., 1938, vol.
83, pt. 7, p. 7960.
82. Interview with Isidore S. Falk. Falk was present at the
talk. No record of the speech has been found in Truman's
senatorial papers, nor is it noted in contemporary literature.

Harry Truman, disappointed as a youth by his inability to pass a West Point entrance physical because of poor eyesight, intensely proud of his bracing World War I experience as an artillery officer in France, and determined in civilian life to ward off middle-age flabbiness by walking a mile or more each morning at 120 paces a minute, doggedly followed the old adage that an ounce of prevention is worth a pound of cure. Understandably, members of Isidore Falk's staff had found Senator Truman willing to read their detailed health proposals and to lend a sympathetic ear.[83]

The Missourian's concern for reform causes supported by organized labor was heightened after his selection as Roosevelt's running mate in 1944, since labor leaders had played a major role in lining up delegates for Truman's candidacy at the Democratic convention. The unions could also take credit following the elections for tipping the electoral balance against Dewey in November by getting out the urban vote for the Democrats.[84] By defeating its enemies and rewarding its friends, organized labor expected to lay the foundation of postwar economic security, and a thankful Truman was not averse to its desires.

As Franklin Roosevelt made plans to revive the New Deal in early 1945, Harry Truman languished in the obscurity of the vice-presidency. He had never been really close to the president, and FDR rarely saw Truman during his vice-presidency.[85] Still, Truman's new position

---

However, many Truman senatorial speeches are missing from the files.

83. Truman's early views on the need for physical fitness and preventative health care are best expressed in Remarks at the National Health Assembly Dinner, 1 May 1948, in Harry S. Truman, *The Public Papers of the Presidents of the United States, 1948*, pp. 241–43, and Harry S. Truman, *Mr. Citizen*, pp. 59–60. Truman's cooperative attitude toward health proposals while in the Senate was described in the interview with Falk.

84. Jonathan Daniels, *The Man of Independence*, pp. 245–47; Schmidtlein, "Truman the Senator," p. 329.

85. Mary Hinchey, "The Frustration of the New Deal Revival" (Ph.D. diss.), pp. 78–80.

made him not only important to reform elements, but also the target of their conservative opponents, for as the scandals associated with the Nixon presidency remind us, in order to protect or to promote their vital interests nearly all the major lobbies seek to influence the executive branch as well as the legislative.[86] As for the American Medical Association after the November elections, it was important that organized medicine obtain a true indication of the Roosevelt administration's blueprint for postwar public health and, if possible, shape the administration's plans in its favor. Therefore, the AMA's Washington lobbyist met several times with Truman to sound him out on the issue.[87] Truman reciprocated; he invited the officers of the American Medical Association to meet with him in a special conference.

The meeting took place on 9 January 1945, three days after President Roosevelt delivered his last state of the Union message. Those in attendance included the president of the AMA, Herman L. Kretschmer of Chicago; the president-elect, Roger Lee of Boston; the secretary and general manager, Olin West of Chicago; the speaker of the AMA House of Delegates, Harrison Shoulders of Nashville; and other notable association leaders. What transpired is best described in a letter one of the participants wrote Truman:

> I want you to know how much every one of the doctors who attended your conference several weeks ago appreciated the opportunity of hearing your views and having the chance to express theirs. . . . You put the question squarely up to them, and this problem of the formulation of a health program for the American people is a large order.[88]

In his reply, the vice-president answered that he enjoyed the meeting and said, "I tried to impress upon them [the

86. For examples of their efforts, see David B. Truman, *The Governmental Process*, pp. 395–436.

87. These meetings were recalled in Joseph S. Lawrence to Matthew Connelly, 16 November 1945, Harry S. Truman Papers, OF 286A.

88. Thomas A. Hendricks to Harry S. Truman, 27 January 1945, AMA folder, Vice-Presidential Files, Truman Papers.

medical profession] that the responsibility is theirs, and I hope it got over."[89] Truman was not saying, of course, that the AMA should take sole responsibility for the health program's development and direction; a few days earlier he had written to the AMA secretary, Olin West, that "I hope that we can find a practical solution to our problems."[90]

When Harry Truman became president on that fateful day in April he made the responsibility for the development of health programs his own, because the American Medical Association wasted no time in making it clear that organized medicine would not agree to federal participation in a prepayment program for medical care. Even though Senator Wagner had invited Secretary West of the AMA to suggest changes in the W-M-D bill slated for resubmission in 1945, West refused;[91] and the *Journal of the American Medical Association* viciously attacked the bill when it appeared in May, claiming that the association had never been consulted on the matter.[92] This blatant falsehood was too much for Wagner to endure, and he tried in June to set the record straight in a note to the *Journal*; but Morris Fishbein responded by calling the senator's letter "rhetorical tripe" and charged that, in spite of Wagner's claims, Wagner and others in Washington had displayed "the apotheosis of stubbornness and obstinacy and with it a complete lack of willingness to confer, to consult or to reason."[93] Could it be that the *Journal* editor had no knowledge of the conference with Vice-President Truman or of Wagner's offer to Secretary West? Hardly. Whatever the case, the AMA Board of Trustees brought the round of charge and countercharge

89. Harry S. Truman to Thomas A. Hendricks, 6 February 1945, AMA folder, Vice-Presidential Files, Truman Papers.

90. Harry S. Truman to Olin West, 2 February 1945, AMA folder, Vice-Presidential Files, Truman Papers.

91. Robert Wagner to Olin West, 7 December 1944 and West to Wagner, 15 December 1944, copies in Social Security General Correspondence, 1944 file, box 2, Cohen Papers.

92. Editorial, *JAMA* 128 (2 June 1945):364–65.

93. Organization Section and Editorial, *JAMA* 128 (30 June 1945): 672–74, 667–68. Quotations are on pp. 668, 674.

to an end by releasing in July its "Constructive Program for Medical Care," which allowed no room for compromise. The core of the AMA's fourteen-point proposal called for expansion of existing private health insurance plans and postponement of "revolutionary changes" in health services while so many medical men were still in the armed forces.[94]

AMA intransigence alone, however, cannot explain Truman's quick decision to press forward with a government-sponsored health program. If anything, it reinforced convictions he already held, as is evidenced by the fact that Truman had talked to Judge Rosenman and another Roosevelt holdover, Budget Director Harold Smith, about expansion of social security to include health just a few weeks after he entered the White House.[95]

Unaccountably, President Truman recorded in his *Memoirs* years later that he first informed Sam Rosenman about his domestic reform plans, including health care, aboard the *Augusta* en route home from Germany and the Potsdam diplomatic conference in early August. HST even quotes his special counsel as saying upon hearing the news, "You know, Mr. President. This is the most exciting and pleasant surprise I have had in a long time."[96] From this moment forward, Harry Truman and an enlightened Sam Rosenman supposedly joined hands to resurrect the New Deal. There is, however, ample evidence to the contrary.

Judge Rosenman and other members of the president's official family knew about Truman's domestic reform agenda at least two months before the conversation

94. "Constructive Program for Medical Care," *JAMA* 128 (21 July 1945):883; *New York Times*, 19 July 1945.

95. According to Mary Lasker, Judge Rosenman told her that the president directed him to "go ahead and prepare what is necessary," when Truman learned of the impending health message shortly after FDR's death. The meeting with Smith was held on 4 May 1945. Mary W. Lasker to author, 14 August 1967; Conferences with President Truman, 1945–1946, Harold D. Smith Papers; Rosenman, *Working with Roosevelt*, p. 515.

96. Harry S. Truman, *Memoirs: Year of Decisions*, p. 483.

aboard the *Augusta*. When congressional health sponsors Wagner, Murray, and Dingell conferred with HST in mid-May on their plans to reintroduce a revised bill, the president told them to "discuss the social security features of the new bill, and in fact the entire subject, with Judge Rosenman."[97] The next day, HST not only informed Budget Director Smith of his plans to send Congress a message on social security expansion, but also sent instructions for gathering materials for the message to the administrator of the Federal Security Agency (now the Department of Health, Education, and Welfare).[98] Indeed, following the reintroduction of the W-M-D bill, the president came very close to endorsing it publicly when asked in a June news conference if he favored the measure. "I am in favor of the principal parts of it," Truman replied. "In fact, I think I was one of the authors of that bill in the last congress. I haven't studied the present draft . . . , and I am not familiar with its details, but in principle I am for it."[99]

There is no evidence that Truman as senator had ever helped to draft the W-M-D bill; as a matter of fact, he later expressed misgivings over its content, complaining that "it was too cumbersome, and it aimed in too many directions."[100] Nevertheless, Harry Truman had already set in motion plans to urge passage of legislation incorporating similar provisions.

As the cool breezes of springtime yielded to the sweltering summer heat of Washington, Judge Rosenman methodically wove together the various sections of the Truman health message. Materials for inclusion poured in from all directions. From the director of the draft, Gen. Lewis B. Hershey, the president's assistant received information concerning the physical and mental defects

97. Quoted in John Dingell to Robert Wagner, 16 May 1945, Wagner Papers.

98. Conference with President Truman, 16 May 1945, Smith Papers; Watson B. Miller to President Truman, 23 May 1945, Truman Papers, OF 7.

99. Press Conference, 1 June 1945, in Truman, *Public Papers, 1945*, p. 32.

100. Truman, *Memoirs: Year of Decisions*, p. 19.

of selective-service registrants. Vannevar Bush, director of the Office of Scientific Research and Development, sent material bearing on postwar medical research needs. Arthur Altmeyer provided a twenty-four-page section on social security expansion. Wilbur Cohen, Isidore Falk, Michael Davis, and Mary Lasker all willingly lent their talents, with Mary Lasker spending long hours working over drafts in the judge's apartment in the Wardman Park Hotel.[101] By late July, before Sam Rosenman joined the president for a brief stay at Potsdam and before their leisurely return home aboard the *Augusta*, Rosenman had completed the first draft of the health message and had started plans for a message on education.[102]

In reality, the meeting aboard the *Augusta* signaled Truman's decision to publicly outline for the first time his entire postwar domestic program. When Rosenman returned to the White House he put aside the individual messages on health and education and began composing what the president later called "the platform of my administration."[103] Against the advice of Budget Director Smith—who cautioned Truman and Rosenman that the comprehensive message shot in too many directions, lacked consideration for sensitive executive-legislative relations, and prematurely committed the president to programs still in the tentative stage[104]—Truman sent Congress

101. Lewis B. Hershey to Samuel Rosenman, 24 May 1945, Vannevar Bush to Rosenman, 25 May 1945, Health Message folders 1, 3, box 1, Arthur Altmeyer to Rosenman, 28 May 1945, Social Security folder, box 3, Michael Davis to Rosenman, 29 June 1945, Health Message folder 2, box 1, author unknown to Rosenman, n.d., Health Message folder 2, box 1, Rosenman Papers; Mary W. Lasker to author, 14 August 1967.

102. This final draft is undated but makes reference to the remaining need for victory over Japan. Japan capitulated a week after Rosenman's return from Potsdam, and it is unlikely that the draft could have been written during this short period. Health Message Draft, Health Message folder 2, box 1, Rosenman Papers.

103. Truman, *Memoirs: Year of Decisions*, p. 481.

104. Harold Smith to Samuel Rosenman, 31 August 1945, September 6 Message folder, Rosenman Papers; Conference with President Truman, 31 August 1945, Smith Papers.

a sweeping twenty-one-point domestic reform package on 6 September that included recommendations on everything from reconversion measures to housing and full employment.[105]

Essentially the twenty-one-point message outlined programs that Roosevelt probably would have advanced singly and with a great deal of preparatory work.[106] Truman, however, preferred to place presidential prestige boldly on the line in one dramatic pronouncement. His motives are not clear. Perhaps it was inexperience. Perhaps it was the spunky nature of a man who kept a sign on his desk reading The Buck Stops Here and who let it be known in his first days in office that if department heads did not stop dillydallying around and start making decisions he would find some that would.[107] Besides this, there were those constant pressures for action exerted upon Truman by organized labor and liberal Democrats in the Senate, the need to outline a reconversion program now that Japan was defeated, and, above all, the Missourian's intense desire to stake out a claim to domestic leadership in the name of Harry S. Truman.[108]

"It's just a plain case of out-dealing the New Deal," howled GOP House leader Joe Martin after the twenty-one-point message hit Capitol Hill,[109] and Harold Smith's forebodings became prophetic as other lawmen joined Martin in a chorus of protest against Truman's domestic agenda. In spite of the president's attempts to maintain a favorable rapport with his former congressional colleagues, his efforts proved for naught as Republicans took an antiadministration tack designed to gain them support in the 1946 congressional elections, and as long-tenured southern and rural Democrats maintained their rigid stance against urban-based, labor-oriented domestic re-

105. Special Message, 6 September 1945, in Truman, *Public Papers, 1945*, pp. 263–309.

106. Richard E. Neustadt, "The Presidency and Legislation: Planning the President's Program," pp. 997–98.

107. Conference with President Truman, 4 May 1945, Smith Papers.

108. Daniels, *The Man of Independence*, pp. 27–28, 297.

109. Quoted in Phillips, *The Truman Presidency*, p. 104.

form. Forming a conservative alliance with the Republicans in key congressional committees, these Democrats blocked major features of Truman's postwar program.[110] In the same committees, the revised Wagner-Murray-Dingell bill—which had been introduced in late May of 1945 after the cosponsors' conference with the president—became stalled.

With some sections dropped and others added, the bill once again included provision for social security to cover medical expenses. Among the changes in the health insurance section was the inclusion of dental and nursing care. An alteration of administrative procedures was also made to protect private medical cooperatives and to allay fears that professionals would be regimented by the government.[111]

Because the measure, like its 1943 version, included a section outlining the system of taxation to be followed if it were enacted, the Senate bill was referred to the Committee on Finance, and the House bill to the Ways and Means Committee. And this is where the rub came in. Even though the chairman of the Finance Committee, Walter George, gave assurances that the bill would get a hearing, it did not. Instead, the committee busied itself with unemployment and tax legislation. Things looked no better in the House committee, for here, too, there was little chance for a hearing, much less for success.[112]

To break the impasse, the health sponsors decided to introduce still another bill in 1945 that would not mention finances and thus would be referred to different committees, possibly to Senator Murray's Education and Labor Committee in the Senate and to a committee in the

110. Hinchey, "Frustration of the New Deal Revival," pp. 91–95, 156–71; James T. Patterson, *Mr. Republican: A Biography of Robert A. Taft*, pp. 304–14; George H. Mayer, *The Republican Party, 1854–1966*, p. 467.

111. Changes in the health insurance section reflect suggestions made by Michael Davis. Davis to Robert Wagner, 18 December 1944, Wagner Papers; S. 1050 and H.R. 395, 79th Cong., 1st sess.

112. *New York Times*, 4 April 1945; Hinchey, "Frustration of the New Deal Revival," pp. 156–74.

House less hostile than Ways and Means. They met with the president on the matter in September and decided to time the bill's reintroduction with his special health message to Congress.[113]

By now the health security idea had moved to the forefront of Harry Truman's thinking on postwar domestic reform needs. The day after his 6 September message stunned conservatives on Capitol Hill, the president brought up the health issue in a cabinet meeting. He talked about the lack of doctors and the poor distribution of medical centers in the country and about how the statistics on draft rejections from the Selective Service System showed that "radical steps" were needed to "re-establish the health of the nation." He knew that the American Medical Association would oppose a federal program, he said, but he still planned to send Congress a special message on the subject.[114]

On the heels of this declaration, Harry Truman received a visit the following afternoon from Mary Lasker. It was their first meeting, arranged by Anna Rosenberg, a Roosevelt confidant and longtime friend of Mary Lasker. As she entered the huge oval office and approached the new president (who opened the conversation saying something apologetic about sitting in President Roosevelt's chair), Mary Lasker was worried. She had heard rumors that Truman might be wavering in his determination to go ahead on health insurance. After a moment, however, her fears were dispelled. The president warmly agreed with her entreaties about health needs and recalled his own experiences in Missouri. Reassured that HST intended to send a health message to Congress, an elated Mrs. Lasker told him, "You will be the first President in history to do anything about the health of our people."[115]

113. Suggested strategy on this is outlined in an unsigned, undated report entitled "Ways In Which The Senate Can Take The Initiative In Social Security Legislation," 1945 folder, box 19, Cohen Papers. See also, Huthmacher, *Senator Robert F. Wagner*, p. 320.

114. Walter Millis, ed., *The Forrestal Diaries*, p. 93.

115. Mary W. Lasker to author, 14 August 1967.

Only a matter of time now remained before President Truman would send his health program to Congress. His head-reeling twenty-one-point message had contained a reference to a promised health message as well as to separate communications on social security and education. But the latter two would have to wait; HST gave priority to the health program. Accordingly, Sam Rosenman returned to his drafting chores, repeating the routine of pulling in information from pertinent agencies and employing many hands in the writing process. All the old personages contributed sections and some new ones also lent assistance, especially the president's personal physician, Dr. Wallace Graham, just recalled from overseas army duty.[116]

By the end of October, Rosenman had pieced together the major outline of the message. From this point on the final drafting stages came in rapid-fire order because the president wanted to send the program to the hill as soon as possible; he was fed up with the Democratic leadership in both houses and had decided to stop wooing the lawmakers and to start prodding them for action. In fact, Truman had called some of them in and told them that all they had accomplished was to set the clock back.[117] On the evening of 30 October, the president spoke on national radio and for the first time criticized certain congressional committees for holding up his recommendations.[118]

A bit of legislative strategy also influenced the timing of the health message. On 1 November, Truman had learned from his Federal Security Agency administrator that a special staff study was under way in the conservative-dominated House Ways and Means Committee. It involved a resolution passed earlier calling for an investi-

116. The Rosenman Papers contain correspondence, memorandums, and suggested drafts from a wide range of sources. Dr. Graham provided advice on references to diseases and medical terminology. Health Message folders 1, 2, box 1, Rosenman Papers.

117. Conference with President Truman, 30 October 1945, Smith Papers.

118. Radio Address, 30 October 1945, in Truman, *Public Papers, 1945*, p. 441.

gation into the need for broadening social security coverage, and the committee's findings were due around the first of December. Sensing that the report would be hostile to social security expansion, the administrator suggested that the health message be sent "at the earliest possible moment," so that it might influence the committee's conclusions.[119] Consequently, after checking a few last-minute details with Altmeyer and Falk, Rosenman sent the latest draft to the president on 12 November with the assurance that he had gone over it carefully with the experts of the Federal Security Agency.[120]

Daily staff sessions were held to whip the message into final shape. At the end of each day Judge Rosenman delivered the latest draft to the president, and it came back each morning with HST's suggestions, which included the request that the section dealing with mental illness be expanded. His experiences back in Jackson County, Missouri, had convinced him, said Truman, that something had to be done to reduce the burden of mental disorders, that too many elderly folks had been committed to mental institutions by their relatives because the relatives lacked the money and desire to care for them at home.[121]

A health conference was held with the president on the afternoon of 16 November, and Truman accepted the draft of the health message presented at this meeting. Rosenman made a few stylistic changes and sent the message to the printers.[122] Congress and the nation received

119. Watson B. Miller to the President, 1 November 1945, Truman Papers, OF 419-B. The president took cognizance of this information and suggestion, since he placed a notation in the margin.

120. Samuel Rosenman to the President, 12 November 1945, Message folder 2, box 1, Rosenman Papers.

121. Wilbur Cohen to author, 11 July 1967; interview with Truman.

122. 3:45 P.M. Appointment, 16 November 1945, Presidential Appointment Book of Matthew J. Connelly, Truman Papers; Connelly to Samuel Rosenman, 14 November 1945, Truman Papers, OF 103; Sixth Draft of Health Message, Message folder 3, box 1, Rosenman Papers.

President Truman's comprehensive national health program on 19 November 1945.

It was the first presidential message devoted exclusively to the subject of health. It was divided into two parts: the first half outlined unmet needs, and the second presented proposals for their solution. Five major health problems were cited. These included maldistribution of professional personnel and medical facilities, inadequate public health services, the need for expanded research and training programs, the high cost of medical care, and the loss of income due to prolonged illness. In order to meet these problems the president urged adoption of a comprehensive national health program to provide federal grants for construction of hospitals and other health centers, to expand public health services, and to assist mothers and children. Grants would also be earmarked for research programs and medical education. To protect against economic insecurity due to illness, the message suggested two systems of social insurance, one covering losses of wages resulting from sickness and disability, and the other providing workers and their dependents comprehensive medical services prepaid through social security taxes.[123]

When Harry Truman accepted Judge Rosenman's final draft of this message and sent it to Congress, he endorsed a controversial policy that had been planned and developed to a great extent before he became president. Had Franklin Roosevelt lived and kept his promise to the health movement leaders, Congress would have received much the same message over his signature. To say this is to recognize the important role that the staff assistants who were carried over from the previous administration played in the formulation of Truman's health policy. Even in normal times a busy chief executive must place great reliance upon his advisers; he cannot possibly detect all the shades of emphasis or deemphasis in their counsel and in their work, and Truman's assumption of

123. Special Message Recommending a Comprehensive Health Program, 19 November 1945, in Truman, *Public Papers, 1945,* pp. 475–91.

the presidency was anything but normal. Yet on the health issue Harry Truman was not taken for a ride down the river of expediency. His early interest in public health matters made him especially sympathetic to the efforts of Sam Rosenman and the others who helped construct the health program.

Truman's interest in, and executive sponsorship of, a national health insurance program represented a major breakthrough, marking the partial culmination of efforts dating back a quarter of a century. For the first time the health reformers had a presidential mandate. As Michael Davis reflected after the president sent his health message to Congress, "There are educational hills, organizational swamps, and political rivers to cross. But a presidential message is a milestone, nevertheless, from which past progress may be measured."[124]

124. Michael M. Davis, "A Milestone in Health Progress," p. 485.

3

An Uncertain Beginning, 1946

Harry Truman's health message—with its advocacy of national health insurance—and the 1946 congressional elections were separated by approximately one year. During the intervening twelve months the president's economic-control policies alienated so much of the electorate that Democratic office seekers declined to use Truman's name in the 1946 campaign, and their Republican opponents ran on a simple and telling slogan, "Had Enough?" A majority of voters responded in the affirmative on election day in November, thus enabling the GOP to capture control of Congress and ending sixteen years of Democratic dominance on Capitol Hill. The Republican ascendancy also capped months of frustration for the proponents of health reform.

At the outset, in late 1945, general reaction to the administration's national health insurance proposal was mixed. The daily press gave guarded treatment to the November health message; for example, the *Philadelphia Record* and the *New York Herald Tribune* muted their long-standing opposition to "compulsory" medicine. If pressure for national health insurance proved irresistible, editorialized the *Herald Tribune*, it hoped that "the spirit of Mr. Truman's proposals will pervade whatever scheme is finally chosen."[1] Public opinion samplings showed a similar tentativeness and fluctuation of interest. Whereas no less than 58 percent of those polled during the war years had favored a tax-supported federal health system, after V-J Day there was no longer a clear-cut answer to the question, What kind of health insurance would you prefer, government or private? The peacetime nation stood evenly divided in its response.[2] Defense em-

1. *New York Herald Tribune*, 20 November 1945. See also, *Philadelphia Record*, 21 November 1945.
2. National Opinion Research Center Poll, August 1944,

ployment had revived the economy. People had money and because of lingering consumer controls could not spend it. Savings accounts bulged; and the popularity of, and participation in, private prepayment medical plans expanded accordingly.

Private arrangements for prepaid health care fell into four broad categories, and each showed remarkable growth during the war. These were: (1) nonprofit, hospital-sponsored "Blue Cross" hospital expense plans; (2) nonprofit, physician-sponsored "Blue Shield" surgical expense plans; (3) commercial insurance coverage sold by insurance companies; and (4) nonprofit, consumer-sponsored medical cooperatives. Between 1940 and 1946 Blue Cross membership more than quadrupled and participation in Blue Shield increased from 370,000 to over 4 million. Commercial insurance policies expanded fivefold during the same period, and cooperative facilities providing comprehensive health services—such as those offered by West Coast industrialist Henry Kaiser—began to flourish.[3]

Both organized medicine and its reform opposition took stock of these developments following Truman's November health message. Claude Robinson of the National Opinion Research Corporation told the National Physician's Committee, "Whichever sponsorship first makes its prepayment plan both widely known and widely available, that sponsorship can count on public acceptance."[4] After conducting an exhaustive opinion survey of its own, the U.S. Bureau of the Budget arrived at much the same conclusion in a confidential report issued in early 1946; respondents to their survey had split right

Gallup Polls, 14 August 1943, 21 November 1945, 10 April 1946, in Hadley Cantril, ed., *Public Opinion, 1935–1946*, pp. 441–43.

3. Franz Goldmann, *Voluntary Medical Care Insurance in the United States*, pp. 93–187; Herman N. Somers and Anne R. Somers, *Doctors, Patients and Health Insurance*, table A-13, p. 548.

4. Quoted in Elizabeth Wilson, *Compulsory Health Insurance*, p. 105.

down the middle over what should be done about the high costs of medical care.[5]

For the Truman administration this indicated that a vigorous educational campaign would be necessary in 1946 to mobilize public opinion behind the president's program. To be successful, the effort would require strong executive leadership, unity of purpose among the promoters of Truman's health plan, and, in view of the temper of the times, a great deal of good luck. The health reform movement, however, lacked all of these essentials.

Support from the White House soon stalled. President Truman, in spite of his initial and decisive endorsement of national health insurance, simply did not follow through with the kind of articulate leadership the movement needed in order to gain additional adherents. Other than passing references to a "national health program" made on three different occasions in 1946, the president never expressed himself in public on the health security idea.[6] The first of the three occasions when he did mention health security was a radio address delivered on the night of 3 January. In that speech, HST asked the American people to override the special-interest lobbies that were blocking his reconversion program in Congress by letting their representatives know about their own feelings concerning postwar needs.[7] This forceful message, so atypical of Harry Truman's past utterances, prompted Robert Sherwood to write Sam Rosenman about his impressions concerning its political import.

Sherwood, a former Roosevelt speech writer, had left

5. U.S., Bureau of the Budget, "National Medical Care—An Opinion Study," 29 March 1946, Records of the Administrator, Federal Security Agency, file 011.4, box 217, Record Group 235, National Archives. Hereafter cited as FSA Administrator's Records.

6. Radio Report to the American People, 3 January 1946, Address to the Federal Council of Churches, 6 March 1946, Address at the Jackson Day Dinner, 23 March 1946, in Truman, *The Public Papers of the Presidents of the United States, 1946,* pp. 6, 143, 166.

7. Radio Report to the American People, 3 January 1946, in Truman, *Public Papers, 1946,* pp. 1–8.

Washington to resume his career as a playwright in Hollywood, and while dining alone at the Beverly Hills Hotel he heard the faint strains of the president's talk come from a radio in an adjoining lounge. Cutting his meal short, Sherwood went in to listen and found that while the hotel's lobby, bar, and dining rooms were all crowded, he sat alone as the only one interested enough to pause for Truman's speech. "It was mighty depressing," he wrote Rosenman. "It is difficult to find anyone who is strongly opposed to Mr. Truman, but even more difficult to find anyone who is violently for him." Supporters of FDR and the New Deal were lukewarm about Truman's leadership, he said, because "the feeling seems to be that Mr. Truman is content merely to put Liberal policies on the record and leave them there." Still, Sherwood surmised, perhaps the president's radio talk would change that impression if it were "followed by some real aggressive action and even an outbreak of vigorous hostilities between the White House and Capitol Hill."[8]

The impression was not altered. New Dealers became even more disenchanted with Harry Truman in the following months, especially as the last Roosevelt holdovers were dropped from the cabinet. What they considered to be a "purge" reached its climax in September when Secretary of Commerce Henry Wallace was fired after delivering a foreign-policy speech (ostensibly approved beforehand by Truman) in which the New Deal stalwart criticized the Truman administration's hard line against the Soviet Union.[9] Health reformers, meanwhile, had also begun to wonder if the president had forgotten about the cause he had championed in November 1945.

In an effort to draw favorable attention to the president's health message, Mary Lasker paid for three-quarter-page endorsements to be published in the *Washington Star* and *Washington Post*, as well as in the *New York Times,* in early December 1945. The ad was signed by

8. Robert Sherwood to Samuel Rosenman, 5 January 1946, box 8, Samuel I. Rosenman Papers.
9. Alonzo Hamby, *Beyond the New Deal: Harry S. Truman and American Liberalism*, pp. 53–85, 121–34.

nearly two hundred prominent men and women from business, professional, and civic circles, including Mrs. Franklin Roosevelt, David Sarnoff of RCA, Foirello La Guardia, and musician Leonard Bernstein.[10] Earlier, Michael Davis had asked for help from the White House but had not gotten it. Explaining in a note to Judge Rosenman that he had been disappointed with the initial publicity given to the special health message, Davis asked, "Could the President, at one of his press conferences this week, refer to the endorsement received from a number of businessmen, as evidence that the economic as well as the humanitarian values of the health program are appreciated?"[11] Rosenman failed to get Truman to bring the subject up in his press conference; instead the president wrote Davis expressing his appreciation to the business group.[12]

Other examples of the president's silence on health security during 1946 demonstrate that Harry Truman contributed very little to public understanding or even awareness of his proposal, although he certainly had ample opportunity to do so. In addition to his weekly press conferences there were numerous ceremonial functions directly related to health care, occasions that provided the president natural forums for bringing the issue before the public. In early February, the president received a delegation representing the National Arthritis Research Foundation and accepted an honorary chairmanship of the foundation's new research facility. The press reported no statement by the president. On the afternoon of 23 May the president and Mrs. Truman gave a garden party

10. Mary W. Lasker to author, 14 August 1967. Lasker also sent a clipping of the ad to the president. See Lasker to Harry S. Truman, 11 December 1945, Harry S. Truman Papers, Official File (hereafter cited as OF) 286A.

11. Michael Davis to Samuel Rosenman, 26 November 1945, Truman Papers, President's Personal File (hereafter cited as PPF) 220.

12. Rosenman to Charles Ross, 27 November 1945, Truman Papers, PPF 220; Press Conference, 29 November 1945, in Truman, *Public Papers, 1945*, pp. 504–14; Truman to Davis, 28 November 1945, Truman Papers, PPF 220.

for veterans hospitalized in Washington. The press reported no statement by the president. In August the president signed into law two health measures, one providing health programs for certain government employees and the other implementing the Hospital Construction Act, which was an important part of his national program. Again, the president made no statement calling attention to the remaining need for national health insurance. Finally, in late September, a delegation of nurses met with the president to publicize the acute shortage of nurses in the nation. The meeting elicited no press release from the White House.[13]

From his public silence on these and other occasions, one might gain the impression that Harry Truman had lost all interest in his health program, or at least that he was out of touch with developments in the legislative movement. But the facts do not support such a conclusion; Truman remained interested and was kept well informed on the subject. Each month the president received, at his request, reports from the federal security administrator appraising him of legislative developments in the social security and health fields and alerting him to national press reaction over his special health message.[14] In addition, Senators Murray and Wagner kept him informed concerning their plans to hold Senate hearings

13. Newspaper and periodical references to these occasions, when noted, reported no statements by the president regarding his national health program. Nelle Morgan, a nurse in attendance at the September publicity meeting on nursing, recalled that the president was similarly mute on the issue. 10:00 A.M. Appointment, 5 February 1946, 4:00 P.M. Appointment, 23 May 1946, 11:00 A.M. Appointment, 8 August 1946, 12:15 P.M. Appointment, 30 September 1946, in Presidential Appointment Book of Matthew J. Connelly, Truman Papers; Statement by the President Upon Signing the Hospital Survey and Construction Act, 13 August 1946, in Truman, *Public Papers, 1946*, pp. 413–14; interview with Nelle Morgan.

14. The bimonthly reports began on 19 October 1945. They were terminated in February 1947. Also included in the file is "Some Indications of Public Interest and Reaction to the National Health Program," FSA Report to the President, 15 December 1945, Truman Papers, OF 419B.

on the health bill, with the latter telling Truman in late 1945, "We may need some more help from you when the going gets tough."[15]

The president already had a good idea of just how tough that legislative effort would be, however; and he showed no signs in private that he intended to back away from the controversial issue. A few weeks after the health proposal went to Capitol Hill, Judge Rosenman furnished HST with a detailed accounting of organized medicine's hostile reception to the president's congressional message.[16] Truman's response to the attacks can be gauged by his reaction to an intemperate letter sent him by the head of the Association of American Physicians and Surgeons. Like the AMA, the AAPS stood unalterably opposed to medical reform, and the letter warned the president that, if national health insurance was enacted, AAPS members would refuse to participate in the system. Isidore Falk, asked to prepare a reply suitable for the chief executive's signature, wrote an equally intemperate draft, labeling the association unpatriotic and warning that the American people would surely condemn its policies.[17] Nevertheless, the president approved Falk's draft with a handwritten notation[18]:

OK
100%
HST

15. Wagner to Truman, 5 December 1945, James E. Murray to Truman, 5 December 1945, Truman Papers, PPF 2252, PPF 200.

16. Rosenman to the President, 27 November 1945, Truman Papers, PPF 200.

17. Harold T. Low to the President, 18 November 1945, Isidore Falk, "Letter Draft for the President," n.d., Rosenman to the President, 6 December 1945, Truman Papers, OF 286-A.

18. The president's notation was placed at the bottom of Falk's letter draft. Upon further reflection, the reply, changed somewhat in wording but not in substance, was sent out over the signature of Surgeon General Thomas Parran. William D. Hassett to Parran, 10 December 1945, Parran to Harold T. Low, 11 December 1945, Truman Papers, OF 286-A.

"I really think that we are on the right track," Truman mused a few days later. "From the sort of opposition that we are getting I am convinced that we will be doing the country a service to implement the program."[19]

The president felt this way in December 1945 and continued to feel as strongly about his program in the weeks and months that followed. While preparing his combined state of the Union and budget message scheduled for delivery in January, HST made sure that a strongly worded statement recommending enactment of national health insurance would again be sent to Congress.[20] Nor did he stop there. In March, Truman instructed the administrator of the FSA, Watson Miller, "to mobilize all the resources within the Federal Security Agency for vigorous and united action toward achieving public understanding of the need for a National Health Program."[21] "The whole matter is rather close to [the president's] heart and he wants to put steam behind it," presidential adviser Hans Klagsbrunn told an interagency staff meeting called at the White House a few days later to discuss the health program.[22] And in October, HST reiterated his determination to expand social insurance coverage to include health in a conversation with James Webb, the administration's newly appointed budget director.[23]

One cannot, therefore, attribute Truman's reluctance to speak out publicly on health care to presidential igno-

19. Truman to Robert F. Wagner, 8 December 1945, Truman Papers, PPF 2252.
20. Wielding a red pencil, the president actually restored major portions of the message's health insurance section slated originally for deletion by Judge Rosenman. "Marked Copy," Budget Message Draft, 2 January 1946, State of the Union Message folder, Rosenman Papers; Message to the Congress on the State of the Union and on the Budget for 1947, 21 January 1946, in Truman, *Public Papers, 1946*, pp. 52, 64, 83.
21. Truman to Watson B. Miller, 19 March 1946, file 031.2, box 31, FSA Administrator's Records.
22. Quoted in Harry Rosenfield to Watson Miller, March 1946, Records of the Chairman, Social Security Board, file 011.1, box 4, Record Group 47, National Archives.
23. Conference with the president, 11 October 1946, box 3, James E. Webb Papers.

rance or indifference. Rather, his hesitancy stemmed from two other factors: the dizzying succession of abrasive events confronting the White House in 1946, and Harry Truman's settled belief that he could not match Franklin Roosevelt's artistry in public oration.

Certainly 1946 was a difficult year for the new chief executive. It began with 1.5 million workers on strike in the steel, auto, electrical, and meat-packing industries; and by May the president was embroiled in a bitter confrontation with the coal and rail unions. While Truman fought to hold the line on wages, rents, and prices, insisting on the continuation of many wartime controls through the reconversion period, labor demanded fatter paychecks; farmers and industrial management agitated for bigger profits; and autoless, meatless consumers became even more restless when controls were lifted at midyear only to be followed by a severe and wild inflation. Petty or significant, imagined or real, public grievances mounted to an ever-increasing disquietude. Liberals and conservatives alike came to view Truman as an inept and temporary occupant of 1600 Pennsylvania Avenue.[24]

The president's difficulties were further compounded by his inability to defend his policies adequately, much less to promote them. Constantly compared to the charismatic, articulately suave Roosevelt, Harry Truman could not escape the gnawing reality that he lacked finesse as a public spokesman. "I may have to become an 'orator,'" he confided to paper prior to his 1948 campaign for reelection. "I heard a definition of an orator once—'He is an honest man who can communicate his views and make others believe he is right.' Wish I could do that."[25] Nor did Truman appreciate at first that what he said or did as president made news. "I dislike headline hunters," he

24. For examples of Truman's difficulties with a broad spectrum of public opinion, see Hamby, *Beyond the New Deal*, pp. 53–85; Mary H. Hinchey, "The Frustration of the New Deal Revival" (Ph.D. diss.), pp. 218–20, 227; "Truman and Labor"; Allen J. Matusow, *Farm Policies and Politics in the Truman Years*, pp. 38–78; Walter Johnson, *1600 Pennsylvania Avenue*, pp. 224–26.
25. Quoted in William Hillman, *Mr. President*, p. 118.

confessed privately, again in 1948. "It is too bad I am not a showman."[26] Although few men had entered the White House with as many personal friends among the press corps as he, the Missourian felt ill at ease in his presidential meetings with reporters. He met with the press only half as often as had his predecessor, and when Truman did hold press conferences he seldom volunteered information; nor did his curt responses to reporters' questions serve to illuminate or to educate.[27] This onetime railroad timekeeper, bank clerk, county administrator, and Senate committee chairman had made his political mark, not as an accomplished speaker, but as a quiet, efficient, and thorough administrator. Harry Truman preferred the role of director to that of actor.

And the president had ample opportunity to exercise his behind-the-scenes talents in his first year in office. "What a time I am having with some of my prima donnas," he complained to Harold Smith in early 1946.[28] The bickering that took place among his administrative officers over policy decisions, whether domestic or foreign, constantly demanded the president's attention. In the health field, as in others, Truman found himself arbitrating disputes between discordant bureaucrats. Before the April Senate hearings on his national health program (as embodied in the Wagner-Murray bill) could get underway, dissension over its scope, content, and urgency erupted, almost predictively, within the administration.

One problem arose from long-festering organizational and philosophical differences separating the Children's Bureau from the Federal Security Agency. The bureau, a product of the progressive reform movement, had been placed in the Department of Labor nearly forty years before, during the Taft administration; and, because of its

26. Ibid., p. 117.

27. Ronald T. Farrar, *Reluctant Servant: The Story of Charles G. Ross*, pp. 175–88; Elmer E. Cornwell, Jr., *Presidential Leadership of Public Opinion*, pp. 161–65; Press Conferences, 8 January–31 December 1946, in Truman, *Public Papers, 1946*.

28. Conference with the president, 31 January 1946, Harold D. Smith Papers.

special humanitarian interest in women and children, it had become a national focal point for social welfare groups and liberals in general. The Federal Security Agency, on the other hand, had been established in 1939 to administer the government's many new, depression-born public health and social security functions. Logically, proposals to transfer the Children's Bureau from the Labor Department to FSA were advanced both then and during the Second World War. But the bureau and its allies looked with horror upon a scheme that would remove it from the Labor Department, with its cabinet status, to an agency of lesser stature.[29] For more than half a decade they had successfully blocked the transfer, and it was Harry Truman's unhappy circumstance to be caught in a showdown between the two warring executive factions in 1946.

Joined to the transfer question, and complicating matters further, was the Children's Bureau's refusal to back the omnibus Wagner-Murray national health bill (S. 1606) as reintroduced in November 1945. The bureau had administered the Emergency Maternity and Infant Care Program, which had provided medical services for thousands of servicemen's dependents during the war, and it now favored a separate Senate proposal to expand these services to the population at large. Called the maternal-and-child-welfare bill and sponsored by Sen. Claude Pepper, chairman of the much-publicized Wartime Health and Education Committee, the bureau's plan enjoyed important bipartisan support. In fact, the American Medical Association had even shown a friendly disposition toward Senator Pepper. Consequently, the Children's Bureau and Pepper did not want to jeopardize their individualized welfare program by having it linked to the highly controversial and wide-ranging S. 1606.[30]

29. Committee on Public Administration Cases, "The Transfer of the Children's Bureau," pp. 17–20.

30. Agnes W. Brewster, ed., *Health Insurance and Related Proposals for Financing Personal Health Services*, p. 34; Isidore Falk to Arthur Altmeyer, 28 February 1946, Social Security General Correspondence, box 3, Wilber J. Cohen Papers; Mi-

But linked it was, for the chief architects of S. 1606 worked within the Federal Security Agency, and they did not share the bureau's narrow and specialized interest in maternal and child welfare, preferring instead to develop comprehensive welfare and health services for all age groups. Hence, the FSA insisted that title 1 of S. 1606 contain provisions for expanded health services for the general public, including maternal and child care, with the added stipulation that only those covered under title 2, the bill's health insurance section, could qualify for such specialized services. This would exclude many mothers and children not covered by social security. To add insult to injury, the national health bill also contained an administrative proviso that, if enacted, would force the Children's Bureau to direct its part of the program through a less prestigious state agency separate from the one to be utilized by the surgeon general in his administration of national health insurance.[31]

This, and other frictions within his official family, greatly troubled Harry Truman. Expecting complete loyalty from his staff, as well as efficient administration, Truman was determined to reorganize the executive process so that he could delegate responsibility and then see to it that his orders were carried out.[32] First, HST made a point to bring up in cabinet meetings any complaints that came from one cabinet member about the performance of another in the hope that it would stop what he called "this back-biting business."[33] Next, following his September 1945 twenty-one-point message, the president sent a directive to all agency heads assigning them specific re-

---

chael Davis to Samuel Rosenman, 29 June 1945, Health Message folder 2, Rosenman Papers; "Council on Medical Service and Public Relations," and "Organization Section," *Journal of the American Medical Association* (hereafter cited as *JAMA*) 127 (10 March, 21 April 1945), pp. 600–601, 1062.

31. Louis Schwellenbach and Watson Miller to the President, 15 March 1946, Truman Papers, OF 286-A.

32. Conference with the President, 4 May 1945, Smith Papers.

33. Ibid.

sponsibility for their portion of his legislative program, stating, "It is my intention that [an] agency will make the necessary studies, prepare material, assist in drafting, present testimony to Congressional committees, and in general follow the progress of the legislation in Congress."[34] The administrator of the FSA, Watson Miller, was charged with overseeing social security expansion and the enactment of the national health program. Miller, along with the others, would send the White House brief biweekly reports citing any problems faced as well as what progress had been made in the legislative effort. To coordinate this activity and to resolve interagency differences that might arise, the president instructed all agencies to work through the Office of War Mobilization and Reconstruction (OWMR), in cooperation with the Bureau of the Budget.[35]

In early March, with no time to lose before the scheduled Senate hearings commenced on S. 1606, the OWMR began policy conferences between representatives of the Children's Bureau and the Federal Security Agency.[36] By midmonth it had obtained a shaky compromise on some of the differences that divided them. Outlined in a joint memorandum to the president, Secretary of Labor Lewis Schwellenbach (speaking for his Children's Bureau) and Administrator Miller of the FSA agreed to jointly support an amended S. 1606. Provision for child and welfare services would remain in the omnibus bill, but those features, such as restricting coverage to only those entitled to social security, so adamantly opposed by the Children's Bureau, would be dropped.[37] Satisfied with the arrangement, Senator Pepper submitted the required amendment.

There was no agreement, however, on the question

34. Truman to Watson Miller, 4 October 1945, Truman Papers, OF 419-B. Similar directives went to other pertinent agencies.

35. Ibid.

36. Lewis Schwellenbach and Watson Miller to the President, 15 March 1946, Truman Papers, OF 286-A.

37. Ibid.

concerning transfer of the Children's Bureau to the Federal Security Agency. While the secretary of labor agreed to integration of administrative functions, he remained opposed to shifting the Children's Bureau to any agency not enjoying cabinet status. His solution offered two alternatives: either the elevation of the FSA to departmental status prior to its acquisition of the Children's Bureau or the Labor Department's retention of the bureau along with the establishment of a federal policy board to coordinate and direct the health program.[38]

In his reply to the joint memorandum, Truman ignored the secretary of labor's suggestion and told Schwellenbach and Miller that the method of executive unification required further study.[39] The president's decision on the transfer came six weeks later. Convinced by his own observations, as well as by Harold Smith's entreaties that administrative reorganization was essential, Truman sent congress reorganization plan no. 2; and, without warning, the Children's Bureau was slated for transfer to the FSA.[40] Under the terms of the Reorganization Act of 1945, the president's plan would become effective in sixty days if not defeated by both the House and the Senate. Ironically, the energies of women's groups from coast to coast, which would have normally been directed toward backing the Truman health program, were rallied immediately to secure a congressional veto of the reorganization plan so as to preserve the integrity of their beloved Children's Bureau.[41] Their efforts failed, however, for the bureau was transferred to the FSA in July 1946. The main loser was the cause of national health insurance.

Another problem, no less serious in magnitude, stemmed from dissension between the Public Health Service and

38. Ibid.

39. Truman to Miller and Schwellenbach, 28 March 1946, Truman Papers, OF 286-A.

40. Harold Smith to the President, 14 March 1946, Files of the Director, Office of War Mobilization and Reconversion, file 011.1, box 163, Record Group 250, National Archives; Committee on Public Administration Cases, "The Transfer of the Children's Bureau," pp. 20, 22–27.

41. *New York Times*, 13 June 1946.

the Social Security Board, both of which were located within the Federal Security Agency. Here, too, there were important differences over the health insurance proposal, the major one being the disinterested attitude of Surgeon General Thomas Parran. And herein lies an interesting paradox. Thomas Parran, the man slated to administer important aspects of the proposed social-insurance system (and because of this the target of much of the opposition's wrath) was actually decidedly cool to the president's health proposal. Even though his entire professional career had been in public health service, Parran preferred a middle-of-the-road approach to national health care. "I'm fundamentally a conservative," Parran once told Michael Davis,[42] and as such the surgeon general gave his support to programs that would provide federal subsidies for construction of medical facilities and for expanded state systems of public health care, but not for compulsory national health insurance.[43] So, despite Parran's public pronouncements in favor of the administration's omnibus health program,[44] in early 1946 the surgeon general stood somewhere in the middle between those groups who advocated the voluntary way and those, like Isidore Falk and Arthur Altmeyer of the Social Security Board, who wanted a compulsory federal insurance system.

Naturally, health security advocates maintained a suspicious attitude toward Parran. When an unfounded rumor circulated in the spring of 1944 that the surgeon general planned recommending that a commission of physicians be set up to study and make recommendations on health insurance, the president of the AFL, William Green, expressed his distrust of Parran in a letter of protest to the federal security administrator.[45] Isidore Falk was equally distrustful. When he and his staff in the So-

42. Michael M. Davis, "Surgeon General Parran . . . an Accounting," p. 360.

43. Wilson, *Compulsory Health Insurance*, p. 6; interview with Isidore Falk; Arthur Altmeyer to author, 10 April 1967.

44. *New York Times*, 19 January 1945.

45. William Green to Paul V. McNutt, 22 May 1944, file 011.4, box 49, FSA Administrator's Records.

cial Security Board drafted the sickness insurance provisions of the first Wagner-Murray-Dingell bill in 1943,
they did so without consulting the surgeon general. In
fact, although Parran was finally brought in on the preparation of the second W-M-D bill introduced in early
1945,[46] the Public Health Service was not consulted, at
least in a formal way, during the FSA's further revision
of the bill later that year.[47] Therefore, friction between
the Public Health Service and the Social Security Board
continued far into the preparatory stages of the administration's campaign for national health insurance; and,
although they later improved, relations between the two
agencies never became completely cordial while Parran
remained surgeon general.[48]

Despite the bickering and distrust that surrounded
him, Administrator Miller of the FSA responded to the
presidential directive that he undertake "a vigorous program of mobilized public understanding" of the national
health bill.[49] In March, Miller's director of information,
Zilpha Franklin, outlined an educational program so ambitious as to be "without Agency precedent." All constituent FSA units should be put in a "state of emergency,"
Franklin advised, with their information personnel
placed at the disposal of the administrator's office for the
duration of the campaign. She calculated that this would
require the drafting of eight or ten top people from FSA
units for full-time lend-lease. Above all else, interagency
cooperation would be essential, since

46. Marjorie Shearon, *Blueprint for the Nationalization of
Medicine*, pp. 21–22; Arthur Altmeyer to author, 10 April
1967.

47. FSA Assistant General Counsel Alanson W. Willcox
complained six days before introduction of S. 1606 that "The
whole bill lies at least as much in the field of the Public Health
Service as it does that of the Social Security Board. It seems to
me awkward to have such legislation drafted within the Agency
but without consultation with the PHS." Willcox to Miller,
file 011.4, box 18, FSA Administrator's Records.

48. Interview with Falk.

49. Miller to Truman, 1 April 1946, Truman Papers, OF
419-B.

This kind of campaign can't succeed on a basis of loose co-operation, however well intentioned, among people trying to maintain 'business as usual' on other fronts. It can't succeed if each interested agency tries to run an independent show of its own competing for interest and treading on each other's toes.[50]

"I know from past experience," Franklin concluded, "that there is no satisfactory middle ground, no way of doing a 'partial' or 'limited' campaign. The alternatives boil down to 'all or nothing.' "[51]

But the administrator was either unconvinced or unable to implement such an ambitious undertaking. For one thing there existed the delicate question of executive lobbying. For another, Miller was aware of the discordant effects produced by interagency dissension between the FSA and the Children's Bureau, as well as by the split between the Public Health Service and the Social Security Board. Instead, after conferring with Parran and Altmeyer, Miller directed Franklin to supervise an information program of far less scope. This program would consist of public statements in support of the president's program by those in the higher echelons of the agency. Also, rather than eight or ten people preparing material and coordinating the program, four would be assigned to the task, and then only on a part-time basis.[52] Strict guidelines of conduct were established to ward off charges of executive lobbying. Social Security Board offices in the field, for example, were instructed to continue their policy of not providing public information on pending legislation on their own initiative, but instead to furnish summaries of the W-M-D bill "as a public service" only upon request.[53]

50. Zilpha C. Franklin to Miller, 7 March 1946, file 011.4, box 18, FSA Administrator's Records.

51. Ibid.

52. These instructions were outlined in Miller to Warren F. Draper, 25 March 1946, file 011.4, box 18, FSA Administrator's Records.

53. W. Oliver Kincannon to Zilpha Franklin, 24 May 1946, file 011.4, box 18, FSA Administrator's Records.

Restraints like these did not apply to proinsurance lobbying activity conducted outside the government; so, building upon the organizational foundation of the Social Security Charter Committee formed two years earlier, Michael Davis and others incorporated on 23 February 1946 the Committee for the Nation's Health.[54] Assured of an initial working budget of around fifty thousand dollars, of which about half came from members of the Julius Rosenwald family (sponsors of the Rosenwald Fund and contributors to Michael Davis's Committee on Research in Medical Economics) and the other half came from Albert and Mary Lasker, the CNH made its public debut in late March by holding simultaneous luncheons in New York City and Washington.[55]

In 1946 the Committee for the Nation's Health was a small and select group, with Michael Davis its guiding light and with a membership of about two hundred, composed of those who had lent their names for the published endorsement of the president's health message back in December.[56] This situation did not dampen the group's enthusiasm, however, since the organization's role in 1946 was restricted primarily to lobbying efforts on the national level. This included four major functions: (1) providing technical information for sponsors of health legislation, (2) preparing and distributing promotional literature to the nation's major news media, (3) coordinating activities among those special-interest groups who already favored national health insurance, and (4), the most important task of all, winning additional support from those national groups still uncommitted to the crusade.[57]

Given the influence of powerful lobbies in America's legislative system, the CNH's need for additional allies

54. Minutes, 29 April 1946, Records of the Committee for the Nation's Health, Michael M. Davis Papers. Hereafter cited as CNH Records, Davis Papers.

55. Davis to the Executive Committee, 19 March 1946, CNH Records, Davis Papers.

56. Minutes, 29 April 1946, CNH Records, Davis Papers.

57. Minutes, 10 April 1946, Davis to the Executive Committee, 5 June 1946, CNH Records, Davis Papers.

was especially pressing. With the exception of organized labor, now rapidly losing public favor because of its post-war militancy, the Committee for the Nation's Health could, in the spring of 1946, count on the backing of only a few national splinter groups whose members represented but a fraction of the larger work force engaged in their respective fields of endeavor. In the medical profession, for instance, the CNH drew support from small groups of liberal doctors such as the one thousand-member Physicians Forum, composed mainly of academic practitioners in the East; the Committee of Physicians for the Improvement of Medical Care with thirty members, nearly all of who held teaching positions; the dissident Dentists' Committee for the Passage of the Wagner-Murray-Dingell Bill; and the National Medical Association, which represented the nation's four thousand black physicians.[58]

A similar situation prevailed outside the medical community. In industry, endorsement of S. 1606 came from only a few business leaders like the retired president of General Electric, Gerard Swope, an honorary vice-chairman of CNH. In agriculture, of the three major organizations representing the nation's farmers, only ultraliberal James Patton's National Farmers Union indicated enthusiasm for the national health bill. Then, too, there were various consumer lobbies like the National Consumer's League that favored national health insurance, with similar endorsements coming from welfare organizations, representatives of ethnic minorities like the American Jewish Congress and the National Association for the Advancement of Colored People, as well as from a newly formed liberal organization, the Union for Democratic Action.[59] Because Michael Davis and his

58. Representatives of these organizations testified in support of S. 1606. U.S., Congress, Senate, Committee on Education and Labor, *National Health Program: Hearings before the Committee on Education and Labor on S. 1606,* pp. 735, 2650, 1036, 787–88. Hereafter cited as Senate, *Hearings on S. 1606.*

59. Ibid., pp. 2682–86, 969–78, 2725–33, 500–508, 2542–44. The National Farmers' Union had sponsored America's first

colleagues on the Committee for the Nation's Health recognized that the national health movement needed much broader support in order to be successful, they developed plans in the autumn of 1946 to seek additional adherents among rural, professional, and business groups.[60]

While the newly formed Committee for the Nation's Health struggled for increased finances, new members, and public recognition, its opposition enjoyed obvious promotional advantages. Within days of the president's special health message, the National Physician's Committee released an "emergency bulletin" couched in the terse phraseology of a telegram:

ANNOUNCEMENT MADE MONDAY OF WHITE HOUSE DEMAND FOR IMMEDIATE CONGRESSIONAL ENACTMENT COMPULSORY HEALTH INSURANCE LAW. . . . . OBVIOUSLY THIS IS BEGINNING OF FINAL SHOWDOWN ON COLLECTIVIST ISSUE. NOT ONE DAY DARE BE LOST. NATIONAL PHYSICIANS COMMITTEE MUST IMMEDIATELY USE ALL FACILITIES, MEDIA, AND TECHNIQUES FOR PUBLIC EDUCATION. DO NOT UNDERESTIMATE THE CRISIS. IF YOU ARE WILLING TO FIGHT FOR PERSONAL FREEDOM AND PROFESSIONAL INDEPENDENCE SEND US EMERGENCY CONTRIBUTION OF $100, $50 OR $25 NOW TO MAKE POSSIBLE MAXIMUM NATIONWIDE EFFORTS.[61]

Of course, the NPC had long before demonstrated its ability to employ its abundant resources in a nationwide

---

cooperative prepayment medical facility organized under the direction of Dr. Michael Shadid in Elk City, Oklahoma, in 1929. See Frederick D. Mott and Milton I. Roemer, *Rural Health and Medical Care*, p. 440.

60. Davis to T. J. Woofter, 24 October 1946, General Classified Files, Federal Security Agency, file 011.4, box 18, Record Group 235, National Archives.

61. National Physician's Committee, "Emergency Bulletin," 23 November 1945, Health Message folder 1, Rosenman Papers.

effort to forestall medical reform. As of 31 October 1945 the committee's expenditures during the six years of its existence totaled nearly 1 million dollars, 90 percent of which had come from business firms manufacturing pharmaceutical and drug supplies.[62] With an annual budget admitted to be now well over two hundred thousand dollars,[63] the NPC could distribute to physicians, for display in their waiting rooms, thousands of pamphlets like *Showdown on Political Medicine*, which, in question-and-answer form, attempted to prove that title 2, the health insurance section of the new Wagner-Murray-Dingell bill, was more socialistic than anything in any country, with the possible exception of the Soviet Union.[64]

The American Medical Association also attempted to influence important segments of public opinion. First through the pages of the *Journal of the American Medical Association*, then in early December at its semiannual national meeting, association spokesmen blasted the Truman proposal as the first step in the socialization of not only American medicine but of all professions, business, and labor.[65] Although the AMA approved of title 1, the grants-in-aid section of the W-M-D bill designed to expand health services for mothers and children and for the needy, *Journal* editor Morris Fishbein argued that title 2, the health insurance section, would make doctors "clock watchers" and "slaves."[66] In like manner, the AMA House of Delegates adopted resolutions in December denouncing the president's health insurance proposal, reaffirming its support of the National Physician's Committee, and urging again that any changes in medical care delivery systems be deferred until service physicians had returned to civilian practice. The AMA delegates also re-

62. Statement by Edward H. Cary (NPC president), in Senate, *Hearings on S. 1606*, p. 862.

63. Ibid.

64. National Physician's Committee, *Showdown on Political Medicine*, inserted for the record in Senate, *Hearings on S. 1606*, pp. 867–73.

65. *New York Times*, 20, 27 November 1945; editorial, *JAMA* 129 (1 December 1945):950–53.

66. Editorial, *JAMA* 129 (1 December 1945):953.

quested that their board of trustees embark upon a public education campaign "giving the widest publicity through every available medium, a warning of what adoption of a system of federal control of the practice of medicine will mean to our fellow citizens."[67]

It would be inaccurate, however, to characterize organized medicine's response to the Truman health proposal as wholly negative. The AMA supported the Hill-Burton Hospital Construction Act of 1946; and, by endorsing a fourteen-point program for medical care in December 1945, the AMA House of Delegates had gone on record, although in vague terms, for the expansion of public health services for the indigent, for expansion of preventive medicine programs, and above all, for extension of hospitalization and sickness insurance on a voluntary basis.[68] Then in February, association officials went further by announcing the formation of its Associated Medical Care Plans, designed to promote and coordinate on the national level the private surgical Blue Shield prepayment plans sponsored and controlled by its constituent state medical societies.[69] By offering the public a unified nonprofit health insurance system while at the same time emphasizing the virtues of social and economic voluntarism in the wake of wartime regimentation, the AMA hoped to convince the nation that "a voluntary sickness insurance system developed with features peculiar to the American way of life is better for the American people than a federally controlled compulsory sickness insurance system."[70]

The Senate hearings on S. 1606, begun in early April, revealed that the American Medical Association was not

67. American Medical Association, *Digest of Official Actions, 1846–1958*, pp. 325–27.

68. Ibid., p. 325; U.S., Congress, Senate, Committee on Education and Labor, *Hospital Construction Act: Hearings before the Committee on Education and Labor on S. 191*, pp. 137–55.

69. *New York Times*, 17 February 1946; "The AMA Health Program and Prepayment Sickness Insurance Plans," *JAMA* 130 (23 February 1946):494–96.

70. Morris Fishbein, "The Public Relations of American Medicine," *JAMA* 130 (23 February 1946):511.

alone in its determination to defend voluntarism. Despite the fact that Senator Murray, as chairman of the Senate Committee on Education and Labor, used his prerogative to schedule hostile witnesses in such a way as to minimize their influence on the national health bill—by sandwiching them in the middle of the hearings agenda—the chairman's strategy backfired on the very first day. Within minutes of the sounding of the opening gavel, Murray and Republican Sen. Robert A. Taft of Ohio, a presidential hopeful and member of the committee's seven-man minority, became embroiled in a heated exchange over whether S. 1606 was, in fact, socialistic. The Ohio Republican had called the substance of Franklin Roosevelt's 1944 economic bill of rights "a combination of hooey and false promises" and had led the conservative opposition to Murray's full-employment bill, passed in greatly watered-down form the winter before.[71] Interrupting Chairman Murray's opening statement in which the Montana senator urged that witnesses refrain from using the terms *communistic* or *socialistic* when referring to the national health bill, Taft exclaimed, "I consider it socialism. It is to my mind the most socialistic measure that this Congress has ever had before it."[72] Murray's full-employment bill had come straight out of the Soviet constitution, continued Taft, and so, too, he hinted, had the national health bill. Flustered, red-faced, Murray refused to allow Taft to continue. Senator Wagner was scheduled to speak first, the chairman retorted, but Taft insisted

71. "Canning the Planners"; Stephen K. Bailey, *Congress Makes A Law*, pp. 113, 195–98.

72. Senate, *Hearings on S. 1606*, p. 47. Speaking before a medical group, Senator Taft later insisted, "It does not necessarily damn a program to call it socialization. We have long socialized primary and secondary education in the United States." But, he argued, whereas "a primary education must be compulsory . . . private schools cannot begin to do the job," medical care could and should be handled by the private sector. See speech draft "Address of Robert A. Taft to the Wayne County Medical Society," 7 October 1946, "Health-Misc-1949" folder, box 575, Robert A. Taft Papers.

that he be allowed to make an opening statement regarding plans to sponsor his own substitute health bill. When Murray would not yield, the Republican leader rose from his chair and stalked out, announcing a boycott on the rest of the committee meetings.[73] With him went any remaining hope that the W-M-D bill would attract significant Republican support.

Off to a dramatic and controversial beginning, the Senate hearings had to be extended beyond the one month originally intended by the chairman.[74] This only served the opposition, because, as the testimony of one pressure group after another soon made clear, the American Medical Association had powerful allies in its attack on S. 1606. For one, the American Hospital Association, sponsors of the rapidly expanding Blue Cross system of prepayment plans for hospital expenses, considered the Wagner-Murray bill as an opening wedge to complete federal control and operation of the nation's health system. The AHA favored, instead, government assistance to encourage enrollment in private insurance programs. The Protestant and Catholic hospital associations followed suit and expressed similar views. Opposition also came from the American Dental Association, whose president maintained that the Wagner-Murray bill (which for the first time included a dental-care section) would create "the greatest bureaucracy the world had ever known."[75]

Outside the medical profession a powerful phalanx of special-interest groups lined up to defeat the president's program. In 1944 the influential American Bar Association had made a legal analysis of the first Wagner-Murray-Dingell bill and in its report had bitterly assailed the measure's health insurance provisions. Nor did the Bar Association alter its position with the passage of time: ABA spokesman William L. Martin testified that S. 1606 was "foreign to our system of government and incom-

73. Senate, *Hearings on S. 1606*, pp. 49–52.
74. Ibid., p. 50.
75. Ibid., pp. 1689–95, 1170–74, 1786–1808, 1020–25. Quotation is from *New York Times*, 7 December 1945.

patible with the adequate protection of the liberties of the people."[76] Other organizations, like the United States Chamber of Commerce, the National Grange, and the woman's auxiliary of the American Farm Bureau Federation considered title 2 of the national health bill, with its provision for compulsory participation and for increased governmental direction in the field of public health, to be alien to the American way.[77]

To make matters doubly worse for the health sponsors, the Veterans Administration now also balked publicly on title 2 of S. 1606. Just as the Children's Bureau feared that a social-insurance scheme would diminish its stature, the VA saw in the president's proposal a threat to its growing complex of medical facilities and services for disabled veterans. Evidence of this fear had first surfaced within weeks of the president's health message when the VA's chief medical director, Maj. Gen. Paul Hawley, made a surprise appearance at the meeting that opened the AMA's fight against the health bill. As Hawley expressed it, American medicine did not need "the government to tell it how to solve its problems."[78]

Senator Murray had tried to obtain VA support prior to the hearings on S. 1606 by asking John Snyder, OWMR director, to bring the Veterans Administration in line with the administration's proposal;[79] and it appeared for a time that, with the help of the president, his efforts had succeeded. "S. 1606 parallels closely my proposals for a national health program, and I am extremely anxious for the bill to be acted on as expeditiously as possible," the president had written the VA administrator, Gen. Omar Bradley.[80] To further satisfy the VA, Truman also sent

76. *Congressional Record*, 79th Cong., 1st sess., 1945, vol. 91, pts. 11, 12, pp. A1598, A3425; Senate, *Hearings on S. 1606*, pp. 214–15.

77. Senate, *Hearings on S. 1606*, pp. 2337–42, 1639–45, 1383–84.

78. "It's Socialized Medicine, All Right, Says AMA."

79. Murray to John Snyder, 26 March 1946, file 011.4, box 18, FSA Administrator's Records.

80. Truman to Omar Bradley, 1 April 1946, Truman Papers, OF 286-A.

a letter (prepared by Bradley's office) to Chairman Murray recommending that when S. 1606 emerged from his committee it should "provide in explicit terms for the preservation of medical and hospital services under the laws administered by the Veterans Administration."[81]

But while Murray agreed to the amendment, and Bradley wrote pledging his support to the president, the general remained uncooperative. Appearing at the hearings on 3 May, the VA administrator refused to commit himself on the president's health insurance program. Complaining to Truman later, Senator Murray reported that those present had gotten the distinct impression that General Bradley believed that the health problems of America's veterans could be met solely by the Veterans Administration.[82]

Even though the president could still predict privately in early May that the administration would soon "jar something loose" from Congress,[83] political realities foreshadowed certain doom for the national health bill. There was no chance for action on the House side,[84] and the Senate hearings had only demonstrated what an explosive and unpopular issue national health insurance could be. Many factors contributed to the bill's demise: lingering executive disunity, disenchantment with Truman's leadership on the part of many liberals, mounting opposition from hostile lobbies, the public's growing antilabor sentiment generated by the rash of postwar strikes, and Tru-

81. Truman to Murray, 30 April 1946, Truman Papers, OF 286-A.

82. Bradley to Truman, 3 April 1946, Truman Papers, OF 286-A; Senate, *Hearings of S. 1606*, pp. 1590–1639; Murray to Truman, 14 May 1946, Truman Papers, OF 286-A.

83. Conference with the President, 2 May 1946, Smith Papers.

84. The House version (H.R. 4730), as introduced by Representative Dingell, had been bottled up in the Committee on Inter-State and Foreign Commerce. Its chairman, independent-minded Clarence F. Lea, Democrat from California, had sponsored the "Anti-Petrillo" bill in the spring of 1946 to curb the power of unions and was anything but an advocate of national health insurance. See *Current Biography, 1946*, p. 334.

man's reluctance to speak out on the health insurance proposal. One by one, former health reform enthusiasts backed away from the measure. Within weeks of the commencement of the Senate hearings, progressive observers noted the conspicuous absence of liberal senatorial support within the Committee on Education and Labor for the national health bill.[85] And in early May the national convention of the League of Women Voters, which had previously endorsed national health insurance by a two-thirds majority, refused to reaffirm its support, notwithstanding determined efforts by a few delegates.[86]

By mid-June the battle for S. 1606 was over. Recognizing the inevitable, Watson Miller, the FSA administrator, unceremoniously dropped the national health bill from his list of priority legislation for the Seventy-ninth Congress, and congressional health sponsors scurried to bring the Senate hearings to a close; continuation would only allow the opposition to record an ever-mounting disquisition on the alleged dangers of S. 1606. Final capitulation came on 9 July, when Senator Murray announced plans to renew efforts on behalf of the health bill during the next session of Congress, following the November elections that year.[87]

Little did Murray realize that the coming Republican-controlled Eightieth Congress would be even more intransigent on the subject of health security. As officials within the Federal Security Agency turned that autumn to revising the administration's health proposal, the American Medical Association moved toward an ever-closer alliance with Senator Taft and other leaders of the Republican opposition, an alliance that would soon pay big dividends.

The post–World War II crusade for national health insurance had gotten off to an uncertain beginning, and from the perspective of late 1946 it appeared that, for the time being, it had reached an inglorious conclusion.

85. "The Battle for the Nation's Health."
86. *New York Times*, 4 May 1946.
87. Miller to Truman, 21 June 1946, file 011.4, box 18, FSA Administrator's Records; *New York Times*, 10 July 1946.

4

A Trying Time, 1947

Following his surprise election victory in 1948, Harry Truman boasted that "the luckiest thing that ever happened to me was the Eightieth Congress."[1] Except for proadministration commitments in foreign policy, however, GOP-directed actions on Capitol Hill seemingly portended anything but good luck for the president in 1947. Passing the antilabor Taft-Hartley bill over Truman's veto, slashing executive appropriations requests, and seeking to equate national health insurance advocacy with an alleged administration-centered communist conspiracy, the Eightieth Congress established a record of defiant opposition to the Democrat in the White House. As the Republican speaker of the House, Joe Martin, later attested, the Eightieth Congress sought to function as "the people's special instrument of control over their government," an instrument determined to halt the abrogation of "its fundamental powers either to the executive or to arrogant bureaucrats."[2] By year's end, the president's domestic reform program had become embroiled in heated partisan debate, emotional in tone, vindictive in character.

Administration opponents wasted little time following the GOP congressional sweep in acknowledging the obvious. The Republican House and Senate steering committees announced in mid-November 1946 that Truman's reform recommendations, including health legislation, were not on their list for legislative action during the Eightieth Congress.[3] From the American Medical Association's viewpoint, this meant that the medical profession could now function "in a different atmosphere . . . an at-

1. Quoted in Jonathan Daniels, *The Man of Independence,* p. 22.
2. Joe Martin, *My First Fifty Years in Politics,* p. 190.
3. *New York Times,* 16 November 1946.

mosphere that approaches freedom."[4] "Physicians know the importance of unimpeded respiration for health and vitality," said Morris Fishbein. "Apparently we may—at least for the moment—breathe easier."[5]

A far different mood prevailed among advocates of medical reform. Sizing up the situation, organized labor turned to collective bargaining in 1947 to secure management-financed insurance protection against sickness and hospitalization. "There is no evidence to encourage the belief that we may look to Congress for relief," explained CIO leader Walter Reuther.[6] Although the courts did not sanction labor's right to bargain for health and welfare agreements until several years later, by 1948 Reuther's United Automobile Workers, as well as the United Steelworkers, had negotiated and won precedent-setting contracts containing health and welfare provisions.[7]

Within the private councils of the Committee for the Nation's Health, its directorate found solace only in that the CNH had been created as a bipartisan organization. Yet, even had they wanted to, Michael Davis and his associates could not deny that their group had formed for one purpose: to promote the enactment of national health insurance. With that goal impossible of attainment in the foreseeable future, the CNH Board of Directors asked itself plaintively in May 1947, "Is a committee like this required during these years to spearhead work for a national health program? Will the existence of such a committee justify itself?"[8]

Legislative prospects looked no brighter from within the Truman administration. An air of hesitancy pre-

4. "Proceedings of the Chicago Session," *Journal of the American Medical Association* (hereafter cited as *JAMA*) 132 (21 December 1946):996.

5. Editorial, *JAMA* 133 (18 January 1947):180.

6. Quoted in Frank G. Dickinson, "The Trend Toward Labor Health and Welfare Programs," *JAMA* 133 (26 April 1947):1286.

7. Raymond Munts, *Bargaining for Health*, pp. 9–12.

8. Minutes, 9 May 1947, Records of the Committee for the Nation's Health, Michael M. Davis Papers. Hereafter cited as CNH Records, Davis Papers.

vailed, especially in matters concerning social legislation. While the president instructed his cabinet members in mid-November to submit material for the 1947 state of the Union message, the Federal Security Agency waited nearly an additional month for like instructions; consequently, the FSA had only ten days in which to prepare its suggested inclusions. Congress did receive a renewed recommendation for national health insurance in each of the president's three messages in January, but in keeping with changed political circumstances, the proposal was limited in each to a few random sentences.[9] Fittingly, FSA administrator Watson Miller suggested in February that "there would be nothing lost" by discontinuing his biweekly legislative progress reports, and the president agreed that they should be terminated.[10]

Though clearly on the defensive in 1947, the Truman administration did not discard its promotion of health security, nor did the Committee for the Nation's Health move toward disbandment. Swimming against the legislative tide was nothing new for health reformers, they had been doing it for over a quarter of a century. Moreover, even in the face of certain defeat, continued advocacy of adding health insurance to social security could serve the president's program by being a valuable method of educating the general public, of holding onto support already gained, and, for political reasons, of delineating sharply Harry Truman's health program from that of the Republicans. In this latter regard, administration forces

9. Watson B. Miller to John R. Steelman, 1 December 1946, Clark Clifford to Miller, 5 December 1946, Records of the Administrator, Federal Security Agency, file o.11.1, box 16, Record Group 235, National Archives (hereafter cited as FSA Administrator's Records); Miller to Clifford, 16 December 1946, Harry S. Truman Papers, Official File (hereafter cited as OF) 419-F; Annual Message to the Congress on the State of the Union, 6 January 1947, The President's First Economic Report, 8 January 1947, Annual Budget Message, 10 January 1947, in Harry S. Truman, *The Public Papers of the Presidents of the United States, 1947*, pp. 5, 8, 37, 58, 72.

10. Miller to Steelman, 12 February 1947, Truman Papers, OF 419-B.

needed a revised omnibus health bill in 1947 to serve as a counterweight to possible enactment of an alternative and, in their view, woefully inadequate health measure sponsored by the Republican opposition.[11]

This substitute health bill had first been introduced in 1946 under the sponsorship of Republican Senators Robert Taft, H. Alexander Smith of New Jersey, and Joseph Ball of Minnesota. With the Democrats in control of the Seventy-ninth Congress, the Republican bill had received little attention, but in 1947 the situation was reversed; Senator Taft had now replaced James Murray as chairman of the Senate Committee on Labor and Public Welfare. Hence, in February, after consultation with representatives of the American Medical Association, Taft, Smith, and Ball, joined by another Republican, Sen. Forrest Donnell of Missouri, filed a new version of the Republican program (S. 545).[12]

Titled the national health bill, S. 545 offered a medical welfare system for the nation's indigent that would be financed through federal grants and administered entirely by the participating states. Also included were provisions for periodic physical examinations for schoolchildren, cancer research funds, the creation of a national health agency to unify government medical activities, and the establishment of a national institute of dental research.[13]

Liberals objected specifically to the bill's health care section. S. 545 provided treatment for only the poor, and recipients had no voice in its administration. Worse, to qualify for services one had to undergo a poverty-means

11. The positive functions of a "dead" bill are described in Bertram M. Gross, *The Legislative Struggle*, pp. 167–69. They were appreciated by the Committee for the Nation's Health. See Minutes, CNH Legislative Committee, 13 February 1947, CNH Records, Davis Papers.

12. Resolutions authorizing consultation with the GOP health sponsors were passed in 1946 by the AMA House of Delegates. See American Medical Association, *Digest of Official Actions, 1846–1958*, p. 327; James G. Burrow, *AMA, Voice of American Medicine*, pp. 348–49.

13. S. 545, 80th Cong., 1st sess.

test whereby the government would satisfy itself that the applicant was truly indigent, a demeaning requirement to social insurance enthusiasts. Taft's bill, argued Senator Murray, would establish a system of "relief medicine, through public charity, under monopolistic [AMA] control." [14] "Adequate medical services on the basis of need, not ability to pay, is the birthright of every American," added Senator Wagner. "It is a matter of right, not charity." [15]

Robert Taft defended his proposal by explaining that the "general theory" that underlay S. 545 was "that the people of the United States shall pay for medical care as they pay for food, as they pay for their clothing, as they pay for all necessities of life." Only those who could not participate in our free-enterprise system should be provided "free" medical care. They alone, insisted Taft, should be subjected to compulsory medicine, and they should "have to take it the way the State says to take it." [16]

Clinging to the proposition that only social insurance could ameliorate the nation's health needs, and determined to block the Republican "charity" program, in 1947 Wagner and Murray sponsored another in their series of comprehensive health bills. Preliminary work on the measure had begun within the Federal Security Agency soon after termination of the 1946 Senate health hearings, and by December a bill had been drafted and placed in the hands of Senator Murray. [17] "A difficult, monumental job—well done," concluded Watson Miller. [18]

Others were not so sure. Michael Davis had hoped that

14. Radio Address, 2 June 1947, box 75, James E. Murray Papers.

15. U.S., Congress, Senate, Committee on Labor and Public Welfare, *National Health Program, Hearings before the Subcommittee on Health on S. 545 . . . and S. 1320 . . .* , p. 1515. Hereafter cited as Senate, *Hearings on S. 545 and S. 1320.*

16. Ibid., p. 49; *New York Times*, 9 June 1947.

17. Harry Rosenfield to Redrafting Committee, 7 October 1946, Michael M. Davis to T. J. Woofter, 24 October 1946, James Murray to Watson Miller, 31 December 1946, file 011.4, box 18, FSA Administrator's Records.

18. Miller to Harry Rosenfield, 3 January 1946, file 011.4, box 18, FSA Administrator's Records.

title 2, the health insurance section, could be written as a separate measure. As it stood, he complained, the FSA's draft included welfare features similar to those contained in the Taft bill. The Budget Bureau, joined by Senator Murray's staff, also had reservations. Sensitive to opposition charges that the administration's health program would be directed by a governmental "health tsar," they noted not only that the revision had failed to prescribe a lay commission to direct federal responsibility in the program, but also that participation of private health groups like the Kaiser Plan on the West Coast had been greatly limited.[19]

The dissatisfaction necessitated further revision; meanwhile, attempts were made to gain wider sponsorship for the bill, both in the House and the Senate. Liberals hoped that a few Republicans might add their names to the measure. This hope failed, but the liberals did gain expanded Democratic sponsorship for their national health insurance and public health bill of 1947 (S. 1320).[20]

In final form, S. 1320 differed from earlier Wagner-Murray-Dingell bills chiefly in its deference to the "health tsar" criticism. Policy determination on the federal level would be vested in an FSA national health insurance board, advised by a council made up of professional and lay members. Other concessions included guarantees that, if they so desired, nonprofit consumer-sponsored medical cooperatives could participate in the program. There was no retreat, however, on the prepaid health care principle;

19. Michael Davis to Rosenfield, 13 January 1947, Records of the Commissioner, Social Security Administration, file 011.1, box 4, Record Group 47, National Archives; Geoffrey May to Mr. Almond, 10 January 1947, Records of the Bureau of the Budget, General Legislation folder, box 72, Record Group 51, National Archives.

20. *New York Times*, 16 February 1947; Watson Miller to John Steelman, 17 March 1947, Truman Papers, OF 419-B. Joining Wagner and Murray were Senators Claude Pepper of Florida, Glen H. Taylor of Idaho, and J. Howard McGrath of Rhode Island. Companion bills were introduced in the House by John Dingell and Emanuel Celler.

national health insurance remained the keystone feature, with, in this instance, coverage extended to encompass groups beyond the purview of social security in 1947, like farmers and the self-employed. Welfare recipients would have their premiums paid by their state welfare agencies.[21]

A conference held in Senator Murray's office in late April ironed out strategy for the bill's introduction, scheduled for 10 May. Murray's plans had to be altered, however, because word arrived that President Truman intended, for a second time, to send Congress a special presidential message on health.[22]

In a very real sense, Truman's 1947 health message marked the beginning of the president's bid for reelection. Made increasingly aware by a group of advisers that his political fortunes in 1948 depended largely upon the enunciation of a bold, clearly-defined liberal position vis-à-vis the "reactionary" Republicans on domestic affairs,[23] the president began by restating his advocacy of national health insurance. What better way to counter the highly touted GOP presidential aspirant Robert A. Taft? For, as Mary Lasker reminded Truman during a White House visit on 24 April, Senate hearings on Taft's "welfare" health bill were to open in a few weeks.[24] With the Ohioan himself directing the proceedings as Labor and Public Welfare Committee chairman, Taft's emergence as *the* national health care spokesman might be assured, that is, unless Truman seized the initiative beforehand by resubmitting his own design for making public health part of social security.

While White House aide John Steelman hurriedly pieced the message together, the president warmed to the

21. S. 1320, 80th Cong., 1st sess.

22. The meeeting is described in Davis to Rosenfield, n.d., Records of the Commissioner, Social Security Administration, file 011.1, box 4.

23. Susan M. Hartmann, *Truman and the 80th Congress*, pp. 71–72.

24. 10:00 A.M. Appointment, 24 April 1947, Presidential Appointment Book of Matthew J. Connelly, Truman Papers; Mary W. Lasker to author, 14 August 1967.

subject in early May by departing from prepared remarks given before a White House conference on fire prevention. After emphasizing that traffic and fire accidents had maimed 23 million Americans in the past year and that he wanted "those people rehabilitated and given their places back in society," Truman told the group, "I am immensely interested in the health and welfare of the people of this country. You will find that this all fits in a pattern which is covered in a health message which I sent the Congress last year."[25] Two weeks later, on 19 May 1947, two days before Taft opened his health hearings, Congress received the president's second appeal for enactment of a comprehensive health program.

"Healthy citizens constitute our greatest national resource," the message began. Reiterating recommendations made in his 1945 health message, the president stated that the heart of his total program was national health insurance. In two obvious references to Taft's bill, Truman maintained that the social security approach was necessary because "the poor are not the only ones who cannot afford adequate medical care" and furthermore contended that national health insurance would prove "far less costly and far more effective than public charity or a medical dole."[26]

On the same day that Capitol Hill received the president's communication, Democratic health sponsors filed S. 1320. "With the introduction of the National Health Insurance and Public Health Act, the legislative battle lines for 1947 are visibly drawn," proclaimed the Committee for the Nation's Health. The year's number one task for health reformers would be to "Defeat the Taft 'Health' Bill." "Fight it on the charity issue," commanded the CNH. "Fight it on the administrative issue. Fight it as a sop which doesn't provide nearly enough to accomplish even its own limited purposes."[27]

25. Address at the Opening of the Conference on Fire Prevention, 5 May 1947, in Truman, *Public Papers, 1947*, p. 234.
26. Special Message on Health and Disability Insurance, 19 May 1947, in Truman, *Public Papers, 1947*, pp. 250–52.
27. Bulletin, 12 May 1947, CNH Records, Davis Papers.

Actually, Taft's health program stood no chance for passage by the Eightieth Congress. In the absence of a serious threat from the administration, the American Medical Association, although preferring the Republican bill to S. 1320, opted contentedly for the status quo, dampening its earlier support for the GOP proposal. Senator Taft demonstrated the same attitude. On the eve of the health hearings, Taft announced that he did not expect Congress to act on any health legislation during that session. Impressed with Taft's position on S. 545, Bernard De Voto suggested in September that the Ohio Senator had sponsored the bill only to gain organized medicine's support in his quest for the presidency.[28]

For personal and political reasons, Robert Taft and his Republican colleagues were far more interested in discrediting the Truman administration's health forces in 1947 than in promoting their own health package. Especially gulling to them had been tactics employed by Democrat Sen. Claude Pepper the year before in behalf of national health insurance. Pepper, satisfied with amendments to include expanded maternal and child health care in the 1946 W-M-D bill, decided that year to reverse his Wartime Health and Education Committee's earlier middle-of-the-road position by seeing that his committee's final report endorsed the president's comprehensive health program. Faced with the prospect that a majority of the committee's nine members would refuse to go along with the change, Pepper circulated the report among the individual committe members rather than calling a meeting to consider the document. When his ploy failed—only four of the nine signed the report, with minority members Taft and H. Alexander Smith dissenting and three others abstaining because they had not been able to study its contents—Pepper undauntedly released the committee's "conclusions" with an accompanying statement claiming that the report enjoyed "bi-partisan" backing and that

28. Burrow, *AMA*, pp. 349–50; *New York Times*, 20 May 1947; Bernard De Voto, "Doctors Along the Boardwalk," p. 222.

this demonstrated "substantial support" for national health insurance.[29]

Moreover, with the 1948 presidential campaign just over the horizon, GOP leaders reasoned that their political cause could best be served by conducting an aggressive congressional probe into the Truman administration's health insurance promotion. It seemed a worthwhile and fruitful undertaking for several reasons. Under the sixteen-year reign by Democratic-controlled congresses, Democratic-appointed executive branch members had enjoyed so much immunity from congressional scrutiny that many of them must surely have ventured beyond their legitimate administrative functions into the realm of legislative salesmanship. If sufficient evidence to prove executive lobbying in behalf of Truman's health recommendations could be found, if the American people could be shown that their tax dollars had been used to influence opinion on pending legislation, public trust in Democratic presidential stewardship would diminish further. Then, too, by 1947 fears of communist subversion within government agencies had become so widespread that Truman's conservative opponents considered the "socialized medicine" "New Dealer" crowd a vulnerable and suspect group. Had not the November elections given the Republicans a mandate "to toss Communists and the New Dealer fellow-travelers out of the Truman Administration?"[30]

29. Compare U.S., Congress, Senate, Committee on Education and Labor, *Interim Report from the Subcommittee on Wartime Health and Education: Subcommittee Report No. 3 Pursuant to S. Res. 74*, pp. 20–22 with *Health Insurance, Subcommittee Report No. 5*, as reprinted in Senate, *Hearings on S. 545 and S. 1320*, pp. 1487–1514. Senator Taft's objections were stated in a letter to Pepper. See Robert A. Taft to Claude Pepper, 18 March 1946, Health 1945–1949 folder, box 574, Robert A. Taft Papers. For other GOP complaints and Pepper's reply, see *Congressional Record*, 79th Cong., 2d sess., 1946, vol. 92, pt. 8, pp. 9701–7, 9858–61.

30. Rep. Charles Halleck of Indiana, "Speech Before the Republican National Committee, April 21, 1947," p. 188. Former Sen. Robert LaFollette, Jr., a Republican from Wisconsin, expressed similar sentiments in an article appropriately titled "Turn the Light on Communism."

Had not Truman himself found it necessary, lest the Eightieth Congress do it for him, to establish the Loyalty Review Board to screen federal employees for communist connections?[31] The Republicans hoped that by associating the president's compulsory health insurance program with a communist conspiracy, they might soon control the White House as well as Capitol Hill.

"The white light of investigation has been put upon public business in order that our people may know of its operations," Sen. Homer Ferguson of the GOP informed his Michigan constituents in early May.[32] The congressional health probe began a few weeks later with a startling accusation: Executive agencies were costing the American taxpayer $75 million a year for illicit activity "in behalf of a nationwide program of socialized medicine." Consequently, an investigation would be made of the Public Health Service, the Social Security Administration, the Department of Agriculture, and the Office of Education.[33]

Conducted by the House Subcommittee on Government Publicity and Propaganda, which was headed by Forest A. Harness, an Indiana Republican, the inquiry's first revelations came on 2 July. Taking its cue from the American Medical Association, which had passed a resolution the previous December condemning Surgeon General Thomas Parran for lobbying activities,[34] the Harness subcommittee cited an identical charge against Parran;

31. A few weeks following the November 1946 elections President Truman appointed the Temporary Commission on Employee Loyalty. Its work was expanded and made permanent by Executive Order 9835, issued in March 1947. Pressure from the Republican Congress played a major role in Truman's action. See Earl Latham, *The Communist Controversy in Washington*, pp. 365–67.

32. Homer Ferguson, "Radio Address."

33. *New York Times*, 28 May 1947. Accusations arising from the investigation became the subject of two *Reader's Digest* articles. See Christian A. Herter, "Our Most Dangerous Lobby," pp. 5–10, and Forest A. Harness, "Our Most Dangerous Lobby —II."

34. American Medical Association, *Digest of Official Actions, 1846–1958*, p. 328.

the surgeon general had exerted "extra-ordinary executive pressure" upon public health officers in order to assure their promotion of national health insurance. As proof, the Harness report revealed that on 10 December 1945 Parran had sent a copy of the president's first special health message to public health officials in the field accompanied by a letter that stated, "Every officer of the Public Health Service will wish to familiarize himself with the President's message and will be guided by its provisions when making any public statement likely to be interpreted as representing the official views of the Public Health Service."[35]

The subcommittee's second accusation concerned the purpose behind a series of public health workshops held the previous year, sponsored by the Public Health Service and private groups such as the National Farmers Union and labor affiliates, and designed supposedly to stimulate discussions on general public health needs and existing services. In reality, claimed the Harness report, PHS consultants had gone beyond providing technical assistance and had, at government expense, instructed workshop delegates in the techniques of group leadership and political action so as "to generate public sentiment in behalf of what certain witnesses and authors of propaganda refer to as socialized medicine."[36]

The evidence? Instructional materials used by government participants during a workshop held in Jamestown, North Dakota, on 27–30 September 1946 included proinsurance publications by the Physicians Forum, labor unions, and the Committee for the Nation's Health. Also, in its hearings, the Harness subcommittee had taken substantiating testimony from an official of the North Dakota State Medical Association who had attended the workshop as an uninvited observer.[37]

35. First Intermediate Report of the Subcommittee of the Committee on Expenditures in the Executive Departments. . . . submitted for the record, Senate, *Hearings on S. 545 and S. 1320*, p. 1197.

36. Ibid.

37. Ibid.; U.S., Congress, House, Committee on Expendi-

There had been executive lobbying, but the evidence did not support the Harness group's final, irresponsible judgment. Its report ended with the "firm conclusion" that "American communism holds this [health] program as a cardinal point in its objectives; and that, in some instances, known Communists and fellow-travelers within Federal agencies are at work diligently with Federal funds in furtherance of the Moscow party line in this regard."[38]

The subcommittee's entire case rested upon the background of one employee on Isidore Falk's staff within the Social Security Administration. This individual had been cited earlier by the House Committee on Un-American Activities for association with communist-front and fellow-traveler organizations and had written a laudatory account of socialized medicine in New Zealand. Without warning, Chairman Harness raised the issue on the House floor two weeks prior to the report's appearance. Naming the employee in question, the congressman charged that the Social Security Administration was about to send the suspected Communist on another New Zealand junket to continue his studies of socialized medicine. Responding to Harness's charges, Administrator Miller of the Federal Security Agency called off the individual's planned trip, ordered an agency investigation into his background, requested the FBI to do likewise, and informed Harness that pending further evidence the employee would be retained. Later, on the basis of the FBI investigation, the FSA's Board of Inquiry on Employee Loyalty dismissed the charges, and the employee kept his job.[39]

Allegations that communists directed the health reform

---

tures in the Executive Departments, *Investigation of the Participation of Federal Officials in the Formation and Operation of Health Workshops: Hearings before the Subcommittee on Publicity and Propaganda*, pp. 97–98, 108–20.

38. First Intermediate Report, in Senate, *Hearings on S. 545 and S. 1320*, p. 1200.

39. *Congressional Record*, 80th Cong., 1st sess., 1947, vol. 93, pt. 6, p. 7098; Watson Miller to Forest A. Harness, 11 July 1947, Isidore Falk to H. Alexander Smith, 29 March 1948, both submitted for the record in Senate, *Hearings on S. 545 and S. 1320*, pp. 1925–26, 1921–22.

movement did not stop with the Harness subcommittee; they became constant fare during Senator Taft's hearings, begun in May, on S. 545 and S. 1320. On the opening day, in an angry exchange reminiscent of the one with Senator Murray the year before, Chairman Taft let it be known that "under present conditions" the Republicans were in charge and that the hearings would be conducted in a manner that best served their needs. "You had your case; we have our case," said Taft.[40] To build that case, the GOP staff allotted the first four weeks to twenty-nine witnesses friendly to Taft's bill and hostile to Murray's S. 1320. After they had had their say, included mysteriously among those witnesses scheduled to testify in behalf of S. 1320 was a representative of the International Workers Order, a well-known Communist organization. Support from such quarters could only prove detrimental to the health security movement; and, although the Republican leadership pleaded innocent to charges that it had known beforehand about the Communist's background, the tone of the GOP questioning demonstrated otherwise.[41]

From this time forward, the health hearings became an inquisition into the formulation and promotion of the "socialized medicine" bill rather than an investigation into the relative merits of the two legislative proposals at hand. By invariably questioning proadministration witnesses about their political motives, personal acquaintances, and group affiliations, the chief GOP interrogator, Sen. Forrest Donnell of Missouri, acted as if he were uncovering a sinister plot against the American way of life. When Albert Lasker appeared in behalf of S. 1320, for example, Donnell went to such lengths to find out about circumstances surrounding Lasker's attendance at a dinner sponsored by the Committee for the Nation's Health that the retired advertising tycoon agreed jokingly to reveal "the whole dark conspiracy, right in the limelight."[42]

Inquiry of this sort seemed far less humorous to Mi-

40. Senate, *Hearings on S. 545 and S. 1320*, p. 45.
41. Ibid., pp. 1037–76.
42. Ibid., p. 1454.

chael Davis. When Davis testified, Donnell's line of questioning turned quickly to a discussion of Davis's associations with Isidore Falk and others in government. Also, the senator wanted such minute details about the membership of the Committee for the Nation's Health that Davis snapped, "I am not sure whether your questions in connection with these lists [of names] are an inquiry or implied indictment."[43] Finally, in an attempt to link Davis and the CNH with communists, Donnell revealed that CNH had supplied material to a communist-front film company that had been used in a filmstrip advocating national health insurance. Because CNH had not investigated the film company's background before providing the requested information, the committee found itself accused of collaboration with subversive elements.[44]

The Committee for the Nation's Health reacted to the charges of communism by taking steps to insulate itself from further criticism. In October, upon the suggestion of an indignant Michael Davis, the executive committee of CNH adopted the following resolution:

> RESOLVED: That the officers of the Committee for the Nation's Health be instructed not to supply bulletins or other material containing legislative information and advice to organizations which are likely to use it against our purposes and to organizations which in the judgment of the officers are associated with the Communist party or led by members of that party.[45]

By this action, the CNH hoped to ward off further accusations.

Exhaustive interrogation of unfriendly witnesses came naturally to Forrest Donnell, an intensely partisan Republican legislator with a legalistic outlook and bitter memories of past political battles with Democrats in his

43. Ibid., p. 1623.
44. Ibid., pp. 1655–76.
45. Minutes, Executive Committee Meeting, 27 October 1947, CNH Records, Davis Papers.

home state of Missouri.[46] But the general thrust and direction of Donnell's interrogation must be attributed largely to the influence of GOP staff "health consultant" Dr. Marjorie Shearon.

Marjorie Shearon held a doctorate in biology and until January 1945 had spent nine years as an employee in the Federal Security Agency, five on Isidore Falk's staff and four on the staff of the Public Health Service. While working in the Bureau of Research and Statistics, Dr. Shearon had developed a deep antipathy toward her boss, Bureau Director Isidore Falk, and upon her departure from government service set about to expose Falk as the mastermind of a subversive plot to nationalize American medicine.[47]

A prolific writer on the subject of national health insurance, Shearon began a series of news releases in early 1946 to inform the medical profession on matters of social legislation. By August of that year, she had branched out to offer her legislative reference services to other groups fighting "socialized medicine."[48] Best known among Shearon's many offerings was a pamphlet entitled *Blueprint for the Nationalization of Medicine*. First printed and sold in January 1947, this forty-one-page exposé claimed that Isidore Falk controlled and directed from within the Social Security Administration a vast conspiracy to nationalize American medicine; a detailed chart graphically outlined spheres of influence and interlocking directorates allegedly emanating from "THE HOUSE

46. Donnell had won the Missouri gubernatorial election in 1940, but the Democrat-dominated Missouri general assembly refused to certify Donnell's election victory. It required a ruling by the state supreme court to seat him. See "Forrest C. Donnell," *Current Biography, 1949*; Paul F. Healy, "The Senate's Big Itch," pp. 36–37.

47. Senate, *Hearings on S. 545 and S. 1320*, pp. 2217, 2731; interview with Isidore Falk.

48. Marjorie Shearon, "Research Material and Professional Services Available to Medical Associations, Chambers of Commerce, and other groups Seeking Information About Plans to Nationalize Medicine," 9 August 1946. A copy of this announcement is in Health Insurance folder, Robert F. Wagner Papers.

OF FALK."[49] Later Shearon distributed a limited number of these charts, which in cold-war rhetoric labeled all national health insurance proponents, including President Truman, "Collaborationists, Fellow-Travelers, Appeasers, Satellites, and Gullible Accepters."[50]

Senator Taft and his GOP colleagues considered Marjorie Shearon's services a political asset. Upon Taft's recommendation, Shearon became research analyst for the Republican Senate Minority Conference in early 1944; and, assigned to Senator Donnell during both the 1946 and 1947 Senate health hearings, she provided Donnell charts and documents with which to interrogate witnesses.[51]

Shearon also assisted the Harness subcommittee. In one of her news releases, issued before the subcommittee had publicly announced its plans to investigate the propaganda activities of the executive branch, Shearon informed her readers:

> At long last there is to be a congressional investigation of several situations in the FSA. The House Committee on Expenditures in the Executive Departments has just set up a Subcommittee on Publicity and Propaganda in such departments. My Blueprint is to be made the basis of the first investigation. Obviously I can be of some real service in this connection.[52]

In August 1947, Shearon reported another bit of startling information:

49. Marjorie Shearon, *Blueprint for the Nationalization of Medicine.* See also, Senate, *Hearings on S. 545 and S. 1320,* p. 2219.

50. Submitted for the record, Senate, *Hearings on S. 545 and S. 1320,* pp. 2803–4.

51. "Senator Donnell and I plug along getting the stuff in the record," Marjorie Shearon wrote Senator Taft in mid-1947. See Shearon to Taft, 3 July 1947, Health and Social Security Legislation folder, box 576, Taft Papers. See also "Invisible Congress: Marjorie Shearon"; *St. Louis Post Dispatch,* 26 April 1946.

52. Marjorie Shearon, News Release, 9 May 1947. Submitted for the record, Senate, *Hearings on S. 545 and S. 1320,* p. 42.

Confidential, for subscribers only—Not to be shown to anyone else. Not to be released to the press. This story will not
"break" for several days. The leads are mine, but the follow-
up investigation has been done by the Harness subcommittee, and I do not wish to steal their thunder. I am sending
this in the hope that some of you may be in position to act
before August 28.

Social security mission to Japan.—Over 2 weeks ago I gave to
Frank T. Bow, of the Harness subcommittee, the information which enabled him to expose the grandiose plans of
Altmeyer, Cohen, and Miss Mulliner (Senator Wagner's pro-
tégé) to socialize medicine in Japan, and to foist a WMD bill
on the defenseless Japanese. It is a brazen scheme which has
been in the making since the end of last year. The War Department has been sucked in. Falk plans; Altmeyer gives
official sanction and accepts leadership of the mission to
Japan; Cohen and Miss Mulliner execute the plans; the
public pays the freight.[53]

These charges and those subsequently leveled by the
Harness subcommittee enraged the health security forces.
The allegation that communists were actively promoting
national health insurance within the federal government
was "a base calumny and a damnable lie," exclaimed
Senator Pepper.[54] And Senator Murray protested, "I
think we are running into a great danger in this country.
It is becoming so that anyone who sponsors a measure for
the benefit of the people of this country is immediately
jumped upon and accused of being a Communist."[55]

To blunt the attack, Murray and Pepper repeatedly
inserted copies of Shearon's publications into the record
hoping that they would serve to discredit the GOP assistant; the results were mixed, however. In May, because
she had published partisan materials while serving on
the staff of the Labor and Public Welfare Committee,
Murray obtained Shearon's dismissal as committee re-

53. Shearon, News Release, 20 August 1947, submitted for
the record, Senate, *Hearings on S. 545 and S. 1320*, p. 1999.
54. Senate, *Hearings on S. 545 and S. 1320*, p. 1194.
55. Ibid., p. 1404.

110

search consultant; but she continued in the employ of the Republican National Committee and merely took on a new role as part-time consultant to Senator Taft and full-time assistant to Senator Donnell.[56] Senator Murray's protests notwithstanding, Shearon remained at Donnell's side throughout the hearings, providing him materials with which to interrogate witnesses.

By the end of July, the cumulative effect of Shearon's publications, the Harness charges, and Senator Donnell's line of questioning forced Isidore Falk to appear at the hearings to defend his activities and those of the Bureau of Research and Statistics. Falk began by citing examples of faulty documentation in Shearon's *Blueprint for the Nationalization of Medicine*. He also produced memorandums from the files of the Social Security Administration that showed that Marjorie Shearon had completely reversed herself on the subject of compulsory health insurance since leaving Falk's staff. These memorandums, written by Shearon in 1938, demonstrated that at that time the GOP health consultant had been extremely unhappy because the bureau's projected draft of the 1939 Wagner health bill did not contain a national system of compulsory health insurance. Even more interesting were Shearon's earlier views on proposals, similar to Taft's S. 545, to provide health care for only the poor; objections to the poverty-means test as a prerequisite to medical care permeated Shearon's 1938 memorandums.[57]

The health hearings recessed until January 1948, at which time Isidore Falk returned to answer the Shearon-Harness charges that the Social Security Administration planned to send a mission to socialize the medical system of Japan. Such an objective was hardly possible, explained Falk, since Japan had initiated a national health insurance system in 1926. Furthermore, Falk produced a cable

56. Ibid., pp. 2222–23; Shearon to Taft, 23 May 1947, Health and Social Security Legislation, 1946–47 folder, box 576, Taft Papers.

57. Shearon to Falk, 2 November 1938, miscellaneous memorandums, 12–14 November 1938, submitted for the record, Senate, *Hearings on S. 545 and S. 1320*, pp. 1807–26.

from Gen. Douglas MacArthur requesting that the mission be sent to Japan.[58]

The controversy over executive lobbying and communist subversion then shifted to a new, and for Isidore Falk and his Bureau of Research and Statistics staff a far more important, arena: the House and Senate appropriations subcommittees. The subcommittees could have slashed the bureau's appropriations to the bone; but after hearing testimony from Harness and Shearon, the chairman of each gave Falk and his bureau a clean bill of health. Chairman Frank Keefe of the House subcommittee, a Republican from Wisconsin, stated, "I am fully aware of the fact that it is very easy to throw about and bandy the word 'Communist' as a term to hang onto any individual with whom you might be in economic disagreement."[59] As to sending missions abroad to study other systems of social legislation, Keefe defended the practice.[60] The chairman of the Senate Appropriations Subcommittee, Sen. William Knowland of the GOP, concurred. Knowledge of foreign systems of social insurance had been most helpful to the California legislature when it considered passage of unemployment insurance, reflected Knowland.[61]

The verbal support did not, however, prevent the Republicans from cutting the president's 1949 budget request for Falk's bureau. In its report filed in April 1948, the House committee appropriated less than 50 percent of the funds requested, explaining that the bureau's development of social-insurance statistics and materials had reached a sufficient level and it therefore no longer needed

58. Ibid., p. 2011; cable from Gen. Douglas MacArthur to the War Department, 31 August 1947, submitted for the record, Senate, *Hearings on S. 545 and S. 1320*, p. 1999.

59. U.S., Congress, House, Committee on Appropriations, *The Supplemental Federal Security Agency Appropriation Bill for 1949: Hearings before the Subcommittee on Appropriations*, p. 535.

60. Ibid., pp. 520–21.

61. U.S., Congress, Senate, Committee on Appropriations, *Supplemental Federal Security Appropriation Bill for 1949: Hearings before the Subcommittee on Appropriations*, p. 277.

a large staff. The Senate committee restored a portion of the cut, making the bureau's fiscal 1949 appropriation 65 percent of their original request; because the Senate's restoration came after Marjorie Shearon had asked the appropriations subcommittee to abolish the Bureau of Research and Statistics, Falk and his associates could consider themselves vindicated, at least partially.[62]

Far more vituperation than reasoned judgment had nevertheless been injected into the debate over national health care. There is no question that Isidore Falk and other FSA officials had long desired national health insurance, had drafted and revised the Wagner-Murray-Dingell bills for the sponsors, and had promoted the measures in numerous ways. Still, the decision to make national health insurance a part of the administration's program had come from Harry Truman, not from the FSA. The president had instructed Administrator Watson Miller of the FSA in March 1946 to "mobilize all the resources within the FSA for vigorous and united action directed toward achieving public understanding of the need for a National Health Program."[63] So long as executive officials are responsible to the president, who in turn has the constitutional authority to recommend and promote legislation, one must conclude with political scientist Bertrum Gross that, short of a constitutional amendment, "there seems to be no formal procedure for limiting executive influence upon the legislative process."[64]

How did Harry Truman react to the Republican fusillade in 1947? He ignored it, choosing to remain aloof while building his platform for the presidential election campaign that lay ahead. In June, the president again outlined his domestic reform aspirations in a talk before war veterans in Kansas City. "A healthy citizenry is the

62. U.S., Congress, House, Committee on Appropriations, *House Report 1821*; U.S., Congress, Senate, Committee on Appropriations, *Senate Report 1444*, p. 12.

63. Truman to Watson B. Miller, 19 March 1946, file 031.2, box 31, FSA Administrator's Records.

64. Gross, *The Legislative Struggle*, p. 433.

most important element in our national strength," he said. "We must develop a national health program which will furnish adequate public health services, and ample medical care and facilities for all areas of the country and all groups of our people."[65] In August, when vetoing a bill to exclude newspaper vendors from the social security system, Truman exhorted, "We must not open our social security structure to piece-meal attack and to slow undermining. We must, instead, devote our energies to expanding and strengthening that system."[66]

More significant for the health movement, the president made two key appointments in 1947. The first came in August when Oscar R. Ewing, an astute and aggressive politician, replaced Watson Miller as administrator of the FSA. While still in high school, Ewing had already become the secretary of the Decatur County Democratic Committee in his home state of Indiana, and since 1940 he had served intermittently as chairman and vice-chairman of the Democratic National Committee.[67] Soon after the Republicans gained control of Congress, Ewing embarked upon the scheme that earned him the epithet "The mastermind of President Truman's [1948] campaign strategy."[68] At Ewing's suggestion, a group composed of six or eight top Democrats close to the president organized to steer Truman upon a course of liberal action in preparation for the 1948 election campaign.[69] "We wanted to create a set of goals," later explained group member and presidential assistant Clark Clifford, "and

65. Address in Kansas City at the 35th Division Reunion Memorial Service, 7 June 1947, in Truman, *Public Papers, 1947*, p. 269.

66. Memorandum of Disapproval of Bill to Exclude Newspaper and Magazine Vendors From the Social Security Act, in Truman, *Public Papers, 1947*, pp. 371–72.

67. Oscar R. Ewing to author, 9 May 1967; *Current Biography, 1948*, p. 194.

68. Tris Coffin, *New York Post Magazine*, 15 April 1948. Clipping contained in newspaper scrapbook, Oscar R. Ewing Papers.

69. Hartmann, *Truman and the 80th Congress*, pp. 71–72; Cabell Phillips, *The Truman Presidency*, pp. 162–65.

we wanted to build a liberal, forward-moving program around those goals that could be recognized as a *Truman* program."[70]

With Ewing's ascension to the FSA post, promotion of the president's health program took top priority. He quickly established close liaison with the Committee for the Nation's Health because, political considerations aside, the committee's objectives harmonized with Ewing's own social philosophy. After working his way through the Indiana University and the Harvard Law School, Truman's new appointee had seriously considered becoming a social worker; but because his application for a social-work position was denied, Ewing had stuck to the law and, following World War I, had become very wealthy as a law partner with Charles Evans Hughes and with Hughes's son.[71]

Harry Truman's second 1947 appointment that pleased health reformers came in October when the president selected his former solicitor general, Sen. J. Howard McGrath of Rhode Island, to be chairman of the Democratic National Committee. First coming to the Senate in January, by March, McGrath had agreed to cosponsor the revised W-M-D bill. He also worked closely with the Committee for the Nation's Health, appearing alongside Michael Davis in June to debate the health issue opposite the president of the AMA and Senator Taft on the national radio program "American Forum of the Air."[72]

Besides this, the junior senator from Rhode Island gave the health security movement a rare moment of

70. Phillips, *Truman Presidency*, p. 164.

71. In October, Ewing solicited Michael Davis's views on 1948 legislative strategy; and, in early November, Davis represented the CNH at a strategy meeting called by Ewing. Davis to Ewing, 17 October 1947, FSA Report, "Informal Conference on National Health Insurance," 6 November 1947, file 011.4, box 49, FSA Administrator's Records; Thomas Devine, "For the Record."

72. Margaret Stein to J. Howard McGrath, 21 March 1947, and reprint, "American Forum of the Air," 3 June 1947, National Health Insurance folder, box 32, J. Howard McGrath Papers.

exultation during the bleak days of the Taft-Donnell-Harness inquisition. In July, McGrath announced that Raymond Rich Associates, a public-relations firm engaged the year before by the American Medical Association to study its public image and to make recommendations for improvement, had resigned in protest against AMA intransigence. The firm broke with the AMA because,

> Stated simply, the association has yet to take unequivocal and effective action on the policies which it adopted on our recommendation last year: to seek the truth on the economic and social aspects of medicine, to put the public first, and to become adequate in its responsibilities.[73]

For the AMA, McGrath's revelation proved embarrassing; for the Committee for the Nation's Health, the senator's zeal indicated further that the new Democratic National Committee chairman would work to make promotion of governmental health insurance an integral part of the Democrats' 1948 campaign. With J. Howard McGrath at the helm of Democratic party politics, affirmed *U.S. News* in November, "the direction of the [1948] campaign is moved into the Senate wing of the capitol. . . . Legislative strategy and campaign strategy can be fashioned together."[74]

GOP leaders of the Eightieth Congress dealt harshly with the proponents of national health insurance in 1947; but, by year's end, the Committee for the Nation's Health had influential friends ensconced securely within the Democratic party's national directorate and had done much to prove that it could be of great help in the fight for a national health insurance program.

73. Telegram, Raymond Rich Associates to Speaker, AMA House of Delegates, 12 June 1947, submitted for the record, Senate, *Hearings on S. 545 and S. 1320*, p. 1518. See also, Burrow, *AMA*, 334n.

74. "Methods of Democratic Chief McGrath," p. 58.

5

Politics and Health: The 1948 Presidential Campaign

In late 1947, on the eve of the second session of the Eightieth Congress, Sen. Robert A. Taft publicly challenged the Democrats to make compulsory health insurance an issue in the forthcoming national election campaign.[1] Taft, hopeful that the Republicans would make him their presidential nominee in 1948 and confident that the health issue would help insure the political defeat of Harry S. Truman, could hardly have imagined the remarkable turn of events that followed his challenge. The Republican party shattered a tradition that had stood since its birth almost a century before by renominating a once-defeated candidate, Gov. Thomas E. Dewey of New York, thus dashing Taft's presidential hopes. Harry Truman compounded Taft's political despair by not only making compulsory national health insurance an issue in the campaign, but by also using it as a prime example of the failure of the "do nothing" Republican Eightieth Congress to enact his domestic reform program. In the process, Truman outmaneuvered all of his political foes on the Left and the Right and won his uphill battle for the presidency.

Several months before Taft's challenge on the health issue, influential Democrats decided that Truman might even gain some political advantage in 1948 by declaring battle with the Republicans over the health needs of the nation. "The issue is real and an excellent one politically. It is ready-made. It has great and easily mobilized popular appeal," J. Howard McGrath and other S. 1320 sponsors had written Gael Sullivan, executive director of the Democratic National Committee, the previous summer. At the same time, the sponsors conceded that their bill would

1. *New York Times*, 26 December 1947.

have to be revised in order to make it "more politically appealing, more popularly worded."[2]

Statesman and Wall Street financier Bernard Baruch unknowingly set the pattern for the W-M-D bill's revision when in November 1947 he told a medical society group of his support for a national system of voluntary health insurance for those in the high-income groups and of compulsory insurance under social security for those in the low-income ranks.[3] The Baruch suggestions were a compromise; if incorporated into a new Democratic health package, they promised expanded backing among businessmen, as well as possible sponsorship from at least some of the conservative southern Democrats on the Hill who had previously refused to endorse the president's program. "Mr. Baruch's speech provides a springboard which can and will be utilized by both progressives and middle-of-the-roaders as a base for winning support for practicable national health legislation," urged Michael Davis in early December.[4] By Christmas, Sen. James Murray had contacted Alben Barkley, Lister Hill, George Russell, and other members of the powerful Democratic southern senatorial contingent, suggesting that they join him in constructing a substitute health bill, a measure with which they could all live, one that would guarantee a united Democratic stance on public health in 1948.[5]

Soon organized labor fell into line with Baruch's plan; indeed, labor agreed to additional concessions. Writing to Senators Wagner and Murray in February, President William Green of the AFL recommended the introduc-

2. Senators Robert F. Wagner, James E. Murray, J. Howard McGrath, Dennis Chavez, Glen Taylor, and Claude Pepper to Gael Sullivan, 28 July 1947, National Health Insurance folder, box 38, J. Howard McGrath Papers.

3. *New York Times*, 20 November 1947.

4. Michael M. Davis to Executive Committee, 1 December 1947, Records of the Committee for the Nation's Health, Michael M. Davis Papers. Hereafter cited as CNH Records, Davis Papers.

5. James E. Murray to Alben Barkley, Lister Hill, Richard Russell, John Sparkman, and Olin Johnston, 19 December 1947, Health Insurance folder, box 65, James E. Murray Papers.

tion of a packet of separate Democratic health bills, including a "simpler" insurance measure with restricted coverage. Citizens earning above five thousand dollars a year, "whom doctors want to retain as luxury-income, strictly private practice patients" would be exempt from compulsory social-insurance protection. Moreover, to further assure expanded Democratic support, Green agreed that because rural areas lacked sufficient medical facilities and personnel, farmers and their families should also be excluded; a separate health bill could be introduced to meet these rural deficiencies.[6]

While Senator Murray made arrangements to meet with Bernard Baruch to sound him out further on the subject, Administrator Oscar Ewing of the FSA organized a national health conference for the spring of 1948 to focus public attention on the health issue. FSA staff discussions on the advisability of recommending a presidential commission to study national health goals had been going on since mid-1946; with Ewing's appearance on the scene, they moved from the speculative stage to the concrete.[7]

Election-year political considerations dominated Oscar Ewing's thinking. "There is no chance of getting a [health] bill through this year," Ewing told the director of the Bureau of the Budget, James Webb, in February. "I am interested in getting something in (for political reasons) . . . , and to talk to him [the president] about it."[8] Specifically, the FSA administrator outlined his objectives in a memo to the White House: "Problems of the Nation's health and the President's proposals for dealing with them are of major importance, not only in terms of national welfare, but also of the coming campaign. On both counts it is important to focus public attention on

6. William Green to Robert F. Wagner and James Murray, 13 February 1948, box 65, Murray Papers.

7. Murray to Bernard M. Baruch, 25 February 1948, and "Plan for Conference on National Health Goals," 12 June 1946, Murray Papers.

8. Memo on telephone conversation with Oscar Ewing, 25 February 1948, Federal Security folder, box 10, James E. Webb Papers.

the question involved and to emphasize the President's interest in finding answers to them." First, the president should send Congress another special health message containing a section placing "particular stress" upon "the differences between his program and Senator Taft's." Second, the president should announce a few days later his decision to hold a national health conference to formulate national health goals. And, finally, one week should be designated by presidential proclamation as citizen's health week, during which time each community would inventory its health needs.[9]

Save for the national health conference idea, Harry Truman ignored Ewing's proposals. Because the administration wanted the American Medical Association and its allies to participate in the planned health meeting, another presidential message, coupled with a call for a community health survey, might be construed as evidence that the president had prejudged the national health assembly's conclusions. Furthermore, Truman's three annual messages sent to Congress in January had already contained renewed and forceful appeals for "a national system of payment for medical care." Then, too, with legislative strategy on revision of the Democrat's omnibus health bill still in a state of flux in early 1948, the White House could not, with certainty, take a strong position on the matter.[10]

Instead, the president instructed Oscar Ewing to embark upon a comprehensive study of national health needs and then to report on ways to remedy those needs. Faced with an economy-minded, antiadministration, Re-

9. "Tentative Proposals for Focusing Public Attention on the Health Issue," FSA Memorandum, n.d., Files of Clark Clifford, Harry S. Truman Papers.
10. The administration announced in January that it anticipated meeting with the AMA in 1948 to work on problem areas in which the two sides were in agreement. See *New York Times*, 29 January 1948. See also State of the Union Message, 7 January 1948, Annual Budget Message, 12 January 1948, and The President's Economic Report, 14 January 1948, in Harry S. Truman, *The Public Papers of the Presidents of the United States, 1948*, pp. 3, 21, 23, 25, 34, 68, 88.

publican-controlled Congress, Ewing arranged for the incorporation in February of a private organization to sponsor the conference; called the National Health Assembly, this organization raised forty-five thousand dollars in contributions from philanthropic sources. Attended by nearly eight hundred invited delegates representing consumer groups, organized labor, farm organizations, and the medical profession, the National Health Assembly began its deliberations in Washington in May.[11]

Beforehand, the American Medical Association feared that the assembly would turn out to be, like the National Health Conference of 1938, the administration's "sounding board" for a radical medical program. When the assembly adjourned, however, the AMA expressed pleasant surprise at the outcome. Of the assembly's fourteen panel-discussion sections, the panel of greatest concern to organized medicine had naturally been the one dealing with the distribution and costs of medical care. The AMA had been outnumbered on the medical-care section's planning committee, but to its delight the group's final report did not contain an endorsement of national health insurance. In fact, motivated by the prevailing spirit of compromise, the AMA's representatives agreed to sign the panel's concluding statement, thereby committing the association to several new positions: they agreed (1) that health insurance (although voluntary) should be the basic method of financing medical care and (2) that existing state laws (passed earlier at the instigation of medical societies) prohibiting nonmedical groups from organizing voluntary health insurance plans should be removed. Also, although the AMA House of Delegates later rescinded the action,

11. Harry S. Truman to the Administrator, Federal Security Agency, on Raising the Level of the Nation's Health, 30 January 1948, in Truman, *Public Papers, 1948*, pp. 117–18. The story of the incorporation of the National Health Assembly and subsequent developments are outlined in U.S., Congress, Senate, Committee on Labor and Public Welfare, *National Health Program: Hearings before the Subcommittee on Health on S. 545 . . . and S. 1320 . . .* , pp. 2400–2420.

one of the points agreed upon by the AMA's delegates contained an implied condemnation of the poverty-means test, the core feature of the Taft health bill.[12]

Michael Davis considered the AMA's concessions to be significant, to have brought a "real advance" to the cause of health security. Moreover, in June, the Committee for the Nation's Health learned that Oscar Ewing intended to go beyond the health assembly's recommendations by publicly advising the president that only national health insurance could solve the nation's health needs.[13]

Nevertheless, for Davis and the CNH, the AMA concessions and the promised Ewing announcement were more than offset by a number of disturbing developments. By early April it had become apparent that plans to revise S. 1320 in order to obtain expanded Democratic sponsorship in Congress were doomed. The president's special message on civil rights sent to the Hill in early February —the first such presidential declaration since Reconstruction—had caused a major break between the administration and the southern Democrats. The civil rights issue, which led ultimately to the Dixiecrat revolt that election year, made it impossible to obtain southern sponsors for a new packet of health bills. "No one representing the White House (nor Senator McGrath) could approach Southern Senators on this matter," Michael Davis commented gloomily.[14] As a result, Senator Murray and the others scrapped their Baruch-inspired compromise

12. Editorial, *Journal of the American Medical Association* (hereafter cited as *JAMA*) 136 (6 March 1948):694. An account of the activities of the section on medical care, including its membership and conclusions, is contained in National Health Assembly, *America's Health: A Report to the Nation*, pp. 191–234. For the AMA's concessions, see *New York Times*, 5 May 1948; "Health and Harmony," p. 60; Michael M. Davis, "Who Will Pay the Costs?," p. 93; American Medical Association, *Digest of Official Actions, 1846–1958*, pp. 330–31.

13. Davis to the Executive Committee, 6 May 1948, and Minutes, Executive Committee Meeting, 29 June 1948, CNH Records, Davis Papers.

14. Davis to the Executive Committee, 6 April 1948, CNH Records, Davis Papers.

scheme, deciding to stick with their omnibus and controversial S. 1320 in 1948.[15]

The next blow came a few days after the close of the National Health Assembly with the release of a health care study by the Brooking's Institution entitled *The Issue of Compulsory Health Insurance*. Coauthored by medical administrator George W. Bachman and insurance expert Lewis Meriam, the investigation had been undertaken at the request of GOP Sen. H. Alexander Smith, Robert Taft's colleague on the Senate Labor and Public Welfare Committee. Statistical analysis had convinced them, wrote the authors, that the selective-service statistics long used to prove low health levels among the nation's youth were not a reliable index, that on the contrary most Americans enjoyed an exceptionally high level of medical care. As for compulsory health insurance, it would require too much government regulation and control, would inject politics into the relationship between physician and patient, and would increase, not decrease, the overall cost of medical care. Even if a compulsory health insurance system was established, warned Bachman and Meriam, complete health coverage could not be made readily available because the nation lacked sufficient medical personnel and treatment facilities.[16]

The reformers quickly denounced the Brooking's report by pointing out factual errors and earlier biases on the part of the authors;[17] but because the study had been conducted and published under the aegis of a private,

15. Minutes, Executive Committee Meeting, 20 April 1948, CNH Records, Davis Papers.

16. George W. Bachman and Lewis Meriam, *The Issue of Compulsory Health Insurance*, pp. 67–70.

17. Michael Davis and Dewey Anderson, director of the Public Affairs Institute in Washington, prepared a thirty-one-page rebuttal at the request of Senators Murray and Pepper. It was printed as a committee print of the Senate Committee on Labor and Public Welfare. Over six hundred reprints were then distributed to the news media by the Committee for the Nation's Health. A copy is on file in the CNH Records, Davis Papers. See also Frederick Robin to the Executive Committee, 2 August 1948, CNH Records, Davis Papers.

prestigious research organization, its conclusions granted organized medicine still another strong indictment against national health insurance.

Finally, the Committee for the Nation's Health failed to obtain the inclusion of the words *health insurance* in the Democratic party's national campaign platform, which was drafted and adopted in July during the party's convention in Philadelphia. The CNH had tried without success the month before to secure a strong health plank in the Republican platform, but given the president's continued interest in the subject, plus CNH's close ties with the chairman of the Democratic National Committee, J. Howard McGrath, a specific platform reference to the administration's insurance program by the Democrats seemed assured. Leaving nothing to chance, Michael Davis conferred with McGrath on the matter in early June; when the convention's platform committee opened its hearings a few weeks later, CNH board member Morris Llewellyn Cook, former head of the Rural Electrification Administration, along with leaders of the CIO and the AFL, appeared to present nearly identical requests for the platform committee's specific endorsement of the health insurance idea.[18]

For a time their efforts succeeded; the first four drafts of the committee's plank on domestic policy contained the words *health insurance*.[19] But then something happened. On the night of 13 July, the president received an urgent telegraphic appeal from Senator Murray:

OMISSION OF PHRASE QUOTE HEALTH INSURANCE UNQUOTE FROM PLATFORM PLANK ON

18. "Suggested Platform Plank on National Health," 16 June 1948, presented before the Republican Platform Committee by Mrs. Gardner Cowles in behalf of the Committee for the Nation's Health, Channing Frothingham to Henry Cabot Lodge, 16 June 1948, Davis to the Executive Committee, 18 June 1948, "Health of the Nation," presented before the Democratic Platform Committee by Morris Llewellyn Cook, 8 July 1948, CNH Records, Davis Papers; *New York Times*, 9, 10 July 1948.
19. "Draft of Platform," Convention Agenda folder, box 62, McGrath Papers.

HEALTH CONSTITUTES A SERIOUS BLOW TO
CAMPAIGN EFFORTS OF THOSE OF US WHO HAVE
SPONSORED LEGISLATION TO CARRY OUT YOUR
PROGRAM RESPECTFULLY REQUEST YOUR IMME-
DIATE INFLUENCE TO PLACE PHRASE IN PLANK.[20]

To further spur Truman to action, Murray added,
"WARREN'S COMMITMENT TO HEALTH INSUR-
ANCE RENDERS IT ESSENTIAL,"[21] a pointed re-
minder that Earl Warren, the Republican vice-presidential candidate, had since 1945 also fought for government-
sponsored health insurance on the state level as governor
of California.

But the president did not intercede with the platform
committee. In 1948 the Democratic party pledged itself
only to the enactment of "a national health program for
expanded medical research, medical education, and hospitals and clinics."[22] Perhaps Murray's telegram arrived
too late. The White House received it at 8:13 P.M., and
by noon the next day the fifty-five-hundred-word platform was before the whole convention. More likely, the
president and his advisers considered it unwise to force
Democrats on the local level to run on an issue that had
become so controversial; the administration backtracked
in the same way on the civil rights issue, seeing to it that
the platform went to the floor with an ambiguous civil
rights commitment designed to forestall an already ru-
mored rupture on the party's southern wing.[23]

One thing is certain. After the thirty-seven-year-old
mayor of Minneapolis, Hubert Humphrey, a U.S. senatorial candidate, settled the civil rights question by leading a successful floor fight for inclusion of a no-compro-
mise civil rights plank in the platform (precipitating as
well the long-feared southern bolt from the party), Harry

20. James E. Murray to Harry S. Truman, 13 July 1948,
Truman Papers, Official File (hereafter cited as OF) 299-C.
21. Ibid.
22. Kirk H. Porter and Donald B. Johnson, eds., *National
Party Platforms, 1840–1956*, p. 433.
23. *New York Times*, 14 July 1948; Irwin Ross, *The Loneliest Campaign*, p. 117.

Truman more than made up for the *health insurance* deletion in his nomination acceptance speech. Directing his wrath against "that worst 80th Congress," the president enumerated his many requests for economic stabilization and domestic reform defeated by the Republicans. Alluding to the Republican party's national platform ratified in their convention two weeks before ("They promised to do in that platform a lot of things I have been asking them to do that they refused to do when they had the power") and insisting that he had a duty to use his executive powers to "get the laws that people need," Truman announced that eleven days later, on 26 July—better known as Turnip Day back home in Missouri —he would call the Eightieth Congress back into special session. He would ask the Republicans to pass pending legislation to, among other things, curb inflation, alleviate the postwar housing shortage, provide federal aid to education, establish a national health program, and, now that the southern revolt had materialized, guarantee civil rights to all Americans.[24]

Oscar Ewing, and several other of the president's political advisers, had opposed the Turnip Day session;[25] now that Truman had decided to go ahead with it, representatives of Ewing's agency and the Budget Bureau met to consider whether the special session of Congress should be asked to vote on national health insurance. They concluded, "It would be unrealistic to recommend action on health insurance, in view of the fact that it has not been reported to [the floor of] either House, and that one House has not even held hearings on it."[26] "It is a close question as to whether we should include a request for health legislation at this session," observed the president's special counsel, Clark Clifford, the same day. "There is

24. Address in Philadelphia Upon Accepting the Nomination of the Democratic National Convention, 15 July 1948, in Truman, *Public Papers, 1948*, pp. 406–10.

25. Ross, *The Loneliest Campaign*, p. 130.

26. Frederich J. Lawton and D. E. Bell, "Memorandum on Health Legislation," 21 July 1948, Frederich J. Lawton Papers.

still a great deal of difference of opinion as to how far we should go."[27]

To ask the Eightieth Congress to pass, in two weeks time, an explosive measure that the president's own party had itself avoided during its many years of dominance on Capitol Hill was indeed unrealistic. But for political reasons Harry Truman decided to include the request for health insurance anyway. What did he have to lose? Public opinion polls forecast almost certain defeat for him in November, and his party's conservative southern wing had denounced him. Truman's only chance for reelection rested in his ability to check the leftist appeal of former New Dealer Henry Wallace's Progressive party candidacy; to win that year his advisers had told him that he would have to gain the allegiance of four major voting blocs: the farmer, labor, the Negro, and the consumer.[28] The promise of national health insurance held appeal for all, except for the conservative elements of the rural population.

The special congressional session began on 27 July with an opening address from the president. "High prices are not taking 'time off' for the election," he said, nor could the nation longer endure an acute housing shortage. Immediate action on his anti-inflation and housing programs was essential; and, although Congress should "not be distracted from these central purposes," if it found time it should enact a number of other measures recommended earlier by the administration. Number one on the list was "a comprehensive health program, based on health insurance."[29] The Eightieth Congress's refusal to pass Truman's sweeping recommendations, including the Democrats' national health bill, became a major theme during the president's campaign for reelection.

27. Clifford to Mary Lasker, 20 July 1948, Files of Clark Clifford, Truman Papers.

28. Cabell Phillips, *The Truman Presidency*, p. 198; Jules Abels, *Out of the Jaws of Victory*, p. 165.

29. Message to the Special Session of the 80th Congress, 27 July 1948, in Truman, *Public Papers, 1948*, pp. 416–21.

Just before the president left Washington in early September aboard his specially equipped railroad car, the Ferdinand Magellan, to launch his campaign in Detroit with an aggressively partisan Labor Day address, he released Oscar Ewing's report on national health goals, *The Nation's Health—A Ten Year Program*. Giving the report a big buildup at his 2 September news conference ("This report is an impressive document. . . . I heartily commend this report to every citizen who looks forward to these goals"), Truman called upon the next Congress to act upon Oscar Ewing's recommendations to provide:

1. Adequate public health services, including an expanded maternal and child health program.
2. Additional medical research and medical education.
3. More hospitals and more doctors—in every area of the country where they are needed.
4. Insurance against the costs of medical care.
5. Protection against loss of earnings during illness.[30]

Ewing's position on health insurance departed radically from the National Health Assembly's position. While acknowledging that the assembly had not recommended health insurance through social security, Ewing stated, "I have re-examined the whole matter as objectively as possible . . . , and I still find myself compelled to recommend it." Each year, he claimed, 325,000 needless deaths occurred because of the lack of proper medical attention due to high costs. Private, voluntary insurance plans covered less than 10 percent of the nation's populace; the only solution was a system of national health insurance.[31]

Ewing's report had been ready for some weeks;[32] by

30. News Conference, 2 September 1948, in Truman, *Public Papers, 1948*, pp. 457–58.
31. Oscar R. Ewing, *The Nation's Health—A Ten-Year Program*, pp. x, xi, 75–114.
32. The CNH had expected the report to be released as early as June. Presidential press secretary Charles Ross was informed of its completion in early August. CNH Press Release, 1 June 1948, CNH Records, Davis Papers; John Thurston to Charles Ross, 4 August 1948, Truman Papers, OF 103.

releasing it on the eve of his campaign for reelection, Harry Truman saw that the document had as much political effect as possible. When the Ferdinand Magellan pulled out of Washington's Union Station on the afternoon of 5 September, a copy of *The Nation's Health* was included among the president's speechmaking materials.[33]

Truman's advocacy of health security in the campaign had been anticipated by remarks he had made in a speech the previous June. Addressing the Los Angeles Press Club while on a fourteen-day "nonpolitical" preconvention tour of the West, a tour taken ostensibly so that the president could receive an honorary degree from the University of California, Truman complained about Congress's failure to enact his health insurance program. The Republican Congress had had plenty of time to study and debate the issue, he said, yet they had done nothing about it. "Now the health of this Nation is the foundation on which the Nation is built. I have made a personal study of that situation. We have got a health and accident situation in this country that is the most disgraceful of any country in the world." There were only two classes of people who could get proper medical attention, insisted the president, "the indigent and the very rich"; and something had to be done to solve the cost problem for "the ordinary fellow who gets from $2,400 to $5,000 a year."[34]

Truman expanded upon this theme after the campaign had formally begun. In September, returning to California, where the supporters of Henry Wallace threatened to throw the state into the Republican camp, the president told a Los Angeles audience, "We worked out a painstaking plan for national medical care. . . . It provided for new hospitals, clinics, health centers, research,

33. The Ewing report was the subject of Truman's entire speech at Rochester, Minnesota, home of the famous Mayo Clinic, on 14 October. Rear Platform Remarks at Rochester, Minnesota, 14 October 1948, in Truman, *Public Papers, 1948*, pp. 777–79.

34. Address Before the Greater Los Angeles Press Club, 14 June 1948, in Truman, *Public Papers, 1948*, p. 351.

and a system of national health insurance. Who opposed it? The well-organized medical lobby. Who killed it? The Republican 80th 'do-nothing' Congress." HST ended his talk with an appeal to the Wallacites: "To these liberals I would say in all sincerity: Think again." The communists run the Progressive party, and it has no chance to gain national power. A vote for Wallace is a wasted vote. "A vote for the third party can only weaken the efforts of the Democratic Party to build a healthy nation and a peaceful world."[35]

Later, talking over a national radio hookup from Indianapolis, Truman emphasized that his health insurance plan was not revolutionary; it was simply a better way to pay for medical care, it was "100 percent American." Then, striking a familiar note, Truman shifted to the offensive.

"What did the Republicans do with my proposal for health insurance? You can guess that one. They did nothing! All they said was—'Sorry. We can't do that. The medical lobby says its un-American.' And they listened to the lobbies in the Congress."

"I put it up to you. Is it un-American to visit the sick, aid the afflicted, or comfort the dying? I thought that was simple Christianity."

"Does cancer care about political parties? Does infantile paralysis concern itself with income? Of course it doesn't."

"The Democratic Party holds that the people are entitled to the best available medical care. We hold that they have a right to ask their Government to help them get it."[36]

The president varied his pitch on the health insurance issue throughout the remainder of the campaign, but one thing remained constant: The Republicans had deprived

35. Address at Gilmore Stadium at Los Angeles, 23 September 1948, in Truman, *Public Papers, 1948*, pp. 557, 558–59. For the threat posed by Henry Wallace in California, see Ross, *The Loneliest Campaign*, pp. 68, 189, 215.

36. Address in Indianapolis, 15 October 1948, in Truman, *Public Papers, 1948*, p. 805.

the nation of a highly essential national health program in the past; and, if restored to power, they would do so again in the future.[37]

All the while, the GOP presidential candidate, Thomas E. Dewey, remained aloof, refusing to counter Truman's statements on health or the president's other oftentimes exaggerated charges against the Eightieth Congress. In February, before the New York governor had won the GOP presidential nomination, Dewey had bitterly assailed those who wanted to "relegate the business of curing sick people to the dead level of government mediocrity."[38] But during the campaign Dewey could not speak out against a government-sponsored health insurance system without calling attention to the conflicting and well-publicized position advocated by his liberal running mate, Gov. Earl Warren of California. Republican strategy dictated a policy of harmony and unity, forcing Dewey to remain silent on the health insurance issue.[39] And it seemed equally ill-advised to respond to the other issues emphasized by Truman. Confident of victory, painfully aware of the negative consequences of his hard-hitting campaign against Roosevelt in 1944, and unwilling to defend (much less to criticize) the actions of a Congress controlled by his own political party, Dewey chose to speak of unity, unity of party and nation.[40]

In Truman's case, inclusion of the health insurance issue in the campaign followed closely the overall strategy outlined earlier by Clifford, Ewing, and McGrath. Also,

37. In addition to national radio audiences, local crowds in Ohio, Minnesota, Wisconsin, West Virginia, Pennsylvania, Indiana, Massachusetts, New York, and Missouri were told that the Republicans, if restored to power, would continue to block passage of a national health bill. See Truman, *Public Papers, 1948*, pp. 727, 777–78, 786, 810, 838–39, 856, 881, 912, 938.

38. *New York Times*, 21 February 1948.

39. In June, *Look* magazine ran an article written by Warren in which the liberal California governor outlined his long-standing recommendations for a state-sponsored health insurance system. Earl Warren, "My Plan for Health Insurance."

40. Abels, *Out of the Jaws of Victory*, pp. 191–94; Ross, *The Loneliest Campaign*, pp. 157–59.

the Committee for the Nation's Health enjoyed direct access to Truman's campaign speeches through the president's chief speech writer, Clark Clifford. In mid-1946 Clifford, a nephew of the crusading *St. Louis Post-Dispatch* editor Clark McAdams, had replaced Samuel Rosenman as the president's special counsel. By 1948, Mary Lasker had become friendly with Clifford, and from June to mid-October that year Lasker sent the president's assistant a steady flow of CNH fact sheets on health care and speech materials for use in the campaign. She also asked Clifford to contact Senator Murray's office to obtain additional speech material on health from Murray's assistant, former CNH officer William Reidy.[41]

Yet, Harry Truman cannot be depicted as putty in the hands of a few close and influential advisers in 1948. Nor were his campaign statements on health security motivated solely by the dictates of election-year political strategy. Truman's responses to three isolated incidents in 1947 and 1948 best reveal the president's true feelings on the subject.

In early May 1947, a short time before Congress received the president's second special message on health, two high-ranking AMA officials called at the White House to invite the president to attend the AMA's Atlantic City convention in June. The convention would be a memorable affair, they said, since it marked the AMA's centennial celebration. Truman declined their invitation to attend, but he did promise to send an appropriate message to the gathering.[42] The Federal Security Agency prepared a draft of the message and sent it to the White House. Pencil in hand, the president pored

41. Clifford, Mary Lasker, and their friend Washington socialite Florence Mahoney often dined together. On one occasion, Clifford jokingly referred to their get-togethers as "our exclusive club." Clifford to Lasker, 21 October 1948, Lasker to Clifford, 28 June, 8, 9 July, 31 August, 19 October 1948, in Files of Clark Clifford, Truman Papers.

42. 11:15 A.M. Appointment, 8 May 1947, Presidential Appointment Book of Matthew Connelly, Truman Papers; Mary Switzer to Charles Ross, 29 May 1947, Handwriting of the President folder, Charles G. Ross Papers.

over the FSA draft, slashing out those passages that ran counter to his own thinking about the AMA. "I have my doubts," he wrote in the margin after deleting a passage that credited the AMA for elevating American medical education to world supremacy and for assuring citizens "a high quality of professional care." Truman also objected to giving the AMA credit for promoting scientific advancement and to statements that implied that governmental social programs should always place their emphasis upon voluntary effort, upon "citizen leadership." When he had finished, HST dashed off a marginal note to his press secretary, Charles Ross: "Charlie, there are some good thoughts in this—some not so good. Let's save the good ones."[43] Little remained to save, however; Harry Truman had deleted more than half the text! The remainder, a generalized statement of congratulations, went out to the AMA by night letter on 10 June.[44]

In sum, Truman's hatchet job on the FSA draft indicates that by 1947 organized medicine's attacks upon the president, his official family, and his health program had enraged the chief executive. Indeed, the Missourian developed such an intense dislike for the editor of the *Journal of the American Medical Association*, Morris Fishbein, that fourteen years later the former president, after making sure that his longtime secretary Rose Conway was beyond earshot, described Fishbein's editorializing in pungent language.[45] Also, when in July 1947 an official of the Oklahoma State Medical Association wrote to chide Truman that his health proposals were "Bismarkian business" and that the president did not qualify to "determine the future of medicine," HST, in a rare personal reply to such a letter, shot back, "It is perfectly

43. "Draft Message from the President to the Centennial of the American Medical Association," Handwriting of the President folder, Ross Papers.

44. "Telegram From White House," *JAMA* 134 (28 June 1947):805–6.

45. Truman told the author that he considered Fishbein's editorial attacks upon himself and his staff unfit to print. He went on to describe Fishbein in terms at least equally unprintable. Interview with Harry S. Truman.

apparent that you are not familiar with the Public Health Program advocated by the Administration. I am sorry that you haven't taken the trouble to enlighten yourself on the subject."[46] Given Truman's attitude toward organized medicine, it is little wonder that, as the AMA delegates gathered for their centennial celebration in Atlantic City, the president, halfway across the continent in Kansas City, was telling his old wartime buddies of the 35th Artillery Division, "We must develop a national health program which will furnish adequate public health services, and ample medical care and facilities for all areas of the country and all groups of our people."[47]

The second incident relating to Truman's thinking on health care occurred in connection with the National Health Assembly in May 1948. Oscar Ewing had written to presidential secretary Matthew Connelly in March to inquire if the president would attend the opening session of the assembly and address the delegates. "I am sure that we can make a draft of a speech that will be extremely effective," Ewing urged. "It can be one of his major speeches this spring."[48] Truman agreed to attend "and say a few words";[49] and the FSA staff, along with White House assistant Charles Murphy, went to work on the president's speech. Their labors were wasted, however; the president addressed the gathering without the aid of a speech draft. Truman knew that when reading from a prepared text his speech delivery lacked appeal; and, anticipating the presidential campaign, his political advisers had urged him to practice speaking extemporaneously.[50] The president's speech to the National

46. Lewis J. Moorman to Truman, 7 July 1947, Truman to Moorman, 16 July 1947, Truman Papers, OF 286-A.

47. Address in Kansas City at the 35th Division Reunion Memorial Service, 7 June 1947, in Truman, *Public Papers, 1947*, p. 269.

48. Ewing to Connelly, 12 March 1948, Truman Papers, OF 103.

49. Connelly to Ewing, 19 March 1948, Truman Papers, OF 103.

50. Copies of the unused speech drafts and relevant memorandums are in the National Health Assembly Dinner folder,

Health Assembly represented a major test in this regard.

The result was a long, disjointed, yet highly effective presentation. Medical care is "something which is closer to my heart than any other one thing in the world except peace in the world," the president began. Recalling how as a young artillery officer thirty years before he had been troubled by the large number of young men found physically disqualified for military service and how the high draft-rejection rate during World War II had further alarmed him, Truman told the assembly delegates that this was one of the reasons he had asked for a universal military training program in 1945. As a former army officer, and as a man who rose early every morning to take a brisk walk to stay in physical shape, Truman deplored the fact that a high percentage of Americans were physically unfit:

> You know, the [*sic*] most of us, the reason we are not physically fit is because we are too lazy to take care of ourselves. We sit down and wait until this paunch comes on, and when we get bent over, then we try to correct it by heroic methods; and 9 times out of 10, if you go along and do what you ought to, in the first place, you wouldn't have that situation.
>
> What I want to do is to have the medical men and the health plant of this country to keep people healthy, not to cure them after they get sick, or after they get beyond the point where they can be cured.[51]

How did the president hope to achieve this goal? His words reveal an attitude of militant paternalism.

> You have got to educate young people. You have got to tell them how to take care of themselves. You have got to tell them what to do in certain emergencies, and you have got to have a medical profession and a hospital organization program that can meet that situation, and that the people can afford to pay for. We have got two things to do in this

---

Charles S. Murphy Papers. See also, Jack Redding, *Inside the Democratic Party*, pp. 50–53.

51. Remarks at the National Health Assembly Dinner, 1 May 1948, in Truman, *Public Papers, 1948*, pp. 239–41.

health program. We have got to improve our technical skill —improve our knowledge; and then we have got to find an economic program that will help us to make use of that information.[52]

The president cited examples of how diseases that plagued American soldiers in the Spanish-American War and the Second World War were now being conquered and of how man had advanced in knowledge and longevity since the days of Caesar. Urging the conferees to come up with a ten-year program to accelerate man's progress against disease, Truman concluded:

> It is a crime that 33 1/3 per cent of our young men are not physically fit for service. Let us see if we can't meet that situation. Let us see if we can't remedy it. I know we can.
> We have met everything else in this mechanical age. Now let us see if we can't make the greatest machine—the machine that God made—work as he intended it.[53]

Before he began his assembly speech, the president had remarked to Mary Lasker, who sat next to him and who had told him that she was looking forward to hearing his talk, "Oh, I'm a dub at speaking!"[54] Afterward, in the privacy of the White House, a more confident Harry Truman confided to paper, "Attend a health meeting and speak extemporaneously. Seemed to go over big."[55]

Finally, Truman's activities on the health front during the summer and fall of 1948 were not confined to political speechmaking. While the pollsters were forecasting his certain defeat in November, HST took time out from his busy campaign schedule to seek a long-range accom-

52. Ibid., p. 242. Truman displayed the same militant paternalism in late 1961 when the author asked his views about the need for social insurance to pay hospital expenses for the aged. People will never lay aside enough money for a rainy day, he said, unless you force them to do it through a payroll tax of some kind. Interview with Truman.

53. Remarks at the National Health Assembly Dinner, in Truman, *Public Papers, 1948*, p. 243.

54. Mary W. Lasker to author, 14 August 1967.

55. Quoted in William Hillman, *Mr. President*, p. 135.

modation with the nation's hospital associations, which
were a key link in organized medicine's phalanx of opposition to his national health program. Although on
record against national health insurance, the American
Hospital Association, along with other hospital groups,
had historically been far less intransigent on the subject
of prepaid health care than had the American Medical
Association. Hospital administrators, on fixed salaries
and largely dependent upon public funds for their operations, lacked the long tradition of unrestrained enterprise that characterized private medical practitioners.
Consequently, since 1933, the American Hospital Association had helped promote the creation and expansion of
nonprofit, private medical insurance plans; by 1940 its
Blue Cross hospital insurance system had become well
established.[56] Government health insurance advocates had
long hoped for a rapprochement with the hospital groups.
There were signs that 1948 might be the year for such an
understanding.

In June, John Connorton, the executive secretary of
the Greater New York Hospital Association, approached
White House secretary Matthew Connelly to suggest that
Truman meet with the president of the American Hospital Association in the hope that "an atmosphere of cooperation" might be established between the administration and the AHA. Connelly turned to Oscar Ewing for
advice; and, in August, Harry Truman agreed to meet
with the presidents of the three major hospital groups—
the AHA, the Protestant Hospital Association, and the
Catholic Hospital Association.[57] Beforehand, Truman
wrote to the president of the AHA, Graham Davis, to assure him, "Nothing I have in mind or in the recommen-

56. Franz Goldmann, *Voluntary Medical Care Insurance in
the United States*, pp. 62–63; Nathan Sinai, Odin W. Anderson,
and Melvin L. Dollar, *Health Insurance in the United States*,
pp. 26–28.

57. John Connorton to Matthew Connelly, 25 June 1948,
Connelly to Ewing, 29 June 1948, Truman to Graham L. Davis,
19 August 1948, Truman Papers, President's Personal File
(hereafter cited as PPF) 172-A.

dations I have made to the Congress looking toward a National Health Program would interfere in any way with the 3,000 or more of our voluntary hospitals which supply so large a part of the hospital care for our people."[58] These assurances were repeated when, on 13 September, the president met with the hospital leaders. Hospitals would remain just as free under his social insurance plan, said Truman, as the banks had remained under the federal reserve system. To continue the dialogue, Truman suggested that the three national hospital representatives form a committee to meet with Oscar Ewing and iron out their differences with the administration.[59]

Later, Truman received word that the hospital groups had agreed to follow his suggestion, they would soon meet with Ewing "to discuss health insurance" and would keep the president posted on the developments.[60] The hospital leaders met with Ewing in December 1948 and twice in the summer of 1949.[61] Of course, if the president had been defeated in November, as so many had predicted, it would have been a far different story.

Truman's meeting with the hospital leaders in September was based upon the assumption that he and his federal security administrator would be around to promote national health insurance for some time to come. When over 24 million voters cast their ballots for Harry Truman in November, making possible the greatest political upset in American history, the president's prophecy came true. By promoting the idea of national health insurance during the campaign, the president had provided

58. Truman to Davis, 19 August 1948, Truman Papers, PPF 172-A.

59. Connelly to Connorton, 1 September 1948, Truman Papers, PPF 2856; 11:30 A.M. Appointment, 13 September 1948, Presidential Appointment Book of Matthew J. Connelly, Truman Papers; "White House Conference."

60. Graham Davis to Truman, 15 September 1948, Truman Papers, PPF 2856.

61. John Hayes, John Barrett, and John Martin to Truman, 21 July 1949, Truman Papers, OF 286-A; Oscar R. Ewing to author, 9 May 1947.

health reformers with an immeasurable amount of free publicity. By winning, Truman and his party had given them much more: the anticipation that health security would be moved to the forefront of domestic debate in 1949.

6

A Testing Time, 1949

During his last major campaign appearance of 1948, Harry Truman promised that a national health insurance program would soon be legislated, "because the Democrats are going back in power, and we are going to see that we get it."[1] Although the president's party did capture control of Congress in the election, and Harry Truman did retain the presidency, it was a promise the president could not keep. Responding quickly to Truman's surprise victory in November, lushly financed and powerfully influential forces moved to block passage of the president's comprehensive health security scheme. Conducting one of the most wide-ranging and imaginative lobbying efforts in the nation's history, the American Medical Association transformed the *socialized medicine issue*, as it had become almost universally labeled by the end of 1949, into a political liability for its proadministration sponsors.

Public interest in health security reached a postwar high during the early months of 1949. In the first five weeks of the new year, the Federal Security Agency received inquiries about health insurance from twenty-seven of the nation's leading periodicals and newspapers. This resulted from the confluence of two major developments: the recent initiation of national health service in Great Britain and the recognition that the president, fresh from victory in November, intended to push again for his social-insurance scheme in Congress. Discussion of one development frequently led to comment on the other, with most of it decidedly critical. "Good Medicine Doesn't Mean Socialism," insisted *Collier's* in March; in April, *U.S. News* criticized the high cost of Truman's program

1. Address at Keil Auditorium, St. Louis, 30 October 1948, in Harry S. Truman, *The Public Papers of the Presidents of the United States, 1948*, p. 938.

in "Free Medicine, How Much?," and a *Reader's Digest* article demanded, "Shouldn't Doctors Have Rights Too?" The month of May saw more of the same with *Life* editorializing against "Health by Compulsion," *Collier's* arguing "Medicine and Politics Don't Mix," *Newsweek* indignantly asking, "What Price the Welfare State?," and the *Saturday Evening Post*, after running two critical articles on the British health system, admonishing its readers in a third, "Do you Really Want Socialized Medicine?"[2]

The issue was aired on radio as well. In January, the NBC "Round Table" discussion broadcast from the University of Chicago considered the subject, as did the ABC debate program "Town Meeting of the Air" the following month. In March, radio commentator Fulton Lewis, Jr., accused Oscar Ewing, the administrator of the FSA, of already enjoying free medical care at the taxpayers' expense at a government hospital. And in April, CBS news analyst Elmo Roper devoted one of his Sunday afternoon broadcasts to the health question. By March, the Federal Security Agency had received so many letters from the public on the subject that for the first time it became necessary to use form letters in reply.[3]

2. Zilpha Franklin to John Thurston, 10 February 1949, Records of the Administrator, Federal Security Agency, file 011.4, box 7, Record Group 235, National Archives (hereafter cited as FSA Administrator's Records); *New York Times*, 30 November 1948; William L. Chenery, "Good Medicine Doesn't Mean Socialism"; "Free Medicine, How Much?"; Henry J. Taylor, "Shouldn't Doctors Have Rights Too?"; "Health by Compulsion"; "Medicine and Politics Don't Mix"; "What Price the Welfare State?"; Steven M. Spencer, "How Britain Likes Socialized Medicine"; Steven M. Spencer, "How British Doctors Like Socialized Medicine"; Steven M. Spencer, "Do You Really Want Socialized Medicine?"

3. University of Chicago, "Should We Adopt Compulsory Health Insurance?"; "Should We Adopt a Compulsory National Health Insurance Program?" Letters regarding the Fulton Lewis broadcast are in the file by that name, Harry S. Truman Papers, Official File (hereafter cited as OF) 7; Elmo Roper, "Where the People Stand," reprint of CBS Radio Broadcast, 17 April 1949, Records of the Committee for the Nation's

Writing to Oscar Ewing the previous December, a friend had wished the FSA director "a very Merry Christmas and a New Year in which the AMA war cry turns to a plea for peace."[4] But rather than seek an accommodation with the administration in 1949, the American Medical Association mobilized the most ambitious lobbying effort of the post–World War II era. Stunned by the president's reelection, the AMA Board of Trustees vowed to exhaust the association's treasury, if need be, to prevent passage of Truman's health insurance scheme. To do battle, the AMA leadership made a special twenty-five-dollar assessment upon each of its members in December to build up a "political war chest," hired the services of a high-powered public relations agency to conduct its campaign, and maneuvered to replace the National Physician's Committee as organized medicine's major militant political action group.[5]

By early 1949, the National Physician's Committee had become more of a liability than an asset to the AMA. The year before, the NPC had received a great deal of adverse publicity by sponsoring a contest to entice cartoonists to draw and print cartoons attacking "socialized medicine." Rules of the contest, in which three thousand dollars in cash awards was offered, required participating cartoonists to submit already-published cartoons depicting "the meaning and implications of political distribution of health care services in the United States." So that interested cartoonists might know just what kind of a portrayal would be expected by the NPC judges, the contest an-

---

Health, Michael M. Davis Papers (hereafter cited as CNH Records, Davis Papers); Harvey Bush to Ruth Thorne and William Martin, 10 March 1949, file 011.4, box 7, FSA Administrator's Records.

4. Mary Harrington to Oscar Ewing, 18 December 1948, file 011.4, box 18, FSA Administrator's Records.

5. "Proceedings of the St. Louis Interim Session," *Journal of the American Medical Association* (hereafter cited as *JAMA*) 138 (18 December 1948):1164; "A Call to Action, Against Nationalization of Medicine," *JAMA* 138 (11 December 1948): 1098–99; "The American Medical Association: Power, Purpose and Politics in Organized Medicine," p. 1012.

nouncement, run as an ad in the press trade journal, *Editor and Publisher,* included a sample cartoon showing "mother" Congress spooning out bitter socialized medicine to its unhappy "public" child, while a group, including a bound-and-gagged physician, mourn in the background at the coffin of "free enterprise."[6] "The contest rules leave no doubt that this is a subtle bribe to cartoonists to support or oppose certain political beliefs . . . and to obtain general circulation for those beliefs in newspapers and magazines," charged the *Editor and Publisher* in a follow-up editorial one week after it had printed the NPC's contest advertisement.[7] Also, in February 1949, the NPC aroused a storm of protest by distributing a letter addressed to "Dear Christian American," containing anti-Semitic undertones, and exaggerating the charge against national health insurance (including the accusation that it would lead to free love) so much that even the AMA had to repudiate the letter. In April, responding to diminishing financial support and the AMA's desire to take direct command of organized medicine's political-action movement, the NPC Board of Trustees voted to end the committee's operation.[8]

At first, the AMA's new militancy aroused a flurry of dissent from some of its members. Several medical societies, including the AMA's largest local unit, the New York County Medical Society, refused to pay the twenty-five-dollar assessment. And in February, 148 prominent physicians lodged a letter of protest with the AMA in which they urged others to refuse to pay the assessment and charged that the association planned to spend too much money on "stand pat propadanda."[9]

6. Reprints of the contest advertisement are in the 1948 folder, CNH Records, Davis Papers.

7. Ibid.; *New York Times,* 15 March 1948.

8. "The National Physician's Committee," *JAMA* 139 (2 April 1949):924; *New York Times,* 17 April 1949.

9. Leonard Engel, "The AMA's Slush Fund"; "The Doctor Gets A Bill"; "A Protest Against the Present Attitudes and Policies of the AMA in Regard to the Problem of Medical Care," *JAMA* 139 (19 February 1949):532.

The protests were of short duration, however, for the AMA had employed an aggressive and highly successful San Francisco public relations firm, Whitaker and Baxter, to win over its dissident elements and to direct its political activities. This resourceful husband-and-wife team had worked for the California Medical Association in 1945 and had taken credit that year for successfully blocking legislative action on Gov. Earl Warren's state-sponsored health insurance proposal. Coming to the national scene in mid-December 1948 following Truman's reelection, Whitaker and Baxter launched the AMA's new "National Education Campaign" from its offices within the AMA's Chicago headquarters.[10]

As explained by Clem Whitaker in February, the national education campaign had both immediate and long-range objectives. The immediate objective was to defeat the Truman administration's health insurance measure in 1949 by distributing millions of pamphlets, making wide use of the press and radio, mobilizing additional pressure groups against government health insurance, writing letters to congressmen, and organizing speakers' bureaus throughout the country. Before the end of February, state and county medical societies had received Whitaker and Baxter's "Simplified Blueprint" outlining their local responsibilities for the battle ahead. Resolutions opposing compulsory health insurance would be adopted by the societies and sent to representatives in Congress within sixty days; every congressman's personal physician would write his patient explaining his opposition to the Truman health plan; a speakers' committee and a press committee would be established in each county medical society to disseminate national-education-campaign materials; and a concerted effort would be made to obtain additional pro-AMA endorsements from farm, business, civic, religious, and veterans organizations, in fact, one of the first Whitaker and Baxter mailings to campaign field directors included a listing of

10. *New York Times*, 17 December 1948; "AMA: Power, Purpose, and Politics," pp. 1012–24.

conventions scheduled to be held in their respective localities in 1949.[11]

Another important Whitaker and Baxter mailing went out in April to doctors all over the country. It consisted of 1 million copies of a foldout pamphlet entitled "Compulsory Health Insurance—Political Medicine—Is Bad Medicine for America!" and designed to be prominently displayed in doctor's waiting rooms for perusal by their patients. Reproduced in color on the pamphlet's cover was Sir Luke Fildes's famous and heartrending nineteenth-century painting "The Doctor," which portrays the family doctor on a house call, devotedly huddled by lamplight over a sick child. The caption beneath warned, "Keep Politics Out Of This Picture!"[12]

Other pamphlets soon followed, the most widely noted being "The Voluntary Way is the American Way," the title of which became the general theme of the AMA's campaign. In question-and-answer form, the pamphlet presented organized medicine's indictment against Truman's "compulsory" health insurance plan. The following excerpts reveal the thrust of the AMA charges; and the juxtaposed rebuttals, which were submitted by the Committee for the Nation's Health during the 1949 Senate health hearings, reveal the tenor of the debate.

AMA pamphlet	CNH reply
What is "compulsory health insurance"?	
It is a multibillion dollar program proposed by the Office of the Federal Security Ad-	It is a pay-as-you-go plan to make good medical care available to everyone. It was pro-

11. "What Will We Do With the Doctor's $25.00?," address by Clem Whitaker, 12 February 1949, reprint from the *Dallas Medical Journal* (April 1949) in CNH Records, Davis Papers; Stanley Kelley, Jr., *Professional Public Relations and Political Power*, pp. 78–79.

12. AMA National Education Campaign, "Compulsory Health Insurance—Political Medicine—Is Bad Medicine for America!," in CNH Records, Davis Papers; *New York Times*, 25 April 1949.

AMA pamphlet	CNH reply
ministrator, which would supplant voluntary health insurance with compulsory health insurance—levying a pay-roll tax to support the new Government-regulated system of medicine.	posed before the Federal Security Agency was ever born.

How much will the tax be?

Estimates range from 3 percent to 10 percent on every pay check up to $4,800, half paid by the employee and half paid by the employer. The self-employed would pay the whole amount.	Employed persons would pay 1½ percent of their wages or salaries, employers would match the 1½ percent contribution of employees, and the self-employed would contribute 2¼ percent of earnings. In each case, the percentage would apply only on the first $4,800 of earnings.

Why should the cost, even for second-rate service, run so high?

Because government-controlled medicine is political medicine. In Germany it took 1 government employee for every 100 persons insured. At that ratio, America would require a million and a half nonmedical employees—clerks, administrators, bookkeepers, and tax collectors—on the Federal pay roll, siphoning off medical funds before they ever bought the patient care of any kind.	Disparaging statements alleging "second-rate" care or that the quality of care has deteriorated under government-initiated health programs in European countries has simply not been substantiated. In fact, some of the AMA's charges have been countered by leaders of the medical professions in those countries. In 1946, and again in 1948, Dr. Charles M. Hill, secretary of the British Medical Association, protested to the AMA

AMA pamphlet	CNH reply
	against these allegations which he termed a "gross libel" on the British medical profession. The correct statement of facts regarding the number of administrative employees under established European systems is more nearly 1 to every 2,000 persons rather than 1 to every 100. We estimate the administrative costs to be 5 to 7½ percent of benefits, which is far less than the administrative costs of any of the existing voluntary health insurance plans.

Is compulsory health insurance really "insurance"?

It is not. And it is gravely unfair to pretend that it is.

Reasons it is not "insurance":
1. Though an arbitrary "premium" is collected, in the form of a pay-roll deduction, benefits are neither specified nor guaranteed. In the exact language of the sponsors, certain services are promised "when funds are available," "in so far as possible," and "when facilities permit." 2. Sound insurance is based on sound actuarial standards—and on contracts clearly setting forth both benefits and costs. Millions of Americans have such guaranties in writing—under

National health insurance is a form of social insurance similar to old-age and survivor's insurance. It differs from commercial insurance inasmuch as premiums are geared to income and ability to pay rather than being fixed in proportion to benefits given and size of family.

AMA pamphlet	CNH reply

voluntary health insurance. But the only guarantee in the compulsory health "insurance" proposal is guarantee of a new pay-roll tax—the amount unpredictable.

Why is compulsory health insurance called socialized medicine?

Because the Government proposes to: Collect the tax; control the money; determine the services; set the rates; maintain the records; direct both the citizens and the doctor's participation in the program; assume control not only of the medical profession, but of hospitals—both public and private—the drug and appliance industries, dentistry, pharmacy, nursing, and allied professions; dominate the medical affairs of every citizen— through administrative lines from the central government in Washington—down through State, town, district, and neighborhood bureaus.

To substitute emotion for reason and to frighten the American people. We are for national health insurance because we are opposed to a system of socialized medicine. The provisions of our national health-insurance bill belie the assertions of Government control and domination over the lives and livelihoods of patients and physicians.

Would socialized medicine lead to socialization of other phases of American life?

Lenin thought so. He declared: "Socialized medicine is the key-stone to the arch of the socialist state." Today,

Is Lenin AMA's authority? He is not ours.
[Later, Senator Murray reacted to this oft-repeated

A Testing Time

AMA pamphlet	CNH reply

much of the world has launched out on that road. If the medical profession should be socialized, because people need doctors, why not the milk industry? Certainly, more people need milk every day than need doctors. On the same erroneous premise, why not the corner grocery? Adequate diet is the very basis of good health. Why not nationalize lawyers, miners, businessmen, farmers? Germany did, Russia did, England is in the process.

quote attributed by the AMA to Lenin by releasing a letter from the Library of Congress's Legislative Reference Service that stated that its researchers were unable to find such a statement in Lenin's speeches or writings.]

How do movements like compulsory health insurance get started?

Because people of short memory for American history, and shorter vision for the American future, proclaim that increasing political control of American lives and work is a "trend." It is a trend only so long as energetic people who like the American way of life above all others look the other way when political controls like compulsory health insurance are proposed.

By failure of the Robin Hood System of medicine—that of soaking the rich to give charity care to the poor—to meet the needs of the vast majority of self-reliant and self-supporting people for adequate medical care.

Under compulsory health insurance, may a patient choose his own doctor?

The compulsory system inevitably means the panel practice

The bill specifically states "persons and their depen-

AMA pamphlet	CNH reply
system, under which doctors are assigned to patients and patients to doctors. There is no guaranty of freedom of choice. Further, if the doctor desired and obtained were not on the Government panel, the patient would pay both his doctor's bill for service, and the Government's bill for no service. Proponents of compulsory health insurance in this country promise that patients would be free to choose their own doctors. But this same promise was made in England. It is an empty promise, never kept.	dents . . . shall be assured full freedom to choose their physicians and to change their choices as they may desire." There is no provision for assignment of patients to physicians, nor will there be any limitation on the number of patients a doctor may serve unless the physicians themselves decide that a limitation is essential to protect the quality of care.

Are the doctors of America "lobbying" against compulsory health insurance?

The medical profession—together with hundreds of other professions and organizations which recognize in Government-controlled medicine a step toward regimentation—are presenting their case before the bar of public opinion in every community in the Nation.[13]	Yes; with a multimillion dollar fund, paying among other, $100,000 a year to their two chief lobbyists [Whitaker and Baxter], and underwriting the costs of a campaign of misrepresentation.[14]

13. American Medical Association, *The Voluntary Way is the American Way*, submitted for the record in U.S., Congress, Senate, Committee on Labor and Public Welfare, *National Health Program, 1949: Hearings before the Subcommittee on Health Legislation on S. 1106, S. 1456, S. 1581, and S. 1679*, pp. 811–19. Hereafter cited as Senate, *1949 Health Hearings*.

14. Committee for the Nation's Health, *Fifty Questions on*

In its first year of operation, Whitaker and Baxter distributed more than 55 million pieces of similar literature and spent over $1.5 million in the process.[15]

Their theme—the voluntary way is the American way—also reflected the AMA's second, and more positive, long-range objective in 1949, that of promoting the expansion of voluntary, private health insurance coverage similar to its physician-sponsored and physician-controlled Blue Shield plans. The idea made sense. President Truman and his supporters claimed that only 3.5 million Americans were adequately protected under private health insurance. If Whitaker and Baxter could sell more of the AMA's kind of insurance, it would help stop consideration of Truman's kind. In February, the association announced a new twelve-point program for the advancement of medicine and public health, including "further development and wider coverage by voluntary hospital and medical care plans to meet the costs of illness." And for the first time in AMA history, its house of delegates gave sanction in June to lay-sponsored private health insurance coverage.[16]

Another AMA decision in 1949 concerned the removal in June of Morris Fishbein from his post as editor of the AMA's journal. Fishbein had held this powerful position for over thirty years, and his ouster was interpreted by some, including President Truman, as an attempt to placate those physicians who objected to the editor's acid attacks on the proponents of national health insurance.[17]

Compulsory Health Insurance, submitted for the record, Senate, *1949 Health Hearings,* pp. 819–28. The letter requested by Senator Murray concerning the validity of the Lenin quotation is W. C. Gilbert to James Murray, 2 May 1949, submitted for the record, Senate, *1949 Health Hearings,* p. 280.

15. *New York Times,* 7 December 1949; James Burrow, *AMA, Voice of American Medicine,* p. 362.

16. Burrow, *AMA,* p. 413; American Medical Association, *Digest of Official Actions, 1846–1958,* pp. 334–35; *New York Times,* 10 June 1949.

17. Milton Mayer, "The Rise and Fall of Doctor Fishbein"; *New York Times,* 8 June 1949; "Activities of the Editor," *JAMA* 139 (18 June 1949):630; The President's News Conference of June 9, 1949, in Truman, *Public Papers, 1949,* p. 281.

Actually, Fishbein's demise resulted as much from a desire to defer to Whitaker and Baxter's direction of the AMA's new public relations program; by midyear its national education campaign worked so smoothly that the editor's powerful pen was hardly missed.

On the other side of the health security debate, the Committee for the Nation's Health could not hope to match the AMA's resources. In contrast with Whitaker and Baxter's $1.5 million budget, the CNH took in a total of $104,000 in 1949, of which about $98,000 went into its working budget. Like the AMA, the CNH and its research branch, Michael Davis's Committee on Research in Medical Economics, published and distributed pamphlets, but not in nearly so large a number. The CNH's pamphlets included "Are Blue Shield Plans Satisfactory?," in which it was argued that they were not; "Restrictions on Free Enterprise in Medicine," in which the AMA stood accused of monopolizing health services through its control over Blue Shield plans; and "Record of the American Medical Association," which chronicled the AMA's shifting attitude on the legitimacy of governmental and private health insurance since the early part of the century. These, along with special condensations of Ewing's 1948 report on national health goals, were distributed primarily to the liberal special-interest press, especially to that of the AFL and the CIO. The CNH counted heavily upon the labor press, and the CIO gave the committee a major assist in 1949. Its department of education and research distributed pamphlets and poster kits on national health insurance, and the August issue of CIO's *Economic Outlook* magazine devoted itself entirely to the subject.[18]

It is the president, however, who commands the great-

18. Minutes of the Annual Meeting, 15 June 1950, Frederick Robin to Executive Committee, 10 September 1948, "Are Blue Shield Plans Satisfactory?," "Restrictions on Free Enterprise in Medicine," and "Record of the American Medical Association," in CNH Records, Davis Papers. The August 1949 issue of *Economic Outlook* is included in Files of Clark Clifford, Truman Papers.

est public attention; and because Truman had forcefully spoken out for his health insurance proposal in campaign appearances the year before, health reformers expected that the president would do so again in 1949. In February, Oscar Ewing told the press that the president intended to do "everything possible" to get his health insurance scheme enacted by Congress; President William Green of the AFL, after emerging from an April White House meeting on the matter, told reporters that Truman would probably go on radio to talk to the people about his health program; and a few days later Senator Murray wrote that the president had "promised to go all out" on the senator's forthcoming omnibus health bill.[19]

But Truman did not make the radio talk; and, just as in 1946, the president confined his public utterances on health largely to formal communications to Congress. These included his state of the Union message in January, wherein HST asked Congress to enact "without further delay" a national health insurance system and to "spare no effort" to improve the nation's health; the president's economic and budget messages sent up a few days later; and, on 22 April, his third special message on health, this time listing four legislative recommendations, with health insurance on the top of the list. Although repeatedly queried by reporters about his health insurance program during press conferences from January to June, Truman refused in each case to provide them with more than a cursory reply; he would not use the press conference as a vehicle for selling national health insurance to the public.[20]

Noting these muted presidential responses to reporters,

19. *New York Times*, 19 February, 16 April 1949; James Murray to J. Howard McGrath, 21 April 1949, box 32, J. Howard McGrath Papers.

20. State of the Union Message, 5 January 1949, The President's Economic Report, 7 January 1949, Annual Budget Message, 10 January 1949, Special Message to the Congress on the Nation's Health Needs, 22 April 1949, in Truman, *Public Papers, 1949*, pp. 5, 26, 27, 226–30; Elmer E. Cornwell, Jr., *Presidential Leadership of Public Opinion*, pp. 168–70.

political scientist Elmer E. Cornwell, Jr., has concluded in *Presidential Leadership of Public Opinion* that Harry Truman's inept handling of the health insurance issue before the press in 1949 exemplifies Truman's weakness as a political leader; unlike Franklin Roosevelt, contends Cornwell, Truman considered the press conference an ordeal rather than a newsmaking opportunity.[21] There is, however, another reason for Truman's hesitancy to go beyond a prepared text when discussing his health program in 1949; legislative strategy dictated that HST not spell out his proposals in precise detail.

Given the president's penchant for administrative orderliness and his distaste for bureaucratic sideshows wherein agency heads jockeyed for power—as in his first few years in office—by the end of his first term Truman had established a legislative clearance procedure, directed from within his Bureau of the Budget, whereby any agency-inspired legislative proposal would be subjected to careful scrutiny to determine whether it conformed to the president's intent as well as to his budgetary policy.[22]

To work effectively, the clearance procedure could not be compromised. So, even though Truman sympathized with Oscar Ewing's desire to seek early congressional action on health insurance, HST sent Ewing a faintly veiled reprimand when, a few days after the November elections, a front-page *New York Times* story quoted Ewing as saying that the president intended, despite AMA opposition, to back a national health insurance bill in 1949.[23] Reminding his zealous FSA administrator that legislative policy had to conform to still-to-be-determined budgetary limitations, the president told Ewing, "Extreme caution must be exercised in making public statements about the speed at which we can move forward toward our goals. . . . I count on you to prevent any premature announcements until we are in a position to know which things must be

21. Cornwell, *Presidential Leadership of Public Opinion*, pp. 168–70.

22. Richard E. Neustadt, "The Presidency and Legislation: The Growth of Central Clearance."

23. *New York Times*, 30 November 1948.

done first and how rapidly they can be done."[24]

"In connection with the above," emphasized Truman, "may I again call your attention to my desire that legislative proposals to be coordinated and cleared within the Executive Branch in accordance with the established procedures."[25] The established procedure required that the Bureau of the Budget allow only those proposals that conformed with the president's fiscal policy to go to Congress stamped "an administration bill." If the measure did not meet budgetary limitations, but Truman still favored it, the proposal went to the Hill with a designation indicating that the president was "generally in accord," but was "uncommitted on matters of detail."[26]

For a number of reasons, reasons that help explain Truman's hesitancy to discuss his insurance program with reporters, Senator Murray and the other health sponsors, after consulting with the president in early April, decided that their 1949 omnibus health bill would go into the congressional hopper with the "generally in accord" designation rather than as an administration bill. "By late March it had become obvious that the kinds of modifications which would be necessary in working out an Administration approved bill, would prove unacceptable and perhaps fatal to the Senate sponsors," explained Bureau of the Budget staff member Richard Neustadt.[27]

This was largely because Senator Murray and the other proadministration members of the Senate Labor and Public Welfare Committee were confronted by a rival, antiadministration group from within the committee headed by Sen. Lister Hill, Democrat from Alabama. Hill chaired the Subcommittee on Hospital Construction and Local Public Health Units, whose five members' views on Truman's health insurance idea ranged from barely luke-

24. Truman to Ewing, 30 November 1948, file 011.4, box 18, FSA Administrator's Records.

25. Ibid.

26. Richard E. Neustadt, "Presidential Clearance of Legislation" (Ph.D. diss.), copy in History of Health Security folder, box 211, Edwin E. Witte Papers.

27. Ibid., p. 176.

warm (Democrats Hill, Paul Douglas of Illinois, and Garrett Withers of Kentucky) to openly hostile (Republicans Robert Taft of Ohio and H. Alexander Smith of New Jersey). Most important, Hill had gained recognition as the successful sponsor of the 1946 Hospital Construction Act and had charted an independent course opposed by the administration when he introduced a bipartisan bill providing federal assistance to the states for purchase of Blue Cross–type health plans for the poor and scheduled subcommittee hearings of his own on legislation to increase hospital construction funds and aid to local public health units. These hearings began in May, several weeks before Senator Murray's Subcommittee on Health Legislation could begin its own hearings on Murray's administration-supported S. 1679 and other related bills.[28]

As explained by Richard Neustadt,

> Given this situation, the pro-insurance forces badly needed to assert and hold the lead on medical education, hospital construction, public health and related features of the Administration's total health program . . . partly in order to spotlight the interrelationships between insurance as a bogey to ease the path of the other features; partly to assure that pro-Administration forces got the credit for whatever committee and floor action was to eventuate.
>
> Hence, the pro-insurance (and pro-Administration) sponsors wanted to introduce and hold hearings on big and dramatic programs in the fields of hospital construction, medical education and public health; programs bigger in scale and more expensive than could have been justified or approved under the President's budgetary and general Administration policies (bigger also than the rival subcommittee had projected).[29]

28. Ibid.; U.S., Congress, Senate, Committee on Labor and Public Welfare, *Hospital Survey and Construction (Hill-Burton) Act Amendments: Hearings before the Subcommittee on Hospital Construction and Local Public Health Units on S. 205, S. 231, S. 614, Title III of S. 1679, and Title IV of S. 1581.*

29. Neustadt, "Presidential Clearance of Legislation," p. 176.

"We have thought that there is nothing inconsistent in pressing for a comprehensive health bill and at the same time supporting measures like the local public health bill," Oscar Ewing had explained to a welfare leader the previous February. "The matter is essentially one of legislative tactics."[30] Ewing's strategy also held that Senator Murray's omnibus health bill (cosponsored by eight other Democrats, including freshman Sen. Hubert H. Humphrey) should be introduced on 25 April, three days after the president sent Congress his third special message on health; in this way the bill would have the appearance of being an administration-approved bill. In reality, of course, each of the bill's seven titles—which taken together covered everything from federal aid to medical education and an expanded hospital-construction program to the controversial health insurance system—remained subject to amendment or even deletion.[31]

Lest the news media and subsequently the opposition discover that Murray's S. 1679 did not enjoy unqualified presidential backing, once the measure was introduced in Congress, Truman had to avoid direct and specific discussion concerning the bill's provisions. When pressed to comment on his overall legislative program at a press conference in May, a few days after Senator Murray had opened his health hearings, the president declared, "I am not answering any questions—specific questions about specific bills." He was in favor of all his program, he said. When asked if he thought his program was making progress in Congress, Truman said "yes" and snapped, "All this conversation is to prevent the making of progress."[32]

Legislative strategy, then, as well as Truman's inclination to respond to reporters' questions in a terse, cryptic, and sometimes flippant manner, explain the president's seemingly insensitive attitude toward the importance of nurturing public support for his health program. Indeed,

30. Ewing to Mrs. Theodore Oxholm, 23 February 1949, file 011.4, box 17, FSA Administrator's Records.

31. Neustadt, "Presidential Clearance of Legislation," p. 177.

32. News Conference of May 26, 1949, in Truman, *Public Papers, 1949*, p. 269.

HST had earlier shown great awareness of the importance of public relations when leaders of the Committee
for the Nation's Health paid him a well-publicized White
House visit in mid-April; this meeting was purposely
timed to cast public attention upon the health issue just
prior to release of Truman's health message and the subsequent introduction in Congress of the Murray-Dingell
1949 omnibus health legislation (S. 1679 and H.R. 4312).

The meeting had been conceived by Nate Robertson,
CNH's public relations director. Writing in late March
to presidential press secretary Charles Ross, Robertson
asked if he could have five minutes of Ross's time to explain two ideas that would greatly help to promote the
president's health program.[33] A few days later, Robertson
and Ross lunched together, and the CNH press agent
gave Ross a detailed memorandum outlining his proposals:

> We need your help to get half a break in the newspapers.
> I think the President can perhaps turn the tide in this pub-
> licity battle by doing one or two things. First, he could help
> us to get a good play on the first of a series of reports we
> have coming out on the health insurance program and the
> need for it, by letting us submit the report to him and re-
> leasing it at the White House. We have a wonderful series
> of reports coming up, but I fear the papers will ignore them
> without some such send off.
>
> Now the second proposition. We have decided it would
> be a good idea to capitalize on the public resentment against
> the AMA and its assessment by starting a campaign to en-
> courage medical consumers, or patients, to send us 25 cents
> each, as voluntary contributions to match the AMA's com-
> pulsory contributions of $25 from each doctor. . . . If the
> President would start the thing off by a public contribution
> of a quarter to the fund, we could get the labor papers, at
> least, to urge their readers to send in quarters. We would

33. Nate Robertson to Charles Ross, 28 March 1949, Truman Papers, OF 286-A.

follow up with similar contributions by Green, Murray, and others.[34]

Ross quickly obtained the president's approval for the meeting, and it was scheduled for 15 April. Included in the CNH delegation were Dr. Channing Frothingham of Boston, chairman of the Committee for the Nation's Health; President William Green of the AFL; and other labor leaders. According to plan, Dr. Frothingham presented the president a report prepared by the Committee on Research in Medical Economics that blamed the AMA for blocking the growth of private health insurance plans that were not controlled by the AMA's constituent medical societies. Robertson got only half of what he had requested, however. The president did not agree to the "penny for a dollar" idea, probably because this would involve him in pressure-group politics. Robertson and the CNH did score on one point, though: The White House meeting rated first-page treatment in the *New York Times*.[35]

Harry Truman also encouraged others to explain his controversial health proposal to the public. On his short return to Independence over the Christmas holidays following the election, HST chatted with an old army friend, Kansas City dentist A. F. Schopper, about his ideas on health insurance. Schopper later wrote Truman that he would be speaking before dental groups throughout the country in the coming months and, if provided the facts, would gladly express Truman's true intentions in order to combat the misquotations of the American Medical Association. The facts were soon on their way to the dentist.[36]

From within the administration, the major part of the promotional effort fell upon the shoulders of the FSA

34. Robertson to Ross, 1 April 1949, Truman Papers, OF 286-A.

35. 11:45 A.M. Appointment, 15 April 1949, Presidential Appointment Book of Matthew Connelly, Truman Papers; *New York Times*, 16 April 1949.

36. A. F. Schopper to Truman, 21 January 1949, Truman to Schopper, 2 February 1949, Truman Papers, OF 286-A.

administrator, Oscar Ewing. Ewing made at least a dozen major speeches in 1949, including an appearance in February alongside the AFL social insurance director, Nelson Cruikshank, on the ABC "Town Meeting of the Air" broadcast to debate the health issue opposite Sen. H. Alexander Smith of New Jersey and AMA spokesman Morris Fishbein. In addition, Ewing's FSA staff supplied administration allies with information detailing the health needs of the nation. In fact, Ewing followed the practice of sending a free copy of his 1948 report, *The Nation's Health*, to those who had written him expressing support for the president's program, while suggesting to those who had written in opposition that they might want to purchase a copy of *The Nation's Health* for one dollar from the superintendent of documents.[37]

The Federal Security Agency also drafted the 1949 version of the Murray-Dingell omnibus health bill, even though the sponsors later decided that the measure would not be introduced as an administration bill. In January, following the president's state of the Union message, Murray and the other sponsors had submitted an insurance measure identical to the one considered by the Eightieth Congress, but then discussions had begun in February between Murray and the FSA on the feasibility of drafting a new bill. Soon the FSA had projected plans to draft an expanded proposal containing seven titles, covering those health needs outlined in Ewing's report on national health goals the year before.[38] In contrast with the intraagency friction that had marked the draft-

37. Copies of Ewing's speeches are scattered throughout the administrator's records. Ewing's policy of providing free copies of his 1948 report to only friendly correspondents becomes evident upon examination of his replies to letters contained in the administrator's correspondence files for April and May 1949. For both, see file 011.4, box 217, FSA Administrator's Records.

38. S. 5, 81st Cong., 1st sess.; Murray to Ewing, 5 February 1949, Memoranda, "Summary of Meeting on Health Insurance," 11 February 1949, John Thurston to George Perrott, 23 February 1949, file 011.4, box 17, FSA Administrator's Records.

ing activities in 1946, the 1949 redrafting went smoothly; Katharine Lenroot's Children's Bureau was now securely ensconced within the FSA, and former Surgeon General Thomas Parran had been replaced by the more coopera- tive Leonard A. Scheele. By early April, the first draft had been completed and Democratic congressional spon- sors met with the president to discuss the proposed legis- lation. The decision was made at that time to pursue a flexible strategy in order to enhance chances of passage for the noncontroversial features of the bill.[39]

And the strategy worked, at least in part. Of the seven titles contained in S. 1679, the Senate passed four in the form of separate measures. These measures covered all the recommendations set forth in the president's special health message, except health insurance. They dealt with federal aid to medical education, the establishment of medical research institutes, amendments to extend and liberalize the Hospital Construction Act of 1946, and federal grants to assist the states to develop and maintain adequate public health systems. However, only one of the four, the amendments to the Hospital Construction Act, obtained House approval and became law in 1949.[40]

Beginning in April, important lobbies fell into line against the president's proposal for national health in- surance. For the first time all the major welfare organiza- tions of the Catholic church announced their united op- position to the idea of government insurance. In a joint statement issued on 17 April the National Catholic Wel- fare Conference, the National Conference of Catholic Charities, and the Catholic Hospital Association declared that Truman's program would make health care "prac- tically a Government monopoly." Like the AMA, they favored extension of existing private health insurance

39. Arthur J. Altmeyer to author, 10 April 1967; "Items Dis- cussed with President Truman as Essential to a Well Rounded National Health Program," 5 April 1949, S. 5 folder, box 139, James E. Murray Papers; Neustadt, "Presidential Clearance of Legislation," p. 177.

40. "Resumé of the Handling of Health Legislation, 81st Congress, 1st Session," box 65, Murray Papers.

plans.[41] The 5-million-member General Federation of Women's Clubs soon followed suit at their annual convention. Before and after the health hearings began in the House and Senate in May, major business groups, conservative farm groups, patriotic organizations, and many posts of the American Legion went on record against the proposal.[42] In August, even the National Medical Association, composed of the nation's black physicians, balked on the issue. Despite their incoming president's warning that "if you support the stand against Truman, you will receive a pat on the back from the AMA, but condemnation from ten million Negroes and the NAACP," delegates to the association's 1949 convention refused to renew the NMA's earlier endorsement.[43]

This rising tide of opposition can be attributed mostly to the effectiveness of the AMA's Whitaker and Baxter campaign to associate the president's program with socialism, the impact of which was greatly magnified by the prevailing fear of Soviet espionage in 1949 and a corresponding concern over socialist threats to American free enterprise. Top leaders of the American Communist party went on trial in January 1949 for conspiring to teach the violent overthrow of the U.S. government; in March, former Justice Department employee Judith Coplon was indicted on espionage charges; in May, accused

41. *New York Times*, 18 April 1949. The Catholic groups feared that the extension of social insurance would result in an encroachment of taxation upon religious and charitable institutions. In January, Senator McGrath exchanged letters with Cardinal Francis Spellman seeking an acceptable solution. None was found. J. Howard McGrath to Cardinal Spellman, 4 January 1949, Spellman to McGrath, 10 January 1949, Robert F. Wagner Papers.

42. *New York Times*, 23, 29 April, 2 May, 15 June, 10, 11, 13 August 1949; American Legion resolutions, Truman Papers, OF 286-A; Senate, 1949 Health Hearings, pp. 756, 1044; U.S., Congress, House, Committee on Interstate and Foreign Commerce, *National Health Plan: Hearings before the Subcommittee on Health on H.R. 4312, H.R. 4313, and H.R. 4918 and Other Identical Bills*, pp. 162–63.

43. Quoted in Donald R. McCoy and Richard T. Ruetten, *Quest And Response*, p. 187.

Soviet agent Gerhard Eisler fled to Europe to escape charges of congressional contempt and passport fraud; and in June, former State Department official Alger Hiss went on trial for perjury in the wake of charges that, as a Communist, Hiss had provided the Soviets with secret diplomatic documents in 1938.

Anything or anyone remotely associated with the word *socialism* became immediately suspect, and health reformers could never rid their national health insurance proposal of that onerous title. "The term 'socialized medicine' is getting to have a nasty ring to it out here on the 'grassroots front,'" an Indiana publisher warned Oscar Ewing as early as December 1948.[44] The successful impact of the AMA's long campaign to identify the president's program with socialism can be best seen in the 1949 correspondence files of Sen. J. Howard McGrath and of the Federal Security Agency. To the chagrin of medical reformers, those friendly to the president's program referred to it as "socialized medicine" when writing for information almost as often as did those who were writing in opposition to it![45] "I have no knowledge of any proposed plans of socialized medicine and we have no literature on that subject for distribution," Oscar Ewing replied plaintively to an Indiana congressman who had passed along a letter from a high school teacher asking, as had so many others, for information on "proposed plans of socialized medicine." Perhaps, suggested Ewing, the educator was referring to national health insurance, since "the two terms are frequently, and incorrectly, interchanged."[46]

Association of the two in the public mind also cost Oscar Ewing promotion to a cabinet-level position in 1949. In June, under the provisions of recently enacted legislation, the president signed Reorganization Plan No.

44. Paul L. Feltus to Ewing, 6 December 1948, file 011.4, box 18, FSA Administrator's Records.

45. See FSA correspondence folders for March, April, and May 1949, file 011.4, box 17, FSA Administrator's Records; National Health Insurance folders, box 32, McGrath Papers.

46. Ewing to Ralph Harvey, 27 January 1949, file 011.4, box 18, FSA Administrator's Records.

1. This plan, if not voted down by either the Senate or the House within sixty days, would automatically upgrade the Federal Security Agency to departmental status as the department of welfare and upgrade Ewing's position to secretary of welfare. On 16 August, however, the Senate, after two days of debate, voted 60 to 32 to reject the reorganization scheme.[47]

The vote was as much a referendum against national health insurance as it was against the president's reorganization plan. During the debate that preceded the Senate's action, opponents repeatedly charged that if the FSA was granted departmental status, Oscar Ewing, as a cabinet officer, would be in a stronger position to push for socialized medicine.[48] Leading the opposition to Ewing, southern Democrat John McClellan warned that if Reorganization Plan No. 1 was not defeated, the FSA's elevation would "lend impetus to and greatly augment efforts of high Government officials to force acceptance of [socialized medicine] through the prestige and power of a cabinet office."[49] Following the vote, the antiadministration *New York Daily Mirror* editorialized that Ewing, "the principal advocate of socialized medicine in this country," had been defeated because he had made the FSA "the center of socialistic concepts of the old New Deal and the new Fair Deal."[50]

Twenty-three Democrats joined thirty-seven Republicans to kill the administration's reorganization plan; and of the twenty-three Democrats, twenty represented southern states. Herein lay the president's legislative dilemma. Despite his party's numerical majority in both the Senate and the House, the southern bloc remained overwhelmingly opposed to his all-inclusive health insurance pro-

47. Message to Congress Transmitting Reorganization Plan No. 1 of 1949 Establishing a Department of Welfare, in Truman, *Public Papers, 1949*, pp. 310–11; roll call vote on S. Res. 147, 16 August 1949, *Congressional Record*, 81st Cong., 1st sess., 1949, vol. 95, pt. 9, p. 11560.
48. *New York Times*, 22 July 1949.
49. *Congressional Record*, 81st Cong., 1st sess., 1949, vol. 95, pt. 9, p. 11522.
50. *New York Daily Mirror*, 19 August 1949.

posal or to any other major new adventures in behalf of labor-supported, urban-oriented social and economic reform. Extension of some existing (and by 1949 much less threatening) New Deal–type programs might win their support, but this, too, proved highly unpredictable because of the president's championing of civil rights. Especially grating to southern sensitivity was Truman's policy of desegregating the armed forces and his continued insistence that Congress reestablish and make permanent a fair employment practices committee charged with policing job discrimination.[51]

The southern bloc's power manifested itself even before Senator Murray and the other proadministration sponsors introduced S. 1679 on 25 April. By that time a group of southern Democrats and conservative Republicans had introduced two competing health insurance bills in the Senate, and a majority of the Labor and Public Welfare Committee's members had associated themselves with one or the other; Murray did not have enough votes to report out of committee anything resembling the health insurance title contained in S. 1679.[52]

One of the two competing measures was a revised version of the Taft-Smith-Donnell bill that, like its predecessors, provided federal funds for medical care for only the poor. The other bill was a bipartisan compromise proposal cosponsored by southern Democratic Senators Lister Hill of Alabama, Herbert O'Conor of Maryland, and Garrett L. Withers of Kentucky, along with GOP Senators George Aiken of Vermont and Wayne Morse of Oregon. Drafted with the assistance of the American Hospital Association and introduced on 30 March, the Hill-Aiken bill, as it was called, provided federal assistance to the states to subsidize premium payments on private plans like Blue Cross for persons unable to pay for them.[53]

51. *Congressional Record*, 81st Cong., 1st sess., 1949, vol. 95, pt. 9, p. 11560; McCoy and Ruetten, *Quest and Response*, pp. 171–99; Richard M. Dalfiume, *Desegregation of the U.S. Armed Forces.*

52. *New York Times*, 28 April 1949.

53. S. 1581, S. 1456, 81st Cong., 1st sess.

In late May, a group of Republicans, including Rep. Richard Nixon and led by Senators Ralph Flanders of Vermont and Irving Ives of New York, introduced still another health insurance bill. Their scheme would establish a locally organized and controlled private insurance system, with premiums scaled to the subscribers' incomes. Any deficiency between the system's cost and income would be remedied by state and federal funds. In contrast to the Hill-Aiken bill, the Flanders-Ives bill did not require recipients to take a poverty-means test.[54] Therefore, while the Taft "charity" bill and the administration's comprehensive health insurance measure represented opposite legislative extremes in the health security debate in 1949, the Hill-Aiken bill and the Flanders-Ives bill sought the middle ground of compromise.

Compromise was necessary if the president wanted some form of health insurance passed during the first session of the Eighty-first Congress. With Murray's bill blocked in the Senate committee, there was little hope that the less liberal House Committee on Interstate and Foreign Commerce would report out its companion measure, especially in the face of southern Democratic opposition and mounting pressure-group hostility.[55]

Of the two compromise insurance proposals before Congress—the GOP Flanders-Ives bill and the bipartisan Hill-Aiken bill—the Hill-Aiken bill had the greater chance of passage; it alone could have attracted sufficient southern Democratic and moderate Republican support. Cosponsor Lister Hill from Alabama had achieved dis-

---

54. S. 1970, H.R. 4918, H.R. 4924, 81st Cong., 1st sess. Besides Nixon, the measure was sponsored in the House by GOP Representatives Christian Herter of Massachusetts, Jacob Javits of New York, and Clifford Case of New Jersey.

55. The House Committee on Interstate and Foreign Commerce was even more antiadministration than the Senate Labor and Public Welfare Committee. In a roll-call vote taken in 1950 on the president's second attempt to elevate the FSA to departmental status only seven of the committee's twenty-six members voted with the administration. See roll-call vote on H. Res. 647 pertaining to Reorganization Plan No. 27, 81st Cong., 3d sess., *Congressional Quarterly Almanac* 6 (1950):560.

tinction as chief sponsor of the federal hospital construction program begun in 1946; and, of the four major health bills to clear the Senate in 1949, only one, Hill's amendments to the Hospital Construction Act, got beyond the House and became law. Had Truman thrown his support to the Hill-Aiken bill, it would surely have attracted many southern votes. Indeed, the entire southern Democratic bloc in the Senate voted the following year to enact the first major upward revision of social security coverage and benefits since 1939, a measure that included a provision whereby states could use federal funds to help pay the doctor bills of public-assistance recipients.[56]

Moreover, the American Hospital Association had helped draft the Hill-Aiken bill, and the other hospital groups favored it.[57] So, too, did the American people. In a public opinion sampling conducted by the Gallup Poll in April, 47 percent favored the limited, government-supported plan to help pay for private insurance as envisioned by the Hill-Aiken bill, whereas only 33 percent backed the comprehensive social security idea.[58] Had the president modified his position and backed the AHA-supported bill, Truman could have achieved his rapprochement with the hospital groups, and the nation might very well have seen the enactment of a compromise system of health security during his presidency.

Instead, as the first session of the Eighty-first Congress wore on, no sign came from the White House to indicate a willingness to compromise. Negotiations begun at the president's request the year before between Oscar Ewing and the leaders of the American, Protestant, and Catholic

56. In his study of the voting patterns of the 81st Congress, David B. Truman has found that the southern Democrats in the Senate did not "as a unit offer continuous, unremitting opposition to the remainder of the party." See David B. Truman, *The Congressional Party*, p. 59. On the Senate social security vote, which was 81 to 2 in favor of the amendments, see *Congressional Quarterly Almanac* 6 (1950):198–99.

57. *New York Times*, 12 June 1949; Senate, *1949 Health Hearings*, pp. 447–48, 469.

58. *Public Opinion Quarterly*, Summer 1949, p. 358.

hospital associations had come to an impasse. John Connorton, executive director of the Greater New York Hospital Association, acting as intermediary between the hospital groups and the White House in 1949, had written presidential secretary Matthew Connelly in June urging that the administration modify its position on health insurance and support "the adoption of legislation which has been agreed upon by all the national hospital associations."[59] The administration's reply came from presidential aide Charles Murphy. "It seems to me," Murphy wrote Connelly, "that it would be out of the question for the President to follow the suggestion of Mr. Connorton. His suggestion is, in effect, that the President openly abandon his recommendation for national health insurance for the time being. I suggest that Mr. Connorton be steered to Oscar Ewing as the Administration spokesman on this subject."[60] The hospital group's reply came in July; after meeting with Ewing on three separate occasions, the leaders of the American, Protestant, and Catholic hospital associations reported to the president that they could not support his health insurance program.[61]

Even after Congress adjourned in mid-October and the S. 1679 sponsors revealed that they had abandoned hope of a showdown on the Senate floor until after the 1950 elections,[62] the administration stood its ground. "The two sides are now at a point where they are more interested in hitting each other than in finding some solution," complained Democrat Sen. Paul Douglas of Illinois in December. If the administration did not yield ground soon, Douglas warned, it would be a long time before any form of government-supported health insurance was enacted. To break the impasse, Douglas an-

59. John Connorton to Matthew Connelly, 21 June 1949, Truman Papers, OF 286-A.

60. Charles Murphy to Connelly, 28 June 1949, Truman Papers, OF 286-A.

61. John Hayes, John Barrett, and John Martin to Truman, 21 July 1949, Truman Papers, OF 286-A.

62. *New York Times*, 27 October 1949.

nounced that he would introduce an insurance bill to cover only catastrophic illness.[63] In an angry retort, Rep. John Dingell protested to Douglas that the junior senator from Illinois had not conferred beforehand with Senator Murray and himself and that Douglas's health insurance scheme would be far less popular than that included in the Taft "charity" bill.[64] Meanwhile, Oscar Ewing toured Great Britain, sending back laudatory reports on the recently inaugurated British system of socialized medicine, while his FSA staff optimistically devised a public information program to be used during the tooling-up period in the event that the national health insurance title of S. 1679 was passed as a separate measure during the second session of the Eighty-first Congress.[65]

Why did the Truman administration remain so intransigent on the insurance issue in 1949? A mixture of three things determined the president's course of action: Hope that the Congress might become more receptive, at least after the 1950 elections; a legislative stratagem whereby the national health insurance proposal served as "a bogey" to stimulate action on less controversial aspects of the administration's program; and, above all, the president's disinclination to retreat before his political enemies. "As I've always said," Truman later reflected to journalist Edward R. Murrow, "the great statesmen you read about were politicians who became statesmen only after they were in their graves."[66] In 1949, Truman felt compelled to stick with his bold, anti-AMA health insurance plan. He could not shift his support to the Hill-Aiken bill without alienating organized labor and other elements of the liberal political coalition that had just elected him. The Hill-Aiken bill did nothing for union members; it contained the poverty-means test considered

63. Ibid., 8 December 1949.

64. John D. Dingell to Paul Douglas, 10 December 1949, John D. Dingell Papers.

65. *New York Times*, 7, 10, 16, 20 December 1949; Harvey Bush to Maurice Robbins, 6 December 1949, file 011.4, box 17, FSA Administrator's Records.

66. CBS Television, 1957, Audio-Visual Collection, Truman Papers.

so repugnant to liberals; and most of all, the measure promoted the very thing that the American Medical Association sought in 1949: Expansion of the private, physician-controlled and hospital-controlled insurance systems.

Straining relations even further between the White House and organized medicine, the AMA began in August to accuse the Truman administration of employing police-state tactics against the AMA's constituent medical societies. Generally, the charge probably reflected the AMA's concern over attempts made in 1949 by White House ally Rep. Frank Buchanan of Pennsylvania to launch a congressional probe into the lobbying activities of powerful special-interest groups.[67] Specifically, the allegation concerned activities of the Justice Department under newly appointed Attorney General J. Howard McGrath. McGrath had placed fifteen of the AMA's state and county medical societies under investigation for seeking to monopolize prepaid medical-care plans in their areas. What the AMA's charge did not include, however, was acknowledgment that such investigations had been conducted periodically ever since the Supreme Court sustained a ruling in 1943 holding the AMA guilty of restraint of trade in the District of Columbia.[68] Truman's support of the Hill-Aiken bill, a measure that would further expand the AMA's brand of physician-controlled health insurance coverage, would have required, in the face of the AMA broadside, a great deal of statesmanship.

67. The Buchanan committee began its work in late 1949, held hearings (mostly on the real-estate lobby) in 1950, and released a judicious, but little-acknowledged final report on lobbying activity at the conclusion of the Eighty-first Congress. See Alonzo Hamby, *Beyond the New Deal*, pp. 322–27.

68. *New York Times*, 23 August, 7, 16 October 1949; "Statement by the Board of Trustees on Investigations of Medical Organizations," *JAMA* 141 (15 October 1949):465; Burrow, *AMA*, pp. 247–49. Later, the editorial director of the AMA's national education campaign resigned in protest, claiming the AMA charges against the Justice Department were greatly exaggerated. See *Congressional Record*, 81st Cong., 2d sess., 1950, vol. 96, pt. 10, p. 13916.

Could the president have switched his allegiance to the GOP Flanders-Ives bill? Hardly. By 1949 the national health insurance issue had become so identified with political partisanship that Truman could not back a Republican measure. The president himself had contributed to this development by his oft-repeated accusations during the 1948 presidential campaign that the GOP, in alliance with the AMA, had blocked his health insurance program. Naturally, following Truman's victory in November, the Republican national leadership struck up a loud chorus of opposition to what they called the Democratic party's attempts to socialize medicine. Defeated GOP presidential candidate Thomas Dewey called the administration's proposal an "evil invention" that would "reduce our doctors to servitude." [69] Dewey, along with other Republicans, also echoed the AMA's widely publicized accusation that Soviet leader Lenin had stated that socialized medicine was "the keystone in the arch of the socialized state." Sen. Arthur Vandenberg of Michigan added his influential voice to the attack on "socialized medicine," as did Senator Taft on numerous occasions.[70] Taft, speaking as chairman of the Senate Republican Policy Committee, accused the Democrats of refusing to take their health insurance bill to the Senate floor for a showdown because "they would rather preserve the issue for the 1950 elections." [71]

In New York, in the fall, the GOP used the issue against former Gov. Herbert Lehman, who was running in a special election to fill the Senate seat vacated by the death of Robert Wagner. Assisted by organized medicine, the Republican attack became so intense that, although Lehman won by a narrow margin over his GOP opponent, John Foster Dulles, he was forced to disassociate himself from the president's health insurance proposal.[72] At year's

69. *New York Times*, 14 February 1949.
70. Ibid., 14 February, 14 March, 20 April, 14 October 1949.
71. Ibid., 20 April 1949.
72. R. M. Cunningham, "Can Political Means Gain Professional Ends?"; Kelley, *Professional Public Relations and Political Power*, pp. 87–99.

end, the *New York Times* announced that the Republican national leadership had decided to make "socialized medicine" a key issue in the 1950 congressional elections, since, "It is the one issue on which Republicans throughout the country are more unified than any other."[73]

The national leadership of the Democratic party also employed the health insurance proposal as a major political theme in 1949. The Democratic National Committee jumped into the debate in April by sponsoring the first in a series of radio broadcasts in support of Truman's health insurance program. By October, India Edwards had outlined for the president a plan to promote his health insurance idea through her Woman's Division of the Democratic National Committee. And in December, Democratic National Chairman William Boyle, Jr., accused the AMA of taking "punitive action" against its members who refused to fight the president's health scheme.[74]

As for the president, the closest thing to a personal public response from him to the growing AMA-GOP onslaught first came in late September in a speech on Democratic Women's Day. Speaking in general terms, Truman complained that "certain people" had forgotten about the welfare clause in the constitution. Later, in November, Truman made a speech in which he attacked the "reactionaries" who had tried to block his Fair Deal legislative program during the Eighty-first Congress. But again the chief executive did not mention his proposal for health security.[75] At one point Truman referred to his election campaign the year before and said, "I did my level best then to explain to the American people the

73. *New York Times*, 2 January 1950.

74. Ibid., 23 April, 8 December 1949; Democratic National Committee Press Release, 24 April 1949, Democratic National Committee Clipping File, Truman Papers: 11:00 A.M. Appointment, 18 October 1949, Presidential Appointment Book of Matthew Connelly, Truman Papers.

75. Radio Address on Democratic Women's Day, 27 September 1949, in Truman, *Public Papers, 1949*, pp. 489–91; Address in St. Paul, Minnesota, 3 November 1949, in Truman, *Public Papers, 1949*, p. 553.

policies I support. No man—no matter how reactionary his views, or how much he may disagree with me—can honestly deny that the American people knew where I stood before the election." [76]

Few could deny that the president had forcefully discussed his health insurance ideas before the American people during the campaign of 1948; by doing so, Truman had set the stage for the protracted political debate that followed. In support of the administration's side of the issue, the public had heard largely from Oscar Ewing and the Committee for the Nation's Health. In support of the opposition, the nation had heard from the popular press and the American Medical Association's $1.5 million national education campaign. It had hardly been a fair contest.

76. Address in St. Paul, Minnesota, 3 November 1949, in Truman, *Public Papers, 1949,* p. 553.

7

Politics, Then Health: The Medicare Compromise

It would take the combined impact of the United States involvement in a war with North Korea and an unfavorable outcome in the November congressional elections in 1950 to move Harry Truman toward advocating the less ambitious plan of providing government hospital insurance for the aged. Even though the southern Democrat–Republican bloc on Capitol Hill had scorned national health insurance during the Eighty-first Congress's first session in 1949, the less inflammatory provisions contained in the administration-backed omnibus health bill had passed the Senate as separate measures. Clearing the upper chamber had been aid for medical education, funds for expanded government research activities, grants to local public health facilities, and a liberalized hospital-construction program. In October, the hospital-construction bill had actually reached the president's desk for signature.[1]

Nor had other administration programs fared so badly on the Hill in 1949. True, there had been disappointing setbacks in the area of civil rights legislation, in attempts to obtain an imaginative and controversial new method of farm supports (called the "Brannan plan"), and in repeal of the Taft-Hartley Act. But these had been offset by House passage of amendments to greatly increase social security payments and coverage, by Senate passage of an aid to education bill, and by final congressional approval of an increase in the minimum wage and of a long-sought-after housing-construction program. Things looked encouraging enough at year's end to prompt Truman to expand his Fair Deal objectives to include a broad-

1. "Resume of the Handling of Health Legislation, 81st Cong., 1st sess.," box 65, Health Bill S-1679 folder, James E. Murray Papers.

ened housing program to aid middle-income groups and provisions for federal assistance to small business.[2] The Democratic-controlled Eighty-first Congress had reversed the "backward trend of the 80th Congress," Truman noted approvingly in the spring of 1950. And, he predicted, "some of the worst obstructionists" on Capitol Hill would be gone after the congressional elections that fall.[3]

Until then, the president and his supporters continued to use the omnibus health bill, S. 1679, as a lever to block passage of antiadministration bills, such as Senator Taft's "charity" proposal and the Hill-Aiken bipartisan bill to subsidize purchase of Blue Shield and Blue Cross insurance for persons unable to afford it. The Federal Security Agency's "general position on S. 1679 should be maintained since retreat or major compromise would confuse and alienate advocates without winning over opponents," Oscar Ewing had written Truman in January. "Approval might later be given to a more limited program, such as compulsory hospital insurance or insurance against catastrophic illness. . . , if there were reasonable chances of adoption," recommended Ewing. In the interim, Ewing advised that a number of "clarifications" or "modifications" be made in S. 1679, ranging from greater emphasis upon the use of private, voluntary prepayment programs,

2. Richard Neustadt, "Congress and the Fair Deal: A Legislative Balance Sheet," pp. 366–72; Alonzo L. Hamby, *Beyond the New Deal: Harry S. Truman and American Liberalism,* pp. 293–342.

3. Address in Chicago at the National Democratic Conference, 15 May 1950, in Harry S. Truman, *The Public Papers of the Presidents of the United States, 1950,* pp. 412–13. About the same time, the president's chief Republican congressional opponent, Sen. Robert A. Taft of Ohio, expressed his own concern over the likelihood of Congress becoming more reform minded in 1951. Writing a British physician in April 1950, Taft observed that while the "present Congress is opposed to [compulsory health insurance] . . . , there is a very strong propaganda [*sic*] for it and it is likely to grow in strength by the time a new Congress meets in 1951." See Taft to J. L. Macaulay, 30 April 1949, S. 1679–S. 1581, 1949 folder, box 575, Robert A. Taft Papers.

to a refusal to authorize payment of health services "if there is evidence that patients abuse the [national health insurance] system."[4]

The president agreed, but only to a point. By crossing out the word *should* in Ewing's suggested modifications of S. 1679 and replacing it with his penciled qualification *might*, Harry Truman indicated a reluctance, if not an outright refusal, to placate those who desired a softening of his position.[5] He resisted yielding ground to his congressional detractors, especially in the face of organized medicine's multi-million-dollar attack upon him; and a renewed request for national health insurance appeared in each of Truman's three annual messages to Congress that January.[6]

As it turned out, there was no need to modify the insurance provisions contained in S. 1679. Senator Murray's subcommittee on health allowed the bill to languish in 1950, turning instead to a study of the country's existing, voluntary health insurance system. In the House, meanwhile, the Committee on Interstate and Foreign Commerce, which had held hearings the year before on Rep. John Dingell's version of S. 1679, busied itself with bills dealing with airline subsidies and interstate shipment of slot machines.[7]

The closest thing to congressional action on health security in 1950 came in July when the House, in a sequel to the Senate's performance in 1949, beat down a renewed administration reorganization plan to elevate the Federal

4. FSA Memorandum, "Discussion and Agreements of Working Committee," 21 January 1950, Records of the Administrator, Federal Security Agency, file 011.4, box 18, Record Group 235, National Archives. Hereafter cited as FSA Administrator's Records.

5. Presidential notation, file 011.4, box 18, FSA Administrator's Records.

6. State of the Union Message, 4 January 1950, Annual Economic Report, 6 January 1950, and Annual Budget Message, 9 January 1950, in Truman, *Public Papers, 1950*, pp. 9, 29, 46, 54.

7. *Congressional Record*, 81st Cong., 2d sess., 1950, vol. 96, pt. 6, p. 7770.

Security Agency to department status by the lopsided margin of 249 to 71. Again the debate preceding the vote centered upon the "dangerous" consequences of Oscar Ewing's promotion to cabinet rank. And, again, members of Harry Truman's own political party refused to follow his lead. Nearly half the negative votes had come from Democrats; still smarting over Truman's position on civil rights, not a single member of the House's ninety-one-man southern Democratic delegation voted with the administration.[8]

Congress's unrelenting hostility to major health-care reform caused a rift among key leaders of the Committee for the Nation's Health, so much so that the CNH nearly closed its books in 1950. Rumblings of discontent had first appeared within the committee during the bleak and uncertain days just prior to the 1948 presidential election, when the organization's chief financial backers, Albert and Mary Lasker and the Rosenwald family, raised objections to Michael Davis's insistence that national health insurance remain the CNH's chief legislative goal. "Davis was unrealistic about what could be accomplished in Congress," Mary Lasker later reflected.[9] The rift healed then, however, largely because of Harry Truman's surprise victory that November. But when favorable action on the omnibus health bill did not develop in 1949, the CNH sponsors renewed their criticism of Davis's leadership. A faction led by the Laskers demanded in November that the committee begin placing primary emphasis upon passing the less controversial aspects of the president's health program, especially federal funding for medical education and research. The other group, led by Davis, maintained that the CNH, while promoting passage of piecemeal legislation in 1950, should continue to place highest priority upon national health insurance. The final impasse came in January after representatives of the AFL and the CIO brought the matter to a head by

8. House vote on H. Res. 647 to disapprove Reorganization Plan No. 27, 10 July 1950, *Congressional Quarterly Almanac* 6 (1950):560–61.

9. Mary W. Lasker to author, 14 August 1967.

throwing their support to Davis. The Laskers and Rosen-walds withdrew their 1950 pledges and resigned from the committee.[10]

The militants had won, but for a few precarious months afterward, the CNH operated on a hand-to-mouth basis. With only fourteen hundred dollars in the bank and expenses running at three thousand dollars a month, urgent appeals went out to organized labor for financial support, and in late March the United Steel Workers saved the committee from financial collapse by contributing two thousand dollars. Other unions followed with various offerings, totaling about twenty-five thousand dollars.[11] By October, Michael Davis could report "a radical and wholesome change in the basic financing of the health insurance movement."[12] Organized labor had become CNH's chief benefactor, a role that labor maintained until the committee's demise in 1956.

The Democratic National Committee provided additional financial support for the CNH in 1950. The president's continued advocacy of health security, plus the AMA's expensive lobbying effort against it, guaranteed that the health insurance issue would be used either in behalf of or against Democratic congressional candidates that year. In May, after hearing Oscar Ewing urge that it back Truman's program, the Democratic National Committee (purged the year before of six southern members who had bolted to the Dixiecrat banner)[13] adopted

10. Lessing J. Rosenwald to CNH Executive Committee, 23 October 1948, Minutes of Executive Committee Meeting, 3 November 1948, Executive Committee to Rosenwald, 8 November 1948, Minutes of Executive Committee Meeting, 25 January 1950, Albert D. Lasker to Michael M. Davis, 23 January 1950, Davis to Executive Committee, 6 April 1950, Records of the Committee for the Nation's Health, Michael M. Davis Papers. Hereafter cited as CNH Records, Davis Papers.

11. Davis to Executive Committee, 14, 30 March 1950, CNH Records, Davis Papers.

12. Davis to Executive Committee, 5 October 1950, and unsigned memorandum, "Cash Receipts and Disbursements for the Year Ended December 31, 1950," CNH Records, Davis Papers.

13. *New York Times*, 16 May 1950; Donald R. McCoy and

a resolution that used a bit of reverse psychology against the AMA and its Republican allies, declaring:

> In order to avoid socialized medicine in the United States, we endorse the President's program for broadened federal activity in the entire field of health and medical care and the adoption of a-pay-as-you-go insurance program to put medical care within the financial reach of all Americans.[14]

Anticipating the endorsement, the chairman of the Democratic National Committee, William Boyle, Jr., had promised Michael Davis a DNC contribution of from fifteen to twenty thousand dollars to be used for publication of campaign literature. Until the money could be raised, India Edwards gave CNH one thousand dollars out of the emergency fund of her Woman's Division of the Democratic National Committee. In return, CNH sent Democratic national headquarters copies of a booklet entitled "Better Medical Care That *You* Can Afford" and of a speaker's handbook on national health insurance for distribution to party leaders throughout the country. In June, CNH's Frederick Robins traveled to Iowa, Minnesota, and Michigan to participate in training institutes organized to brief Democratic congressional candidates.[15]

All in all, 1950 proved to be a busy year for the revived Committee for the Nation's Health. In addition to sending out fourteen informational bulletins and sixteen special mailings to cooperating organizations, CNH prepared forty-six thousand pieces of material for the liberal, special-interest press; distributed three hundred fifty thousand pieces of its own literature; participated in one hundred fifty conferences with members of the adminis-

Richard T. Ruetten, *Quest and Response: Minority Rights and the Truman Administration*, p. 182.

14. "Democratic Party Resolution on Platform," Chicago, 17 May 1950, copy in CNH Records, Davis Papers.

15. Davis to Executive Committee, 7 April, 6 June 1950, Minutes of Executive Committee Meeting, 15 June, 6 July 1950, CNH Records, Davis Papers; Democratic National Committee Press Release, 1 May 1950, Democratic National Committee Clipping File, Harry S. Truman Papers.

tration and Congress; furnished materials to the Democratic National Committee, Americans for Democratic Action, the Liberal party, and the CIO Political Action Committee; and provided speeches for a number of Congressmen. By year's end, CNH had spent about thirty-six thousand dollars.[16]

In marked contrast, the American Medical Association's "National Education Campaign" for 1950 cost over $2.25 million.[17] "The first skirmishes were ended and won," an AMA spokesman told the press in late 1949. "Unfortunately, the war was not."[18] To continue the battle against Truman in 1950, doctors were again beseeched to rally against the enemies of free enterprise; for, as the chairman of the AMA Board of Trustees warned physicians in May, "If twenty more radical Congressmen and five or six radical Senators are elected this fall, the fight will be over and we will have socialized medicine."[19]

Although the AMA, as a nonprofit, tax-exempt organization, could not enter directly into the election contest of 1950, member physicians acting as individuals could participate and did so by forming local committees to defeat candidates considered dangerous to organized medicine. Success came early in Florida when Sen. Claude Pepper lost to George Smathers in the state's Democratic primary in May. To help defeat Pepper, many doctors over the state donated one hundred dollars apiece, their wives staged parties to raise more funds, and medical political-action committees labored against Pepper in every Florida county. Prior to the election, patients in a Tallahassee hospital actually awoke one morning to find cards placed on their breakfast trays reading "This is the season for canning Pepper!" In Wisconsin, doctors or-

16. "CNH Activities in 1950," January 1951, "Cash Receipts and Disbursements for the Year Ended December 31, 1950," CNH Records, Davis Papers.

17. Report of Coordinating Committee," *Journal of the American Medical Association* (hereafter cited as *JAMA*) 147 (22 December 1951):1692.

18. *New York Times*, 7 December 1949.

19. Ibid., 9 May 1950.

ganized as Physicians for Freedom pitted themselves against another arch rival of organized medicine, Rep. Andrew Biemiller.[20] The same held true in the Far West. "The doctors have now moved into Idaho and Utah," wrote embattled Sen. Elbert Thomas from Utah to Oscar Ewing in July. "We will have all of the opposition that has been showing itself so strong in other places. But here is hoping."[21]

On the national level, the AMA organized a $1.1 million newspaper and radio advertising campaign to start the week of 8 October. Although the campaign was ostensibly launched to stimulate enrollment in private health insurance plans and to develop an "articulate public opinion" that the "socializers in Washington" could not ignore,[22] its intensity and timing were designed to influence the voter's response to congressional candidates, to serve, as Elmer Davis observed in one of his radio commentaries, "as an adjunct to the Republican campaign."[23] Beforehand, the AMA ran ads in trade magazines urging sympathetic businesses to purchase tie-in advertisements of their own in the AMA October marathon. Businessmen could choose from twenty-seven varieties of layouts, of which one would be designed to conform to their particular type of enterprise. Participating firms merely added their names to precast mats made available by the AMA to local newspapers. During the selected two-week period, 8–22 October, every bona fide weekly and daily newspaper in the United States (10,033 in all) carried a five-column-wide, fourteen-inch-deep ad from the AMA or from one of its business allies decrying the enemies of free enterprise, while 1600 radio stations broadcast spot announcements and 35 magazines carried similar adver-

20. R. Cragin Lewis, "New Power at the Polls: The Doctors," in Henry A. Turner, ed., *Politics in the United States*, p. 181; "The American Medical Association: Power, Purpose, and Politics in Organized Medicine," p. 1016.

21. Elbert D. Thomas to Oscar Ewing, 12 July 1950, file 011.4, box 217, FSA Administrator's Records.

22. *New York Times*, 27 June 1950.

23. Elmer Davis Radio Broadcast Transcript, 13 October 1950, in CNH Records, Davis Papers.

tisements. Banks, insurance companies, druggists, even restaurant owners purchased tie-in ads to the tune of an estimated $2 million, bringing the total two-week expenditure to well over $3 million.[24]

Friends of the administration made a feeble effort to blunt the October campaign. Senator Murray called a press conference to label the campaign's cost "a tragic waste" of money that could better be spent for tuition fees for up to nine thousand medical students. Representative Dingell asked concerned citizens to each ask ten people to help counter the campaign and to urge that they in turn ask ten others. The CIO ran a full-page ad in seventy-seven newspapers portraying a mother, with a sick child by her side, writing an open letter to her family doctor. It read, "I am pleading with you, Doctor, to join on my side—on our side—on the side of the people!"[25] But, as CNH's Frederick Robins admitted, given the limited finances of those backing the president's program, trying to counter the AMA's saturation advertising campaign was "like trying to put out a forest fire with a sprinkling can."[26]

John Dingell decided finally that only President Truman could counter the AMA's October campaign. In September, Dingell wrote Truman to ask that he deliver a radio address in order to directly answer the AMA's attack.[27] "I have felt for some time that this is the way to answer the propaganda of the AMA," the chairman of the CNH, Dr. Channing Frothingham, wrote Dingell after learning of the congressman's plan. "I am glad to know that there is a practical way of putting pressure

24. *New York Times*, 15 September 1950; reprint from *Editor & Publisher*, 16 September 1950, in CNH Records, Davis Papers; "The President's Page," *JAMA* 146 (23 September 1950):319; "AMA: Power, Purpose, and Politics," p. 1015.

25. *New York Times*, 17 September 1950; *Congressional Record*, 81st Cong., 2d sess., 1950, vol. 96, pt. 17, pp. A6536–37; CIO ad reprint, CNH Records, Davis Papers.

26. Frederick Robins to Matthew Connelly, 14 September 1950, Truman Papers, Official File (hereafter cited as OF) 286-A.

27. John D. Dingell to Harry S. Truman, 28 September 1950, John D. Dingell Papers.

upon the President."[28] The president of the AFL, William Green, also liked Dingell's idea: "You are right in your conclusion that no one except President Truman could reach the people of the nation and make a convincing answer to the propaganda," wrote Green in October. He, too, planned to urge the president to speak out against the AMA.[29] India Edwards joined in and, in a visit to the White House, asked Truman to make the speech.[30]

Earlier that year, in a style remindful of his 1948 reelection campaigning, the president had lashed out against what he labeled his "reactionary" or "alarmist" opposition. In March, responding to a GOP election-year platform statement that "the major domestic issue today is liberty against socialism" and to Sen. Joseph McCarthy's mushrooming demagogic crusade to expose an unspecified number of Communists in the State Department,[31] Truman told reporters bitingly, "The Republicans have been trying vainly to find an issue on which to make a bid for the control of the Congress for next year. They tried 'statism.' They tried 'welfare state.' They tried 'socialism.' " Now, he said, they were trying "to sabotage the bipartisan foreign policy of the United States." He was "fed up" and determined to provide "the facts" as he saw them.[32] In May, on a whistle-stop tour of northwestern states, undertaken, as he expressed it, "to make things more plain and understandable" for the people,[33] the president defended his Fair Deal objectives,

28. Channing Frothingham to Dingell, 18 October 1950, Dingell Papers.

29. William Green to Dingell, 18 October 1950, Dingell Papers.

30. 10:45 A.M. Appointment, 11 October 1950, Presidential Appointment Book of Matthew Connelly, Truman Papers; India Edwards to Dingell, 18 October 1950, Dingell Papers.

31. *New York Times*, 7 February 1950; Hamby, *Beyond the New Deal*, pp. 396–97.

32. The President's News Conference at Key West, 30 March 1950, in Truman, *Public Papers, 1950*, p. 235.

33. Address at the Dedication of the Grand Coulee Dam, 11 May 1950, in Truman, *Public Papers, 1950*, p. 369.

including government health insurance. Speaking in Minot, North Dakota, Truman told his railside audience that Blue Cross and Blue Shield insurance were fine, but in order to provide better protection for more people, and at a cost they could afford, it was necessary "to pool insurance risks on a nationwide basis." Those who attacked his program simply did not have the facts; there would be no doctors on the public payroll, and the hospitals would remain free of government control.[34]

Nor could the AMA's multi-million-dollar lobbying effort have been far from Truman's mind when, in June, he spoke before a gathering of Better Business Bureau representatives: "There are books, and columns, and advertisements, and pamphlets, and broadcasts, and chain letters, all telling us that the Republic is in peril, and that we are on the last mile, that socialism lies just ahead," but, the president insisted, it had all been said before during the depression thirties by the reactionary and defeatist Liberty League, and the results of government programs initiated then to help farmers, labor unions, and American business had proved the alarmists wrong. He pointed out that American economic productivity had risen from less than $60 billion in 1932 to over $260 billion in 1950. Moreover, Truman said, those who argued against a social security system and federal hydroelectric power projects during the early days of the New Deal should have known better; private insurance policies had increased 50 percent since 1936, and private power companies had expanded their kilowatt output by 60 percent since 1933. The president concluded, "Today, we have learned that these Government activities—such as social insurance and hydroelectric development—do not harm business. Instead, they increase the wealth of all, and in that way they increase the opportunities of all business."[35] Three weeks later, the president of the American Medical Association called Truman's administration "a Gov-

34. Remarks at Minot, North Dakota, 13 May 1950, in Truman, *Public Papers, 1950*, p. 396.

35. Address at a Dinner of the Better Business Bureau, 6 June 1950, in Truman, *Public Papers, 1950*, pp. 460–61.

ernment which is sick with intellectual dishonesty, with avarice, with moral laxity and with reckless excesses."[36]

Aside from political rhetoric, Harry Truman had also given Congressman Dingell and the other health reformers encouragement by his behind-the-scenes labors to pry loose an aid-to-medical-education bill from its House committee during the summer and to win final congressional approval of amendments to liberalize the Social Security Act. The president failed on the medical education bill, after trying for forty-five minutes to persuade the House committee's members to report it to the floor;[37] but in August he won passage of the social security amendments. It had taken Congress a year and a half of debate and compromise, and nearly five thousand pages of testimony, to enact the first major revision of the social security system since 1939. Old age and survivor's insurance coverage was expanded to include about 10 million additional workers, and OASI payments were increased by an average of 80 percent. But opposition by the American Medical Association, the U.S. Chamber of Commerce, most employer groups, and casualty insurance companies helped eliminate a provision providing benefits before age sixty-five to those who became permanently and totally disabled.[38] "To initiate a Federal disability program would represent another step toward wholesale nationalization of medical care and the socialization of the practice of medicine," charged the AMA spokesman at the Senate's hearings on the legislation.[39] However, another feature relating to governmental health financing remained intact in the 1950 amendments. This concerned a liberalized arrangement whereby states could use federal matching funds to make "vendor" payments to doctors and others who dispensed medical services to welfare recipients.[40] Modest in scope in the beginning, the

36. *New York Times*, 28 June 1950.
37. Hamby, *Beyond the New Deal*, p. 349.
38. Arthur J. Altmeyer, *The Formative Years of Social Security*, pp. 179–89.
39. Quoted in Ibid., pp. 185–86.
40. Ibid., p. 281.

"vendor" payment program expanded greatly during the following decade.

The president made a short statement about the need for further improvements in social security when he signed the 1950 amendments into law in August.[41] But, except for one political speech in November, it would be Truman's last major reference to the subject that year. He ignored the appeals from John Dingell and the others that he go on radio to offset the AMA's October campaign. The president "is not making any political speeches," explained a disappointed India Edwards in mid-October; it would be highly unlikely that he would "be able to take a crack at the AMA."[42] The reason? On 25 June 1950, only a few weeks after Truman's free-swinging Better Business Bureau speech, hostilities had broken out in Korea. By mid-September, American and allied United Nations troops were embroiled in a full-scale counteroffensive against the North Korean Communists. "I had hoped to make some speeches in this campaign of 1950," Truman reflected in his only political appearance that fall, but "the critical international situation" had made it impossible.[43] War in the Far East now concerned the president far more than printed attacks by the American Medical Association. In fact, Truman's Wake Island war strategy talks with U.N. Commander Gen. Douglas MacArthur came during the midpoint of the AMA's two-week October publicity extravaganza. Also, about the time the AMA's campaign wound to a close, reports began coming in concerning the intrusion of thousands of Red Chinese "volunteers" into the Korean fighting. When the reports proved true, the war took on a different, and far more ominous, dimension.[44]

41. Statement by the President Upon Signing the Social Security Act Amendments, 28 August 1950, in Truman, *Public Papers, 1950,* pp. 600–601.

42. India Edwards to Dingell, 18 October 1950, Dingell Papers.

43. Address in Kiel Auditorium, St. Louis, 4 November 1950, in Truman, *Public Papers, 1950,* p. 698.

44. John W. Spanier, *The Truman-MacArthur Controversy and the Korean War,* p. 114.

The outcome of the November elections weakened the health security movement even further. Sen. Elbert Thomas and Rep. Andrew Biemiller (cosponsors of the omnibus health bill) were both defeated; while, symbolically, Sen. Robert Taft won reelection in Ohio by a landslide. Although the Democrats retained control of Congress, they suffered a net loss of five seats in the Senate and twenty-eight seats in the House. The conservative coalition became even more powerful on Capitol Hill.[45]

Continued advocacy of national health insurance now seemed absurd. The war in Korea and the election results forced Michael Davis and other leaders of the Committee for the Nation's Health to accept what they had refused to acknowledge one year before: To be at all effective in the foreseeable future, the CNH would have to reorient its lobbying activities, placing greatest emphasis upon passage of the aid-to-medical-education bill and other limited health proposals. On 7 January, the group issued a press release proclaiming, "War Danger Leads Committee to Renew Work for Truman Health Program." In it, CNH stressed the need for additional wartime medical personnel.[46]

For the first time in five years, rejoiced the *Journal of the American Medical Association*, Congress felt no pressure "to look into President Truman's compulsory health insurance suggestions."[47] Accordingly, the AMA's lobbying expenditure for 1951 would be five hundred thousand dollars, $2 million less than the previous year.[48] This did not, however, signal a softening of the AMA position concerning Fair Deal–type liberals. Elmer Henderson, president of the AMA, asserted in February, "Certainly we cannot afford to retire to our ivory towers now and politely disparage the work of the surgeons who cut out the

45. Hamby, *Beyond the New Deal*, pp. 421–22; McCoy and Ruetten, *Quest and Response*, pp. 283–85.

46. Michael Davis to Executive Committee, "Suggested Program for 1951," n.d., CNH Press Release, 7 January 1951, CNH Records, Davis Papers.

47. "Legislative Notes," *JAMA* 145 (20 January 1951):34.

48. "Report of Coordinating Committee," *JAMA* 147 (22 December 1951):1692:

cancer of socialized medicine."[49] Caught up by the prevailing anticommunist rhetoric of the time—especially by Sen. Joseph McCarthy's search for Reds in government and society—and determined that "the right people" be elected to political office in 1952, the American Medical Association began speaking out on domestic concerns beyond the immediate purview of health care.[50] The AMA House of Delegates asked Congress in June to investigate the nation's "entire school system" in order to expose "teachers and authors of textbooks advocating overthrow of the American system of free enterprise by infiltration of un-American fallacies of collectivism."[51] In December, the AMA again called attention to "the dangerous inroads on our national thinking already achieved by the insidious philosophy of collectivism" and demanded the removal of those educators who would "pervert our school system."[52] Moreover, President Henderson of the AMA had charged the previous February that the Committee for the Nation's Health had a "pinkish pigmentation."[53] Despite written protests signed by various CNH members, including Eleanor Roosevelt and future Supreme Court justice Abe Fortas, Henderson expanded upon his accusation over the next two years until, in the eyes of the AMA, the CNH directorship had taken on definite hues of red.[54]

As for Harry Truman, his reaction to legislative affairs following the 1950 elections was that nothing had changed. He was "not blue" over the results, he told re-

49. "The President's Page," *JAMA* 145 (24 February 1951): 567.

50. James G. Burrow, *AMA: Voice of American Medicine*, p. 384.

51. American Medical Association, *Digest of Official Actions, 1846–1958*, pp. 339–40.

52. Ibid., pp. 340–41.

53. "The President's Page," *JAMA* 145 (24 February 1951): 567.

54. *New York Times*, 15 April 1951; Committee for the Nation's Health to Elmer L. Henderson, 15 March 1951, Channing Frothingham to Louis H. Bauer, n.d., Bauer to Frothingham, 17 November 1952, Frothingham to Bauer, 10 December 1952, CNH Records, Davis Papers.

porters. The outcome reflected local issues, and he did not see it as a mandate to go slow on pushing for his Fair Deal program. "I will continue to press for it as long as I am President," he insisted. Furthermore, he expected the incoming Congress to act on all the proposals he would set before it: "I expect to get it all done. . . . I wouldn't be trying to get it if I didn't expect to get it. I hope to get everything I ask for."[55] When he went up to the Hill to deliver his state of the Union address in January, the president, while emphasizing national security matters, nevertheless reminded lawmakers of the "need to provide insurance against the loss of earnings through sickness, and against the high costs of modern medical care."[56] Did the omission of health insurance in the president's budget message mean that it had "been dropped for the time being"? a reporter asked Truman a few days later during a budget news seminar. "No, it has not," the president answered tartly, it could be found on page M56 of the budget; and he added, "Better watch out, you may get a speech out of me on that."[57] Sure enough. On page M56, Harry Truman had included, under the item "Medical Care Insurance Trust Fund," $275 million to cover initial expenses for his health insurance proposal in the event Congress approved the plan.[58]

This seems to have been mostly political bravado, because, at the end of January, Truman explained apologetically to the CNH chairman, Dr. Channing Frothingham, that "legislation to meet the present national emergency must necessarily take precedence in national consideration at this time."[59] Within the administration, Oscar Ewing had begun searching for a substitute for na-

55. The President's News Conference of November 16, 1950, in Truman, *Public Papers, 1950*, pp. 713–15.
56. Annual Message to the Congress on the State of the Union, 8 January 1951, in Truman, *Public Papers, 1951*, p. 12.
57. The President's News Conference on the Budget, 13 January 1951, in Truman, *Public Papers, 1951*, p. 55.
58. Annual Budget Message to Congress: Fiscal Year 1952, 15 January 1951, in Truman, *Public Papers, 1951*, p. 100.
59. Truman to Channing Frothingham, 31 January 1951, Truman Papers, OF 286-A.

tional health insurance, "something," as he put it, "that we might save out of defeat."[60] Having cocktails at the home of publisher William Randolph Hearst, Jr., one winter afternoon, Ewing talked to Hearst about the Truman insurance idea; and Hearst asked if it would not be possible to try a more limited, "pilot plant" approach, such as providing a prepayment program for a small segment of the population. He suggested that this program could be used to test the workability of the administration's all-inclusive approach to health care.[61] Shortly afterward, Ewing visited with another friend, Louis Pink, head of New York's Blue Cross hospital-insurance system. "There is one phase of this whole [health] problem where I think government might be helpful," Pink told Ewing. "It's the over-65 group. We really have no actuarial experience or data upon which we could formulate a program covering them."[62]

In the spring of 1951, putting Hearst's and Pink's suggestions together, Ewing proposed to the president that he advocate a hospital insurance plan for the aged financed through social security. Harry Truman balked at first, he did not want to settle for anything short of his entire national health insurance program. However, after two or three conferences, the FSA director persuaded the president to shift to a program wherein government would insure the over-sixty-five age group and their dependents against hospital expenses.[63]

The federal hospital insurance concept was not really new, it had been considered within the Social Security Board as a possible alternative to a comprehensive prepayment scheme as early as 1942, during Roosevelt's presidency. Furthermore, by the time Oscar Ewing began casting about for a limited, "pilot plant" approach to prepaid health care, those working for Arthur Altmeyer in the Social Security Administration—including Altmeyer's

60. Oscar R. Ewing Memoir, Columbia University Oral History Project.
61. Ibid.; Ewing to author, 9 May 1967.
62. Ewing Oral History, 26 August 1966.
63. Ewing to author, 9 May 1967.

assistant, Wilbur Cohen, and Isidore Falk of the Bureau
of Research and Statistics—had, themselves, been considering ways to modify the sweeping and controversial S.
1679. Since 1949, Falk's staff had devoted increasing attention to the medical costs endured by elderly Americans. Consequently, when Arthur Altmeyer asked Falk
for a statement on hospital insurance to be sent to Oscar
Ewing, Falk could submit a cogently argued summary of
a staff memo he had prepared originally in mid-1950 entitled "Proposals for Providing Hospitalization Benefits
to Beneficiaries Under the Federal Old-Age and Survivors
Insurance System."[64]

In June, after Ewing had held various conferences with
the social security staff, the president and Ewing decided
to test public opinion before seeking congressional sponsorship of a bill incorporating the hospital insurance
plan.[65] In a speech carried on radio that he made while
dedicating a National Institutes of Health clinical
research center in Bethesda, Maryland, Truman, after de-
fending his efforts since 1945 to meet "skyrocketing medical costs" through a system of national health insurance,
said, "This proposal has generated a great deal of controversy. I still believe it is sound, and that the Nation
would be greatly strengthened by its adoption." Then
came the retreat: "I want to make it clear, however, that
I am not clinging to any particular plan." Although he
wanted a workable program that would allow "all Ameri-

64. "Hospitalization Payments Under Old-Age and Survivors
Insurance: Summary of Discussion of Meeting of Social Security Board Staff with Special Committee of the Board of Trustees,
American Hospital Association, and Joint Advisory Committee
of the American Hospital Association, Protestant Hospital Association, and Catholic Hospital Association," 3, 4 September
1942, box 28, Social Security: Hospital and Health Insurance,
1942–1950 folder, Wilbur J. Cohen Papers; Wilbur J. Cohen
to author, 11 July 1967; interview with Isidore S. Falk; Arthur
J. Altmeyer to Oscar Ewing, 24 January 1951, and I. S. Falk,
"Proposals for Providing Hospitalization Benefits to Beneficiaries Under the Federal Old-Age and Survivors Insurance System," 17 July 1950, as amended 10 January 1951, box 7,
Hospital Benefits, 1951 folder, Arthur J. Altmeyer Papers.

65. Interview with Oscar R. Ewing.

cans" to pay for their medical expenses, he offered, "If the people who have been blocking health insurance for 5 years will come up with a better proposal—or even one that is almost as good—I'll go along with them. I want to get the job done, and I am not concerned in the slightest with pride of ownership." Truman insisted, however, that any program produce results. "Medical care is for the people and not just for the doctors—and the rich."[66]

Three days later, Oscar Ewing called reporters in to announce that he was recommending that the president include in his Fair Deal proposals hospital insurance coverage (up to sixty days of confinement per year) for social security pensioners and the widows and children of deceased pensioners. The aged were caught in a dilemma, emphasized a printed handout Ewing circulated among the press. The blessings of medical science, while enabling Americans to live longer, had also left them confronted in old age with chronic illness, low income, and decreased insurability because of high risk. While about half of the general population carried some form of private health insurance, only about 10 to 15 percent of those over age sixty-five could afford such protection.[67]

Truman and Ewing knew, of course, that the American Medical Association would not back even a limited prepayment plan sponsored by the government. President Henderson of the AMA responded to Truman's challenge that his opponents "come up with a better proposal" by claiming that a better plan already existed, "the American medical system, which has made this the healthiest great nation in the world."[68] Nor did the AMA's continued opposition to federal aid to education,

66. Address at the Dedication of the National Institutes of Health Clinical Center, 22 June 1951, in Truman, *Public Papers, 1951*, pp. 352–53.

67. Statement by Oscar Ewing, Press Conference, 25 June 1951, copy in Truman Papers, OF 7; Federal Security Agency, "Background Statement on Old-Age and Survivors Hospitalization Insurance," 25 June 1951, copy provided author courtesy of Isidore Falk.

68. *New York Times*, 23 June 1951.

disability insurance through social security, and other peripheral government health schemes lend encouragement.[69] The White House also knew that retreat from national health insurance would not translate into easier going for proadministration Democrats the following year in the 1952 political campaign. Health insurance would be a major issue, "whether by choice of the Democratic Party or not," presidential aide David Stowe wrote Truman in October. The impact of the AMA's effective "propaganda machine" made this a certainty. Therefore, recommended Stowe, the president should choose "without further delay" one of three courses of action:

1. Soft pedal the health issue and rely upon the record to date.
2. Embark upon an effort to push all features of the health program including the Ewing proposal for medical aid to the aged with the use of OASI funds. . . .
3. Initiate a comprehensive study of the health needs of the nation as a means of re-evaluating the Administration's program.

Option number three was the "most desirable," Stowe counseled, because soft-pedaling the issue would merely give the initiative to the opposition, and an all-out effort would meet with no success in Congress.[70]

Stowe's memo culminated nearly a year of on-again, off-again talks among White House staffers over ways to avoid political repercussions in 1952 over the administration's controversial stance on medical care. John Connorton, the hospital association leader, had helped spark the discussion following the 1950 elections by suggesting to Truman's special counsel, Charles Murphy, that the president appoint a commission to investigate anew the health needs of the nation. Connorton predicted that if such a commission conducted its inquiry in a judicious

69. Altmeyer, *Formative Years of Social Security*, p. 196; Burrow, *AMA*, pp. 375–84.

70. David H. Stowe to the President, 12 October 1951, David H. Stowe Papers.

manner, it would "remove the issue of socialized medicine from the 1952 campaign."[71]

The presidential staff, and ultimately Harry Truman, decided that Connorton's idea had the greatest merit. David Stowe's October memorandum to the president included a draft of an executive order establishing a commission on the health needs of the nation, as well as a roster of possible commission members should Truman agree to his staff's conclusions.[72] "The attached looks all right to me," the president responded. "I think the best thing to do is to go ahead with it. Let's see if we can find the right people for the commission."[73]

Several days later, Truman spoke briefly to the board of trustees of the conservative, pro-AMA American Dental Association assembled in the White House rose garden. The medical rejection rate among draftees during the second world war had "startled" him, the president explained, and when he had tried to do something about it, he had met with "all sorts of accusations . . . about my intending to turn the country into a socialistic state, and all that sort of business." If the dentists would just study his health recommendations, they would "find that there never has been a program more widely and completely misrepresented." Not revealing his decision to appoint a health commission, Truman stressed the need to discover "the facts and the truth" about national health problems. "Now, if somebody has got a better way than

71. John V. Connorton to Charles Murphy, 13 November 1950, Truman Papers, OF 286-A.

72. Stowe to the President, 12 October 1951, Stowe Papers.

73. Truman to Stowe, 15 October 1951, Stowe Papers. In his study of presidential leadership of public opinion, Elmer Cornwell, Jr., implies that the Stowe memorandum and Truman's reply reveal that in this instance the White House staff established broad strategy with "minimal presidential involvement." Yet, as Cornwell himself acknowledges, documents like Stowe's often represented the end product of a staff effort initiated at the president's request. In light of Truman's various other activities and statements relating to the subject prior to the October 1951 memo, the latter explanation seems more valid. See Elmer E. Cornwell, Jr., *Presidential Leadership of Public Opinion*, pp. 240–41.

the one I propose," he said, "I am perfectly willing to accept it. . . , all I want you to do is get the facts, and don't believe what you see in certain magazines and papers."[74]

To provide those facts, facts that might take Democratic candidates off the hook in 1952 and that might even prove embarrassing to organized medicine and to his political opposition in general, Truman announced at year's end his establishment of the President's Commission on the Health Needs of the Nation. A thorough examination of the country's total health requirements was needed, he said, because the "bitter opposition" engendered by his attempts to solve the many shortcomings in national health services had "confused" the public. Nor, Truman claimed, had this opposition come forth with counter-proposals to his suggestions. The commission would, therefore, after gathering the facts over the next twelve months, submit its own recommendations on what should be done to remedy the health situation. In a transparently political maneuver, the president also stipulated that the commission submit interim reports on its findings throughout the twelve-month period of its work, which just happened to be 1952, a presidential election year.[75]

Reformers and conservatives alike expressed disenchantment with the commission idea. Within the government, Isidore Falk felt that the president's decision was unwise; that it only played into the hands of the AMA; and, moreover, that existing evidence amply chronicled the need for national health insurance. Michael Davis of the CNH worried about the philosophical bent of most of the commission's fifteen members and questioned whether, in the time available, the commission could do an adequate job of assessing national health needs. But the loudest and most intense criticism came from the officers of the American Medical Association. In a dra-

74. Remarks to the Officers and Members of the Board of Trustees, American Dental Association, 16 October 1951, in Truman, *Public Papers, 1951*, p. 580.

75. Statement by the President on Establishing the Commission on the Health Needs of the Nation, 29 December 1951, in Truman, *Public Papers, 1951*, pp. 655–56.

matic display of defiance, Dr. Gunnar Gundersen, an AMA trustee, resigned his commission seat before the group had held its first meeting. The commission was merely "an instrument of practical politics," charged the doctor. The president-elect of the AMA, Dr. Louis Bauer, wrote the commission chairman that after looking up the backgrounds of some of the commission members he had become convinced that the chairman faced an impossible task, that the commission surely could not issue an unbiased report. The AMA president, John Cline, went further, describing the commission as "the latest maneuver in the President's campaign to socialize the medical profession."[76]

In most respects, the AMA's criticism was valid. As public health lobbyist Mary Lasker later admitted, the commission had been conceived as "an instrument of practical politics."[77] Although President Truman named Dr. Paul Magnuson—a distinguished surgeon, formerly chief medical director of the Veterans Administration, and an outspoken foe of bureaucratic red tape and compulsory health insurance—as commission chairman,[78] most of the commission's other fourteen members were either moderates on the need for government health funding or openly critical of organized medicine. Among the former group were five members associated with medical schools, "institutional types" who tended to favor federal aid for medical research and education.[79] Among the group that

76. Interview with Falk; Davis to Executive Committee, 13 December 1951, 6 February 1952, CNH Records, Davis Papers; *New York Times*, 13 December 1951; Louis Bauer to Paul B. Magnuson, 31 December 1951, Records of the President's Commission on the Health Needs of the Nation, Truman Papers (hereafter cited as Magnuson Commission Records, Truman Papers); "The President's Page," *JAMA* 148 (19 January 1952): 208.

77. Mary W. Lasker to author, 14 August 1967.

78. "For the Nation's Health," *Time*, 29 December 1952, pp. 32–33.

79. These were Joseph C. Hinsey, Ph.D., dean of the Cornell University Medical College; Russel V. Lee, M.D., clinical professor of medicine, Stanford University; Charles S. Johnson, president of Fisk University; Lowell J. Reed, Ph.D., vice-

could be identified as probably hostile to the AMA were two labor representatives, Walter Reuther of the United Auto Workers and A. J. Hayes of the Machinists International; famed southern journalist Clarence Poe; Elizabeth Magee of the National Consumer's League; and Dr. Dean Clark, general director of Massachusetts General Hospital in Boston. Indeed, even though the president claimed in early 1952 that Chairman Magnuson had himself appointed the commission members,[80] Mary Lasker (who had helped nurture the commission idea through her White House contacts with David Noyes) had—unknown to Magnuson—contributed names for the membership roster.[81]

Another thing that smacked of political gamesmanship to the AMA was the president's announced intention of having the commission release interim reports on its findings throughout election year 1952.[82] On this, however, Truman relented. As finally organized, the commission conducted its inquiry without much fanfare and released its one and only report in December, after the elections.[83]

Chairman Magnuson went to great lengths to gain the AMA's confidence. By showing restraint in the face of AMA charges, and through personal assurances and appeals to the AMA leadership, Magnuson, although not gaining the association's official endorsement, did obtain permission from the AMA Board of Trustees to draw upon the AMA's collection of medical data. As the commission's work progressed in 1952, the AMA's informa-

---

president of Johns Hopkins University and Hospital; and Ernest G. Sloman, D.D.S., president-elect of the American Association of Dental Schools.

80. White House Press Release, 3 January 1952, Truman Papers, OF 103-G; The President's News Conference of January 3, 1952, in Truman, *Public Papers, 1952–53*, pp. 3–4.

81. Lasker to author, 14 August 1967.

82. John Cline to Paul Magnuson, 23 January 1952, Magnuson Commission Records, Truman Papers.

83. Statement by the President on the Report of the Commission on the Health Needs of the Nation, 18 December 1952, in Truman, *Public Papers, 1952–53*, p. 1087.

tional bureaus cooperated fully with Magnuson and his staff.[84]

Harry Truman had, meanwhile, made a decision. He would speak out on the health security issue in 1952 as never before. Prior to appointing the commission, HST had told Chairman Magnuson that, although he wanted to give Magnuson's group a great deal of independence, as president he would not allow its work to tie his hands, if he desired he would advocate health legislation during the commission's deliberations.[85] Writing to Oscar Ewing in December, Truman had acknowledged that "we have had set-backs and disappointments" and that the defense emergency had made it necessary to curtail efforts in the social security field. "But this is nothing to be discouraged about," he said. "Sooner or later we will get the legislation and find the resources to do the bigger job that lies ahead."[86] Going even further a few weeks later, Truman topped the list of those domestic items he wanted included in his 1952 state of the Union message with the admonition "No backing off—Health Insurance."[87] Amidst reports that Congress would do nothing on health care until the president's commission had completed its studies, Truman stated in his annual message in January, "I have repeatedly recommended national health insurance. . . . So far as I know, it is still the best way. If there are any better answers, I hope this commission will find them. But on one thing I am sure: something must be

84. White House Press Release, 15 January 1952, Truman Papers, OF 103-G; Magnuson to John Cline, 15 January 1952, Cline to Magnuson, 23 January 1952, H. A. Press to Magnuson, 29 January 1952, George F. Lull to Magnuson, 13, 15 February 1952, F. H. Arested to H. A. Press, 2 April 1952, Magnuson Commission Records, Truman Papers. The Committee for the Nation's Health also cooperated. See Michael Davis to Magnuson, 6, 18 February 1952, Magnuson Commission Records, Truman Papers.

85. Interview with Falk.

86. Truman to Ewing, 5 December 1951, Truman Papers, OF 7.

87. "HST's Views on State of the Union," 20 December 1951, Files of David Lloyd, box 26, Truman Papers.

done, and done soon."[88] He did not, however, include health insurance in his budget message. When asked about the omission by a reporter, Truman snapped, "My mind hasn't changed on it." It had not been included, he said, because he was waiting for more information on the subject.[89]

In March, the president gave the FSA permission to seek sponsors for a bill encompassing the administration's proposal for hospital insurance for the aged and for beneficiaries who survived them.[90] Senators James Murray and Hubert Humphrey, along with Representatives John Dingell and Emanuel Celler, introduced the bill the following month.[91] Little fanfare accompanied the legislative introduction of this precursor to medicare. Although Oscar Ewing suggested that the president endorse the bill in a special presidential message, Truman, after reviewing the pros and cons of the proposal,[92] decided against it, apparently because a specific presidential statement on the bill would allow the AMA and its allies to charge that the president had compromised his commission's search for a solution to health costs.

Rather than give organized medicine a chance to further attack him, Truman, after announcing in late March his decision not to seek reelection in 1952, sought to "expose" the medical lobby. Having become a lame-duck president, and confronted with legislative stalemate on Capitol Hill, Truman began expressing his mind about "pullbacks" in Congress and about the rich lobbies behind them in a manner more forceful, certainly more specific, than in 1948. In two speeches in May, one to a veteran's group and another on public power, the president blasted big-business lobbies in general and the

88. Annual Message to the Congress on the State of the Union, 9 January 1952, in Truman, *Public Papers, 1952–53,* p. 15.

89. The President's News Conference on the Budget, 19 January 1952, in Truman, *Public Papers, 1952–53,* p. 62.

90. Interview with Falk, interview with Ewing.

91. S. 3001, H.R. 7484, 82d Cong., 2d sess.

92. Ewing to Truman, 22 January 1952, David Stowe to Matthew Connelly, n.d., Truman Papers, OF 286-A.

American Medical Association in particular. "I am going to do a little preaching," he told the veterans in an understatement.[93] Truman then blamed the defeat of a bill just voted down in the House—which would have granted, among other things, social security credit to veterans for time spent in Korea—upon "that great organization which hates the administration worse than it hates the devil, called the American Medical Association." The AMA had helped kill the social security bill, he said, by charging that it contained socialized medicine. The president insisted, "There was nothing in that bill that came any closer to socialized medicine than the payments that the American Medical Association makes to the advertising firm of Whitaker and Baxter to misrepresent my health program."[94] In his speech to the public-power group, Truman lumped the AMA with those who had fought against such government projects as the Tennessee Valley Authority in the 1930s by spending millions to label the projects as socialistic. New Deal and Fair Deal opponents had chosen scare words like *socialism*, he said, because they had no real issues upon which "to hang their hats." "And these power companies, and the American Medical Association, are just tickled to death to have a thing like [socialism] and go around talking about that, but they don't tell you the facts."[95]

The AMA's success in delaying and then emasculating the amendments to the Social Security Act in 1952 enraged the president. Election-year pressures almost certainly guaranteed a modest upward revision of social security payments, but the American Medical Association successfully defeated a provision allowing persons who became permanently and totally disabled before age sixty-five to escape penalty for those years of being unable to work and, consequently, unable to pay social security

93. Remarks to Members of the National Advisory Committee of the Veterans Administration Voluntary Services, 21 May 1952, in Truman, *Public Papers, 1952–53*, p. 358.

94. Ibid., pp. 357–58.

95. Address Before the Electrical Consumers Conference, 26 May 1952, in Truman, *Public Papers, 1952–53*, pp. 371–72.

taxes. By sending telegrams to the House membership and opposing this "disability freeze" provision as socialistic because it made the government responsible for determining a person's medical disability, the AMA's Washington office helped bottle the bill up in the Ways and Means Committee.[96] Even though the Ways and Means chairman, Rep. Robert L. Doughton, an original sponsor of the Social Security Act, pleaded that "This is probably the last social security bill which I will ever introduce for, as you know, I am going out of Congress and what political motives could I have?" and that there was "no more socialized medicine in [this provision] than there is frost in the sun,"[97] the opposition took its toll. The House's original version, as finally reported out of Doughton's committee, retained the "disability freeze" provision; but, after Senate passage of the bill, the House refused to accept the Senate's revision. When the bill emerged from conference committee for final action, the conferees had eliminated the feature opposed by the AMA.[98]

During debate over the social security amendments, and after the enactment of the amendments, the president criticized the American Medical Association for its obstructionism. In the spring Truman observed, "there are a lot of people in Congress who jump when the American Medical Association cracks the whip";[99] and in June, the White House released a letter written by Truman to a lady whose appeal for increased social security benefits had been picked by random from the president's mail. The president wrote that he agreed that social security payments were inadequate and that he blamed the Republicans for delaying passage of the pending legislation,

---

96. Burrow, *AMA*, p. 377; Altmeyer, *Formative Years of Social Security*, p. 196.

97. Quoted in Altmeyer, *Formative Years of Social Security*, pp. 196–97.

98. Ibid., pp. 197–99.

99. Remarks to Members of the National Advisory Committee of the Veterans Administration Voluntary Services, 21 May 1952, in Truman, *Public Papers, 1952–53*, p. 358.

and he explained, "They saw the word 'physician' in the text of the bill and on the advice of the American Medical Association began screaming about 'socialized medicine.'"[100] When the bill reached his desk for signature in July without the "disability freeze" provision, Truman took pains to outline for the nation how the AMA had maneuvered the feature out of the bill. He claimed,

> The net result of the medical lobby's maneuvering was the impairment of insurance protection for millions of disabled Americans. What the lobby could not engineer outright, it won by delay. And be it noted that this victory for the lobby, at the people's expense, was accomplished by a great majority of the Republicans in the House. They were perfectly willing to deny to millions of Americans the benefits provided by this bill in order to satisfy the groundless whim of a special interest lobby—a lobby that purports to speak for, but surely fails to represent, the great medical profession in the United States.[101]

A week later the Democratic National Convention in Chicago nominated Gov. Adlai Stevenson of Illinois as their presidential candidate for 1952. Stevenson had not been Harry Truman's first choice. Some months before, HST had told his staff that he did not favor "the Stevenson type of candidate. I don't believe the people of the United States are ready for an Ivy Leaguer."[102] But when he could not find a better candidate, and especially after Gen. Dwight Eisenhower entered the race for the Republican nomination, Truman backed Stevenson.[103] For his part, Adlai Stevenson, once the campaign got underway, tried to minimize his identification with Truman's Fair Deal,[104] particularly with health insurance. Although

100. Letter to Elizabeth Cochrane on the Need for Increasing Social Security Benefits, 13 June 1952, in Truman, *Public Papers, 1952–53*, p. 419.

101. Statement by the President Upon Signing the Social Security Act Amendments, 18 July 1952, in Truman, *Public Papers, 1952–53*, p. 487.

102. Quoted in Margaret Truman, *Harry S. Truman*, p. 527.

103. Ibid., pp. 530, 541–43.

104. Bert Cochran, *Adlai Stevenson: Patrician Among the*

he was aware of the controversial nature of health care, Stevenson did not have strong feelings about its costs, nor about the need for stepped-up medical research. He once told Mary Lasker, who had come to know him as a result of her donation to his 1952 campaign, "Oh listen, I really believe in herbs and roots." [105] And one of Stevenson's first pronouncements after receiving the nomination was that he did not see eye to eye with Oscar Ewing on the solution to national health needs. [106] In August, to add insult to injury, the Illinois governor responded to a charge by Eisenhower that Truman had wanted to socialize American medicine by meekly observing that the general's attack was "obsolete," that neither the Democratic platform nor the party's candidates had recommended the Truman program. [107]

While Stevenson sparred, the president fumed. Donald Cook, chairman of the Securities and Exchange Commission, sent Truman some statistics in August that revealed that 14 to 17 percent of the loans made the year before by the nation's three largest small-loan companies had been granted for payment of medical, dental, and hospital expenses. Cook's figures also showed that these loans, made at very high interest rates, had gone mostly to people whose annual income stood below thirty-six hundred dollars. [108] "You certainly have gotten right at the meat of the situation," the president wrote Cook:

Politicians, pp. 210–23; Stephen A. Mitchell, "Adlai's Amateurs," pp. 82–84.

105. Mary Woodard Lasker Memoir, Columbia University Oral History Project.

106. *New York Times*, 31 July 1952. Ewing tried to repair the damage the next day, stating that the president and he had stated many times that they were not intransigent on the health issue. See *New York Times*, 1 August 1952.

107. *New York Times*, 22 August 1952. Stevenson was technically correct. The Democratic platform did not mention health insurance. See Kirk H. Porter and Donald B. Johnson, eds., *National Party Platforms, 1840–1956*, pp. 484.

108. Donald C. Cook to Truman, 7 August 1952, Truman Papers, OF 286-A.

My objective in a health insurance proposition is to meet the very difficult situation with which people in the two thousand to six thousand group are placed when it comes to health services. These "skin flint" loan companies, who charge the people from twenty-seven to fifty percent interest on small loans, I think are the worst vultures we have to contend with—they and the American Medical Association are the very reason there has been such a howl about health insurance. One of their sources of ill-gotten income would be dried up. I can see very well why these loan companies wouldn't want health insurance but for the life of me I can't get the doctor's point of view because the objective is to help these people have a nest egg so the doctors and the hospitals can be paid.[109]

Thanking Cook for the information, the president told him, "It will be exceedingly useful to me in the coming campaign."[110]

Several days later, Truman reminded Stevenson that he stood ready "to help win the election."[111] When the campaign began officially in September, the president revived his attack upon organized medicine. Addressing the annual meeting of the American Hospital Association in Philadelphia, he first outlined his administration's past achievements, describing the gains that had been made in the Veteran's Administration's medical program and in federal aid to medical research and hospital construction since 1946. Then he bore down on Eisenhower and the AMA. Quoting from one of the general's recent speeches, wherein Eisenhower had said that government should provide only "indigent medical care," Truman declared caustically that this was like saying "we don't need any form of social security except the county poor house." As to the leaders of organized medicine, they were "pullbacks—they don't want to move ahead at all, no matter how it's done." Injecting a little humor into his

109. Truman to Cook, 14 August 1952, Truman Papers, OF 286-A.
110. Ibid.
111. Truman, *Harry S. Truman*, p. 543.

attack, HST recalled that Mrs. Millard Fillmore had installed the first bathtub in the White House and that a Cincinnati medical group had passed a resolution labeling Mrs. Fillmore "an indecent person" for doing it. The president explained, "This medical association in Cincinnati said that it was unsanitary, that it was unhealthy, that no person should take all his clothes off at one time." Well, he observed, the White House had progressed in the bathtub department over the years, and despite such opposition it now contained more bathtubs than the local Benjamin Franklin Hotel. So, too, he said, had medical knowledge progressed.[112]

Coincidently, shortly after the president's Hospital Association speech, the AMA announced an end to Whitaker and Baxter's national education campaign. When asked at a news conference what he thought about the development, Truman claimed that his recent health speech had caused the AMA to admit that it was wrong and to disband its propaganda effort. The president knew better, of course. The intensity of the AMA's campaign against his health program had diminished greatly since 1950. Also, the same news item announcing Whitaker and Baxter's departure from the AMA pointed out that the agency planned to organize and conduct a national professional committee for Eisenhower and Nixon.[113]

Truman seized upon this latter development during a month-long whistle-stop tour begun in late September. Crisscrossing the country's rail network, first to the West Coast, then back to New England, and finally home, the president told various audiences about the medical lobby that had just joined hands with Eisenhower and Nixon. Claiming that Eisenhower was ignorant and insensitive to health matters, HST warned, "The Republican candidate has a sign on the back of his train that says 'Look

112. Address in Philadelphia at the American Hospital Association Convention, 16 September 1952, in Truman, *Public Papers, 1952–53*, pp. 571–73.

113. The President's News Conference of September 25, 1952, in Truman, *Public Papers, 1952–53*, p. 588; *New York Times*, 23 September 1952.

Ahead Neighbor.' But when it comes to meeting the health needs of the people, that sign ought to say 'Look Out Neighbor.' You can't expect much help from him." Eisenhower, he said, followed the lead of special-interest lobbies like the American Medical Association, whose "outfit" had just joined Eisenhower in an effort to "keep health from being an issue in this campaign. Well, they can't, for I am going to make it an issue."[114]

In a speech at the Palace Hotel in San Francisco, Truman gibed "the dinosaur wing of the Republican Party" for refusing to nominate liberal Gov. Earl Warren of California as their vice-presidential candidate that year (referring to Richard Nixon, he said that instead they "chose another Californian who is not worthy to tie Governor Warren's shoes"),[115] and Truman minced no words in condemning the medical lobby's link to the GOP opposition. What was the medical lobby? It was simply a "reactionary faction" within the American Medical Association, "a few men and an advertising agency." Holding up a newspaper clipping, the president showed his audience the methods of "this little clique" that had "moved over to run a national professional committee for Nixon and Eisenhower." The clipping, from a Nashville newspaper, described how a local doctor sought support from his fellow physicians for a Nixon parade. The doctor's letter, reprinted in the news item, said, "In order to make the best impression on the general public, we are asking you to use a small car if that is at all possible." Truman loved that statement. He recited it twice and concluded, "They are so well off they can't find a little car that the poor man has to ride around in."[116]

The president used the clipping again during rear-platform remarks a few days later in Sedalia, Missouri. The Republicans held "the big car vote," and they could keep it, he said. "We Democrats will be content to get

114. Rear Platform Remarks in Cut Bank, Montana, 30 September 1952, in Truman, *Public Papers, 1952–53,* pp. 641–42.

115. Address at the Palace Hotel in San Francisco, 4 October 1952, in Truman, *Public Papers, 1952–53,* p. 705.

116. Ibid., pp. 704–5.

the small car vote, from the genuine small car people."
And the GOP could also have "the generals and the colo-
nels" on its side, because, he claimed, the Democrats
would win the election with "the corporals and the
privates."[117]

But 1952 was not 1948. The Democratic candidate,
Adlai Stevenson, lost to Dwight Eisenhower by over 6
million votes. President Louis Bauer of the AMA commented about the GOP victory, "As far as the medical
profession is concerned, there is general agreement that
we are in less danger of socialization than for a number
of years."[118] Another AMA leader described the November election results as "a reissue of the Declaration of
Independence."[119]

Michael Davis and the Committee for the Nation's
Health also knew that the GOP sweep would bring an
end to their movement for health security. Although the
CNH did not disband for another three years, the committee functioned increasingly as organized labor's health
information office, providing data on medical-care programs for use by union groups. This lasted until the AFL
and CIO moved toward merger in 1955 and indicated
their intent to establish a health information office within the union. After a decade of activity, during which
hope had turned to despair, the Committee for the Nation's Health closed its books in January 1956.[120]

For Harry Truman, the November elections signaled
the beginning of the final phase of his presidency. But
the public had not heard its last on the health subject
from HST. Speaking at a meeting of the Association of
Military Surgeons on 19 November, exactly six years
after he had sent his first special health message to Con-

117. Rear Platform Remarks in Sedalia, Missouri, 8 October 1952, in Truman, *Public Papers, 1952–53*, p. 747.

118. "The President's Page," *JAMA* 150 (27 December 1952):
1675.

119. "Organization Section," *JAMA* 150 (27 December 1952):
1695.

120. Minutes of Executive Committee Meeting, 6 November 1952, Michael Davis to Cooperating Organizations, 28 December 1955, CNH Records, Davis Papers.

gress, the president admitted that, although opposition to his health program had had its effect, he was proud of the progress made in the field during his administration. He hoped that the next administration would consider seriously the Magnuson commission's forthcoming report on the health needs of the nation.[121]

During August and September, while the public's attention had been focused upon the election campaign, the president's commission had quietly gathered testimony in regional hearings around the country. On 18 December, the commission issued its report. On the question of financing personal health services, the commission upheld Truman's claim that too many citizens lacked the means for proper medical care. However, the commission did not agree with the chief executive's solution to the problem. Although it recognized that the federal government had a large role to play in the medical field, it did not recommend adoption of national health insurance. Instead, the report called for a cooperative federal-state program wherein each state would establish its own health insurance plan (subject to the approval of a federal agency) with federal matching funds providing the payments for those who could not afford the premiums. Social security beneficiaries would be covered through payments to the states out of the OAIS tax mechanism.[122]

This scheme represented a compromise between the two extremes of the Taft health-care-for-only-the-poor proposal and the administration's comprehensive program; and it was to Harry Truman's credit that, in the closing days of his presidency, he accepted the commission's findings. On 9 January, the president sent Congress the first volume of the group's projected five-volume report along with his last health message. Commending the commission's work, Truman conceded that its proposal

121. Address Before the Association of Military Surgeons, 19 November 1952, in Truman, *Public Papers, 1952–53*, pp. 1055–56.
122. U.S. President's Commission on the Health Needs of the Nation, *Building America's Health: A Report to the President*, 1:42–44.

to give federal grants-in-aid to establish private, state-sponsored plans was probably the best solution to the nation's health needs. The commission, he said, had pointed the way "to a fresh and constructive approach in meeting the health needs of the all-important health field."[123]

Eleven days later, Harry Truman boarded the train for the trip home to Independence and retirement. Congress would never enact legislation establishing a prepayment system like that envisaged by the Magnuson commission. But the commission's work had drawn renewed attention to national health care problems. When these problems became intensified over the next decade, especially among the growing numbers of retired persons living extended lives and trying to cope with chronic ailments on restricted budgets, Harry Truman's idea of government health insurance for the aged attracted increasing public acceptance. What had been a politically explosive issue in the years following the Second World War was about to become, at least in its restricted and less inclusive form, the subject of serious deliberation. Congressional Republicans and Democrats alike would agree by the end of the Eisenhower presidency that some type of subsidized health care for the aged was necessary; in final form, medicare, the plan Congress approved in 1965, was the fruition of the compromise Harry Truman made, belatedly, in the final stages of his presidency.

123. Special Message to the Congress Transmitting Volume One of the Report of the President's Commission on the Health Needs of the Nation, 9 January 1953, in Truman, *Public Papers, 1952–53*, pp. 1166–67.

8

The Reality: From HST to LBJ

Dwight Eisenhower's political and economic philosophy matched closely that of organized medicine. "I have found, in the past few years, that I have certain philosophical bonds with doctors," Ike assured an appreciative American Medical Association assembled in convention shortly after his presidential inauguration in 1953.[1] Moreover, in contrast with the Truman years, the AMA now enjoyed entrée to the White House.[2] Yet, ironically, rather than marking an interlude in the battle over public health policy, Eisenhower's eight-year Republican presidential stewardship witnessed a noticeable decline in organized medicine's ability to forestall expansion of government involvement in the health field. By the time John Kennedy came to the presidency and made Truman's health program part of his New Frontier domestic reform agenda, eventual congressional approval of some form of publicly financed health care plan for the aged seemed assured.

First of all, it became obvious early in the Eisenhower presidency that private prepayment health plans, despite their continued expansion among middle-class Americans, were beyond the purview of the very poor and the aged. Republican congressional leaders, as well as White House staffers, concluded in 1954 that, in order to fore-

1. Remarks to the Members of the House of Delegates of the American Medical Association, 14 March 1953, Dwight D. Eisenhower, *Public Papers of the Presidents of the United States, 1953*, p. 98.
2. Various meetings between AMA officials and President Eisenhower are acknowledged in Edward J. McCormick to Dwight Eisenhower, 10 December 1953, George F. Lull to Sherman Adams, 21 December 1953, and Nelson A. Rockefeller to Adams, 23 December 1953, Dwight D. Eisenhower Papers, Official File (hereafter cited as OF) 156-C.

stall pressure for direct federal intervention into the health care sector, some scheme was needed to expand both commercial insurance and insurance of the Blue Cross and Blue Shield type. Consequently, the Eisenhower administration promoted a $15 million federal "reinsurance" program to insulate health insurance companies from abnormal losses, thereby enabling them to broaden their benefits and coverage. But in July 1954, the House defeated a bill embodying the plan. The reinsurance concept rankled many Democrats who opposed federal subsidization of private insurance companies, while the American Medical Association surprisingly attacked it as a foot-in-the-door approach leading ultimately to socialized medicine.[3]

Dwight Eisenhower had tried unsuccessfully to gain the AMA's confidence and support on the issue. Just prior to House action on the administration's bill, Ike arranged a meeting between the AMA and a group of insurance-industry leaders favoring the reinsurance approach. But organized medicine would not yield. Lamenting the AMA's intransigence following defeat of the bill, insurance company executive Frazar Wilde, a participant at the White House gathering, wrote President Walter Martin of the AMA, "The vote confirms my worst fears." Wilde conjectured that, should the Democrats regain control of government, they would "insist on an elaborate governmental Health Program. Then we will have socialized medicine in a large way." He concluded that it was indeed unfortunate that the AMA could not "see

---

3. U.S., Department of Health, Education, and Welfare, "Summary of Proposals," 18 November 1953, Eisenhower Papers, OF-236; Special Message to the Congress on the Health Needs of the American People, 18 January 1954, in Eisenhower, *Public Papers, 1954*, pp. 70–72; Arthur J. Altmeyer, *Formative Years of Social Security*, pp. 252–55. President Eisenhower discussed the polarized liberal and conservative opposition to his reinsurance plan in Address at the Alfred E. Smith Memorial Dinner, New York City, 21 October 1954, in Eisenhower, *Public Papers, 1954*, p. 940.

this danger and the wisdom of taking modest steps which might postpone it."[4]

When opposition to the reinsurance bill would not subside, Eisenhower abandoned it in 1956 in favor of a "pooling plan" whereby the private insurance groups would pool their resources to allow an expansion of their health coverage. The pooling idea received even less attention on Capitol Hill than had the reinsurance plan, however.[5]

Other developments troubled organized medicine during the Eisenhower presidency. Two days after Ike's inauguration in 1953, the AMA's secretary and general manager, George Lull, sent the new president a Chicago newspaper clipping describing the White House scene on the general's first day in office: "On his desk were a dozen yellow roses and a leather bound gold-lettered volume 'Building America's Health'. This was a recent report by a Truman advisory commission proposing more federal medical aid."[6] The clipping was "self-explanatory," Lull told Eisenhower, and he enclosed an AMA Board of Trustees policy statement condemning the Truman commission's findings as an attempt to establish a socialist state.[7] Presidential assistant Sherman Adams assured Lull that "there is no reason to attach great significance to the incident," that many reports "pass over the President's desk every day,"[8] but the AMA remained on

4. Frazar Wilde to Walter B. Martin, 15 July 1954, Eisenhower Papers, OF 117-C7.

5. Hazel Holly, "Reinsurance Has No Magic"; Special Message to the Congress on the Nation's Health Program, 26 January 1956, in Eisenhower, *Public Papers, 1956*, pp. 200–201; Congressional Quarterly Service, *Congress and the Nation, 1945–1964*, 1:1153.

6. *Chicago Tribune* clipping, n.d., contained in George Lull to Dwight Eisenhower, 22 January 1953, Eisenhower Papers, General File (hereafter cited as GF) 131-X.

7. Board of Trustees, American Medical Association, "Statement on Report of the Truman Commission on the Health Needs of the Nation," in Lull to Eisenhower, 22 January 1953, Eisenhower Papers, GF 131-X.

8. Sherman Adams to Lull, 25 February 1953, Eisenhower Papers, GF 131-X.

guard. Through various meetings with Ike during his first year in office, President Edward J. McCormick of the AMA further emphasized his organization's opposition to changes in the social security system, which included the addition of federal disability insurance and government medical services for dependents of military draftees.[9]

On both these issues the AMA met defeat. In 1954 Congress added to social security the disability provision (opposed successfully by the AMA during Truman's last year in office) guaranteeing those who became permanently disabled before age sixty-five their future old-age insurance rights without penalty. In 1956, legislation sponsored by Eisenhower established a "medicare" program (the first use of the term) providing civilian hospital and physician services for certain dependents of military personnel. The same year, the Democratic-controlled Congress passed amendments to the Social Security Act to give monthly benefits to disabled workers aged fifty or older.[10]

After Eisenhower signed the 1956 social security measure into law, a former president of the AMA, Elmer Hess, in a letter to the White House, called it "the worst piece of legislation that has been foisted on a decent man by an opposition party" and provided Eisenhower assistant Sherman Adams with a statement for use by the president in order to help Hess "get the physicians pacified."[11] The statement was not used, although assurances were sent Hess that the White House had tried beforehand to strike the disability feature from the bill.[12] "They're attacking us piecemeal," another AMA leader complained the following year. "Truman was easier to handle because he came at you head-on. . . . The kind of

9. Edward J. McCormick to Eisenhower, 23 December 1953, Eisenhower Papers, OF 156-C.

10. Altmeyer, *Formative Years of Social Security*, pp. 282–84.

11. Elmer Hess to Eisenhower, 13 August 1956, Eisenhower Papers, OF 156-C.

12. Sherman Adams to Hess, 23 August 1956, Eisenhower Papers, OF 156-C.

flanking attack we're being subjected to now is more difficult to fight off." [13]

Partly as a cooperative, goodwill gesture toward Eisenhower and partly in response to societal forces beyond its control, the AMA had itself contributed to a loosening of organized medicine's grip on national health policy. It supported Eisenhower's successful request that the Federal Security Agency be elevated to Department of Health, Education, and Welfare status in 1953 and did not object too strenuously to the administration's policy (embraced by Congress in 1956, 1958, and again in 1960) to greatly increase federal funds for the state-directed vendor payment system for welfare recipients. By the end of Eisenhower's presidency, the AMA had even come to support, as a counter to growing pressures for government health insurance for all those over age sixty-five, implementation of the Kerr-Mills program (named after its Democratic congressional sponsors) to pay health care costs for the elderly poor. [14] Nor could the AMA, confronted by escalating price tags for sophisticated modern research techniques and equipment, resist expansion of federal medical-research activity. After 1955 government funding in the research field rose dramatically. "The Federal Government's medical activities are on a massive scale and they continue to grow," stressed a special report by the AMA's Washington office in 1958. [15] By 1960 HEW medical-research funds had reached $392 million, seven times the appropriations of ten years before. [16]

This accelerating infusion of government involvement in national medical affairs produced another, unexpected

13. Quoted in Richard Carter, *The Doctor Business*, p. 215.
14. James G. Burrow, *AMA, Voice of American Medicine*, pp. 386–87; George Lull to Eisenhower, 13 February 1956, Eisenhower Papers, OF 117; James L. Sundquist, *Politics and Policy: The Eisenhower, Kennedy, and Johnson Years*, p. 306.
15. American Medical Association, Washington Office, "Special Report," 14 November 1958, copy in Files of Special Assistant and Special Consultant Relating to Joint Federal-State Action Committee, Eisenhower Papers.
16. Seymour E. Harris, *The Economics of American Medicine*, p. 39.

side effect, it contributed to a widening of the ideological gulf separating the free-enterprise-oriented private practitioner, as represented by the AMA, from those who depended upon public funding: the medical educators, researchers, and hospital employees. In 1955, after a two-year study, a private commission sponsored by the American Hospital Association concluded, "It does not seem likely that voluntary prepayment can on any broad scale cover such groups as the nonworking aged, the unemployed, or the low income groups without assistance from government."[17] And the AHA Board of Trustees, although stopping short of endorsing the social security approach, recommended federal subsidization of prepaid health services for older persons.[18] In a complete break with the AMA, the American Nurses Association endorsed the medicare concept in 1958.[19] Even within the AMA itself one could detect growing dissension over the health security issue. The 1964 AMA presidential address, for example, was entitled, "Unity in Medicine." Its content concerned the lack of it.[20]

This, plus two other factors, contributed to a renewed, and this time highly viable, health security movement. The other factors were disturbing deficiencies in private health insurance coverage and benefits, and the rise of public concern over problems endured by its senior citizens. As to the former, the *Saturday Evening Post* acknowledged serious problems in the private health insurance sector in a three-part series run in the summer of 1958. Critical of abuses to the system by patients and doctors alike, the *Post* cautioned that the entire voluntary prepayment structure faced collapse.[21] "Voluntary health insurance was created in large part to prevent compulso-

17. Agnes W. Brewster ed., *Health Insurance and Related Proposals for Financing Personal Health Services*, p. 12.

18. Ibid., pp. 13–14.

19. *New York Times*, 14 June 1958.

20. Norman A. Welch, "Unity in Medicine," *JAMA* 189 (20 July 1964):223–25.

21. Milton Silverman, "The Post Reports on Health Insurance," *Saturday Evening Post*, 7 June 1958, pp. 25–26.

ry, Government-controlled health insurance," the *Post* quoted a notable insurance company president as saying. "Now it is in great peril. If it collapses, it will inevitably bring the one thing it was supposed to prevent—Government control of the practice of medicine."[22]

The voluntary system did not collapse, but for most retired Americans it remained far beyond their financial means. In 1956 President Eisenhower had responded to growing public awareness of the elder citizen's needs by appointing the Federal Council on Aging. Two years later, Ike signed H.R. 9822, providing for a White House conference on aging to be held in January 1961. Speaking before the AMA's annual meeting in Atlantic City, New Jersey, in 1959, Eisenhower referred to the medical problems of a greatly expanded aged population. He observed that in 1900 life expectancy was forty-eight years, in 1959 it was over seventy. In 1910 there were 3 million Americans sixty-five years or older, now there were 15 million.[23]

However, with the exception of his reinsurance plan, Eisenhower's approach to the health insurance question harmonized with AMA policy throughout his presidency. He sent Congress three special health messages, one each year between 1954 and 1956; and all stressed the president's conviction that, with minimal government support, the private sector could handle the nation's medical economics problem.[24] *Business Week* applauded, "Patent-

22. Ibid., p. 127.

23. Memorandum Concerning Establishment and Functions of the Federal Council on Aging, 3 April 1956, Eisenhower, *Public Papers, 1956*, pp. 357–59; U.S., Department of Health, Education, and Welfare, *The Nation and Its Older People*, p. 3; Address at the Annual Meeting of the American Medical Association, 9 June 1959, in Eisenhower, *Public Papers, 1959*, pp. 454–55.

24. Special Message to the Congress on the Health Needs of the American People, 18 January 1954, Special Message to the Congress Recommending a Health Program, 31 January 1955, Special Message to the Congress on the Nation's Health Program, 26 January 1956, in Eisenhower, *Public Papers, 1954*, pp. 70–72, *Public Papers, 1955*, pp. 216–23, *Public Papers, 1956*, pp. 196–204.

ly, Eisenhower's health ideas take a different tack from the old Truman national health insurance plans."[25] From Sen. James Murray's liberal and partisan view, this resulted from Eisenhower not having been personally confronted with high medical expenses because he had received "free, socialized medical care" throughout most of his adult life as a military man.[26] The general-turned-president expressed his motives differently. He told a medical group, "This is one profession [that] we don't want to get under the dead hand of bureaucracy."[27]

Until 1957 Eisenhower and the AMA paid no attention to the Truman-style hospital-insurance bills introduced each new congressional term by the small coterie of Democrats on Capitol Hill led by James Murray and John Dingell. After that time, a legislative movement gained momentum behind a new AFL-CIO inspired old-age-insurance bill drafted jointly by Professor Wilbur Cohen of the University of Michigan and Professor Isidore Falk of Yale University. Rep. Aime Forand, a Democrat from New Jersey, became its chief sponsor.[28]

The Forand bill, which differed from the Murray-Dingell proposals in that dependents and survivors of OAIS recipients were dropped from coverage and in that nursing-home and surgical benefits were added, became the focal point of a drive embraced by Harry Truman and led by John Kennedy during his 1960 presidential race against Richard Nixon. Before the campaign got underway that year, the Eisenhower administration offered its alternate proposal, called "medicare," a term Democratic liberals later picked up and attached to their own, far different health care plan. Eisenhower's program, sponsored in slightly modified form by Sen. Jacob

25. "Welfare, Eisenhower Style."

26. Quoted in Richard Harris, "Annals of Legislation: Medicare," *New Yorker*, 9 July 1966, p. 34.

27. Remarks on Receiving the Frank N. Lahey Award From the National Fund for Medical Education," 16 November 1954, in Eisenhower, *Public Papers, 1954*, p. 1053.

28. Harris, "Annals of Legislation: Medicare," *New Yorker*, 9 July 1966, pp. 35–77. *New York Times*, 22 July 1959.

Javits of New York—and endorsed by the GOP candidate, Richard Nixon—called for federal matching grants to enable participating states to provide medical benefits to aged persons earning less than three thousand dollars a year. Neither the Kennedy-backed Forand bill nor the Nixon-backed Javits bill won congressional approval in 1960, but the compromise Kerr-Mills program to assist the medically needy aged was enacted.[29]

This did not still the clamor for a Forand-type program to cover all the elderly, however. In 1961 the new Kennedy administration labeled it "must" legislation, while the National Council of Senior Citizens for Health Care (jointly financed by the AFL-CIO and the Democratic National Committee and headed by retired Aime Forand) began lobbying in behalf of the new, Forand-type King-Anderson bill, named after cosponsors Rep. Cecil King, Democrat from California, and Sen. Clinton Anderson, Democrat from New Mexico. While Wilbur Mills of Arkansas, the powerful Democratic chairman of the House Ways and Means Committee, blocked floor action in the lower chamber, other Democrats, led by President Kennedy, made the King-Anderson bill a major issue in the congressional election of 1962. The liberal-conservative makeup of the new congress that followed differed little from before; but after the assassination of John Kennedy in November 1963, Capitol Hill opposition to the martyred president's New Frontier program diminished noticeably. The Senate, during its next session, reversed its two earlier rejections of medicare and passed an amendment embodying the medicare program. This was the first time either house had voted passage of national health insurance. Although the amendment died in a House-Senate conference committee that fall of 1964, President Lyndon Johnson's landslide victory in November, accompanied by a massive influx of successful liberal Democratic candidates into Congress, assured

29. Harry S. Truman, *Mr. Citizen*, pp. 139–40; Sundquist, *Politics and Policy*, pp. 296–308; Arnold Rose, *The Power Structure: Political Process in American Society*, p. 429.

early passage of some form of medicare legislation by
both houses.[30]

Lyndon Johnson had been one among only several
southern Democratic senators who had voted in favor of
Harry Truman's reorganization plan to elevate Oscar
Ewing's FSA, tainted by charges of "socialized medicine,"
to departmental status back in 1949 and had expressed
himself in favor of the King-Anderson legislation while
serving as Kennedy's vice-president. During the first year
of his presidency, Johnson had also employed his skill at
legislative persuasion, helping win Senate approval in
1964 of the medicare amendment. Now, flush with fifty-
eight new Democrats in the House, of whom most had
already indicated support of King-Anderson, and with
enough votes in the House Ways and Means Committee
to make Chairman Wilbur Mills hedge his opposition,
Lyndon Johnson moved quickly for final action on medicare. In his state of the Union message, he called medicare
the first order of legislative business in 1965 and three
days later underscored his determination to have it enacted by sending the Hill a special message on the subject.
By July, the president, with the aid of a now-converted
Wilbur Mills, had outmaneuvered not only the American Medical Association and the Republican minority,
but also a few powerful opponents in his own party to
gain enactment of a health insurance bill far more comprehensive than its most ardent proponents had hoped
for.[31]

"Year after year, we have seen a piece of political
quackery called Medicare die in Congress," the AMA's
president had observed angrily in February. "After each
of those beatings, we thought Medicare would not dare
show its false face again. We were wrong. It came back

30. Harris, "Annals of Legislation: Medicare," *New Yorker*,
16 July 1966, pp. 35–91; Sundquist, *Politics and Policy*, pp.
308–9, 314–18.

31. *Congressional Record*, 81st Cong., 1st sess., 1949, vol. 95,
pt. 9, p. 11560; Harris, "Annals of Legislation: Medicare," *New
Yorker*, 16 July 1966, p. 74; Rose, *The Power Structure*, pp.
446–47.

during the next election."[32] In a last-ditch attempt to prevent its passage, two substitute proposals were introduced in the House in early 1965, one, tagged "eldercare," was drafted by the AMA and the other, tagged "bettercare," was sponsored by a group of Republicans headed by Rep. John Byrnes of Wisconsin. Eldercare, introduced in behalf of the AMA by Florida Democrat A. Sydney Herlong, Jr., and Missouri Republican Thomas Curtis, along with other conservatives in both parties, promised comprehensive medical treatment, including doctor's office services, for the indigent aged. Bettercare, the Byrnes bill, offered a "complete" health care package to those social security recipients who agreed to pay a small fee from their monthly OAIS checks for purchase of federally subsidized private health insurance plans. Of the two, Byrnes's proposal was the more liberal, for eldercare's services, although comprehensive, would be provided through the existing Kerr-Mills mechanism, restricted to those states where the legislature decided to adopt the plan (and help pay for it), and only available to those aged within participating states who passed a poverty-means test. Whether they favored the AMA plan or the Byrnes plan, opponents of the administration took the tack in early 1965 that Johnson's medicare bill did not provide enough health services, that it was a halfway measure paying only hospital costs for the aged.[33]

But this line of criticism boomeranged with unexpected results for the pro-AMA forces. Wilbur Mills, satisfied by early 1965 that a medicare system could be made financially solvent, adroitly added the opposition's widely heralded extended-service features to the original King-Anderson measure. When the restructured medicare program—now called the Mills bill—emerged from the House Ways and Means Committee, it not only included hospital insurance for persons over age sixty-five whether under social security or not (the King-Anderson plan), but

32. Donovan F. Ward, "Are 200,000 Doctors Wrong?," *JAMA* 191 (6 February 1965), p. 662.
33. Rose, *The Power Structure*, pp. 448–49; "Comparison of Johnson, GOP, AMA Medical Care Bills."

also a voluntary insurance program purchased by the elderly for three dollars a month to cover doctor's office fees and other nonhospital related costs (the GOP Byrnes plan), and a greatly augmented Kerr-Mills program for the state-operated old-age assistance system (the AMA plan).[34]

After fifty years of intermittent struggle against government health insurance proposals, the American Medical Association, its societal influence diminished, its ranks thinned, and its final alternative program preempted by the liberals, faced defeat. The House passed medicare on 27 July by a vote of 307 to 116. The Senate followed suit the next day, sending the measure to President Johnson for signature by a vote of 70 to 24.[35]

The final drama in this half-century battle over health security took place on the auditorium stage of the Harry S. Truman Library in Independence, Missouri, on the afternoon of 30 July 1965. The former president, sitting at a table with President Lyndon Johnson, accepted four pens used in the ceremony in which medicare was signed into law. Fifty years earlier, almost to the day, a small band of social workers and liberal-minded economists had launched the first American legislative campaign for health security by adopting the slogan "Health Insurance—the next step." Twenty years earlier, Harry Truman had given the movement its first presidential endorsement. Many, like Jane Addams, Isaac Rubinow, John Andrews, Abraham Epstein, Robert Wagner, Sr., James Murray, and John Dingell, Sr., were no longer around in 1965 to enjoy the fruits of victory. Others, like Arthur Altmeyer, Michael Davis, Isidore Falk, Samuel Rosenman, Wilbur Cohen, Mary Lasker, and Oscar Ewing, were, however; and they shared the sentiment expressed by eighty-one-year-old Harry Truman that summer day when he told the gathering at his library that he was glad to have lived so long.

34. Harris, "Annals of Legislation: Medicare," *New Yorker*, 23 July 1966, pp. 39–62.
35. *Congressional Record*, 89th Cong., 1st sess., 1965, vol. 111, pts. 13, 14, pp. 18393–94, 18514.

9

Conclusion

About the time medicare became law, the first scholarly historical assessments of Harry Truman's presidency were published. After an initial round of critical but generally favorable monographs, a spate of revisionist studies sharply critical of the Missourian's leadership in domestic and foreign affairs appeared. Labeled the *New Left* school, this group described Truman's domestic policymaking as inept, devious, and overly deferential to conservative, middle-class values. Expanding upon journalist Samuel Lubell's 1952 contention that Harry Truman's "place in history is . . . as the man who bought time," as a president who happily staked out a position in the "dead center of stalemate,"[1] the New Left historians of the 1960s rejected Truman's brand of liberalism (and Franklin Roosevelt's as well) as being too centrist, too moderate for the demands of an urbanized, industrial society.[2]

At first glance, Harry Truman's erratic and lackluster public promotion of his health reform package lends credence to the New Left critique. HST was not an effective salesman. Except when actively campaigning in 1948 and 1952, he failed to use the presidency's unique opinion-shaping opportunities to full advantage; in addition, when he did discuss the health issue, Truman's utterances were usually terse and uninformative, rigidly formal and uninspiring. Before, and to a degree after, the presidential race in 1948, HST lacked a sense of, and talent for, political showmanship, venting energies behind the scenes like a workhorse rather than seeking public following in the manner of a showhorse. The strut and gait

1. Samuel Lubell, *The Future of American Politics*, p. 24.
2. For a thorough critique of Truman historiography, see Richard S. Kirkendall, ed., *The Truman Period As a Research Field: A Reappraisal, 1972*; Robert Griffith, "Truman and the Historians: The Reconstruction of Postwar American History."

of the Missourian's early morning walks and the cocki-
ness of his bearing belied the fact that Harry Truman
was at base a bookish, clerkish individual, more at ease
out of the public limelight than in it.

But Truman's advocacy of national health insurance
during the immediate postwar period was anything but
centrist or moderate. Whether viewed from the perspective of the American Medical Association and its many
powerful allies or from that of the Taft Republicans,
Harry Truman's plan was radical. To organized medicine,
the president's scheme carried the threat of a frightening-
ly alien intrusion by government into the delivery of
health care services and warranted the expenditure of
millions of dollars to finance the most expensive and
most extensive lobbying effort ever waged to defeat a
legislative proposal. To those Republican congressional
leaders who seized upon the issue beginning in 1946 with
a rhetorical looseness and zeal that anticipated the Mc-
Carthy era, the Democratic president's adherence to such
a radical reform idea seemed a political windfall. Labeling HST's insurance plan "socialized medicine" and FSA
staffers as "followers of the Moscow Party line," GOP
spokesmen of the Eightieth Congress hoped to link the
issue in the public's mind with a communist collectivist
conspiracy against the American free-enterprise system,
thereby helping to insure a Democratic defeat in the 1948
elections.

Even had Truman not been confronted with such a
vociferous and well-organized opposition, the political
mood in the country spelled almost certain defeat for the
extremist features of his health program. "Though it
may be conceded that Kennedy and Johnson were better
salesmen of Truman's wares," Samuel Rosenman and his
wife observed in a recently coauthored study of presidential leadership, "it would not have been possible for
them to have achieved his goals in the milieu that followed the war."[3] Organized labor, the chief lobby pro-

3. Samuel I. Rosenman and Dorothy R. Rosenman, *Presidential Style: Some Giants and a Pygmy in the White House*,
p. 509.

moting health security, lost public favor during the period because of its postwar militancy. The popular press opposed the insurance idea; and, although public opinion favored it immediately after the war, support dissipated quickly when the widely anticipated postwar economic depression failed to materialize. "In this country, when all is said and done, social security seems to be a child (and somewhat of an orphan child) of depression," a dejected Arthur Altmeyer wrote his mentor, Edwin Witte, in 1948. "However," he surmised, "I suppose we ought not measure progress in terms of years but in terms of decades."[4]

Certainly these prosperous yet tense Cold War years were not a time to build a public mandate for major social innovation. Indeed, Rosenman's and Altmeyer's former boss, the articulate and charismatic Franklin Roosevelt, had shied away from the health insurance proposition during the previous depression-stricken decade. Dropping it from the original social security bill in 1935 because it threatened to delay or even prevent passage of the bill's less controversial features, Roosevelt lost his only good chance to legislate national health insurance. Shortly afterward, FDR confronted a cross-party, conservative coalition in Congress with enough votes to block further New Deal proposals and enough longevity to outlive not only his presidency, but also the presidencies of Truman, Eisenhower, and Kennedy.

Seen in this broader economic and political context, Harry Truman's failure on the health insurance front cannot be blamed on his failings as a legislative leader alone; for the greatest restraint upon Truman was not a lack of oratorical skill or philosophical conviction (Presidents Roosevelt and Kennedy had both and could not legislate health insurance), or even the tenor of the times. Like FDR and JFK, Truman's greatest obstacle was a legislative situation wherein a sizable faction within his own political party differed from him ideologically and

4. Arthur J. Altmeyer to Edwin E. Witte, 20 January 1948, box 35, Social Security Correspondence, 1945–1948 Folder, Edwin E. Witte Papers.

voted with the opposition party in Congress to defeat their ostensible leader's proposals. While the Democrats enjoyed a numerical voting advantage in six of the eight congressional sessions during Truman's presidency (and throughout all of Roosevelt's and Kennedy's), the party's southern contingent throttled domestic reform. This anti-union, antiurban voting element, alienated from Truman especially by his civil rights policies, lined up almost to a man with the Republicans to block floor action on the Wagner-Murray-Dingell bills and to defeat HST's reorganization plans to elevate Oscar Ewing's FSA to departmental status. By 1949 the pro-Truman, northern, liberal Democratic health sponsors in Congress were exerting almost as much energy to defeat those less inclusive insurance bills sponsored by their southern counterparts as they were in overcoming the mounting AMA lobbying blitz.

The potential for, and reality of, such intraparty feuding and resultant legislative stalemate had, of course, predated Truman's presidency. Because of sectional, social, economic, psychological, and institutional variances, our major political parties emerged through history as loosely organized, quarrelsome, multi-ideological conglomerates, their members bound together fleetingly only on partisan election-year issues or during crisis situations. Consequently, after the economic emergency that had given rise to the New Deal had abated, Franklin Roosevelt confronted, starting in 1937, a fragmented Democratic party and the domestic legislative logjam that factionalism had produced and that would be inherited by Harry Truman in 1945.

Alarmed by this lack of party cohesion, and attesting to the harsh legislative realities faced by Truman, the American Political Science Association organized the Committee on Political Parties in 1946, HST's first full year in the White House. In 1950 this committee of scholars issued its report, entitled *Toward a More Responsible Two-Party System*. Noting the absence of "sufficient internal cohesion" within the Democratic and Republican parties—a fragmentation that allowed inordinate legislative influence by a few senior members in Congress and by special-interest lobbies—the political scientists called for major reform of the nation's electoral apparatus and of Congress's organizational structure.[5]

Later, Stephen Bailey, a consultant to the APSA Committee on Political Parties, published an award-winning study of congressional passage of the Employment Act of 1946. This legislation, which institutionalized governmental apparatus to ward off another 1930s-style depression, had been enacted in the atmosphere of economic anxiety that was felt by conservatives and liberals alike on Capitol Hill during the months following V-J Day. How did Harry Truman perform in the legislative contest? Bailey demonstrates that the process wherein this legislation moved from inception to passage was so "unbelievably complex," so "hopelessly splintered by the power struggles of competing political, administrative, and private interests," that the American voting public could hold no one individual or group responsible for the program's final form, not President Truman, since "the forces which shaped and modified the legislation were far beyond his control"; not the political parties, rife as they were with internal fragmentation; not even the special-interest lobbies involved, for their influence was too diffuse to gauge.[6] It follows logically that any chief executive who tried to pilot the ambitious national health insurance reform program through such turbulent and unpredictable legislative channels in 1946, no matter how adroitly he maneuvered, would have found his proposal scuttled.

Could Truman have floated a scaled-down, less comprehensive health insurance package through Congress

5. Committee on Political Parties of the American Political Science Association, *Toward a More Responsible Two-Party System*, pp. 1–84. For a recent negative assessment of the committee's conclusions, see Evron M. Kirkpatrick, " 'Toward a More Responsible Two-Party System': Political Science, or Pseudo-Science?"

6. Stephen K. Bailey, *Congress Makes a Law: The Story Behind the Employment Act of 1946*, pp. 233–40.

in 1946? Perhaps, because Congress did legislate a bipartisan hospital-construction bill that year, cosponsored by Lister Hill, Democrat from Alabama, and Harold Burton, Republican from Ohio. But for Truman to abandon the Wagner-Murray-Dingell bill for something more modest, yet almost certainly opposed by the American Medical Association, would have required, given the new Democratic president's temperament, a major intellectual metamorphosis. He would not have been the compulsive Harry Truman, determined in the months following the war to demonstrate that he could resurrect and expand his predecessor's New Deal, overcoming Goliaths like the American Medical Association even while faced with the necessity of putting his divided administrative house in order on the question of national health care policy. HST also would have had to possess far keener foresight than most of his contemporaries in order to see that reconversion to a peacetime economy in 1946 would not result in a much-feared return to hard times, that, ironically, rather than smoothing the path for social reform, reconversion's attendant frustrations would result in the election of an even more conservative, Republican-dominated Congress in November 1946.

However, when the Taft Republicans made advocacy of the W-M-D bill such a partisan and inflammatory issue in 1947, Truman and his advisers, while deciding that the best defense is an offense, did seek a compromise alternative. Feigning unrelenting commitment to the president's original, controversial proposal, the White House—along with its small liberal coterie in Congress, the AFL, and the Committee for the Nation's Health—agreed in early 1948 to shift support to the limited Bernard Baruch–inspired catastrophic health insurance scheme, hoping to defuse the issue as a political bombshell and to woo back conservative southern Democrats to the Democratic party. But to southern Democrats, promises of moderation on the health reform front were more than offset by the civil rights (to them, radical rights) message that President Truman sent to Congress in February 1948. Unable to unite his party on the politics of health reform, much less on his own candidacy for reelection that year, Harry Truman yielded nothing to his detractors during the presidential race. His fiery campaign rhetoric against his domestic reform opponents helped HST win an upset victory over Thomas E. Dewey, but it also helped create in the next Congress an even more rigid, uncompromising division on the health insurance issue.

By April 1949, this legislative deadlock had crystallized visibly on Capitol Hill. Hence, Sen. James Murray, Rep. John Dingell, and the other pro-Truman health sponsors devised, in concert with the White House, a "trick gun strategy" to circumvent it. With President Truman's cooperation, Murray and Dingell defied both the AMA's massive lobbying onslaught and those many alternative health reform measures drafted in various antiadministration subcommittees by brandishing their weighty, seemingly singular, omnibus weapon, S. 1679-H.R. 4312. And, by foregoing the "an Administration Bill" label on their legislative blunderbuss, they deftly avoided an irreversible welding together of its seven component parts. Of the seven health programs contained in this new Murray-Dingell bill, four passed the Senate as separate measures; and for a time the strategy seemed highly successful. In the end, however, only one, a bill expanding federal aid to hospital construction sponsored chiefly by Sen. Lister Hill, a Southern Democrat, passed the House and became law.

Of the many separate health insurance bills vying for support in Congress during these legislative sessions of 1949 and 1950, only the Hill-Aiken bill, sponsored by southern Democrats and Republicans, could have generated enough votes to become law. In form it differed little from the scheme recommended by the Magnuson commission and endorsed by Truman in the closing days of his presidency. Had organized labor, the Committee for the Nation's Health, Murray and Dingell, and especially Harry Truman been willing to back the bill in early 1949, the Eighty-first Congress would have probably

legislated the Hill-Aiken program to subsidize Blue
Shield–type insurance coverage for the nation's poor.
But before the outbreak of the Korean War and the so-
beringly harsh realities that accompanied the outcome of
the 1950 congressional elections, a mixture of pride of
authorship, resentment over past southern Democratic
intransigence, deep-seated objections to the Hill-Aiken
bill's poverty-means test requirement, and a refusal to
bow before organized medicine's monumental lobbying
effort, dictated President Truman's and his supporters'
negative reaction to the middle way. Had Truman followed the middle way, he would have indeed justified the
New Left's claim that he should be labeled a centrist.

It would be a mistake, however, to interpret this stubborn but ill-fated health security campaign strategy in
wholly negative terms. Even in defeat the omnibus Murray-Dingell bill served its supporters in numerous ways.
While it aroused violent opposition and heated debate,
the proposal also drew public attention to America's
postwar health needs. Responding to some of those needs,
congressional action during Truman's tenure provided
federal funds to initiate a hospital construction program,
to expand medical aid to the needy, and to encourage
medical research. Also, because organized medicine considered national health insurance a menace to its professional autonomy, it promoted an alternative scheme. Initially opposing even private health insurance, by 1948
the American Medical Association had begun reacting
to the president's health reform idea by fervently promoting expansion of Blue Shield surgical and Blue Cross hospital prepayment plans. As Harry Truman himself
expressed it, his advocacy of national health insurance
had given "a kick" to Blue Shield and Blue Cross.[7] And
it was a mighty hard kick. Whereas Americans held about
28 million Blue Shield and Blue Cross insurance policies
when Harry Truman became president in 1945, over 61

7. Rear Platform Remarks at Minot, North Dakota, 13 May
1950, in Harry S. Truman, *The Public Papers of the Presidents
of the United States, 1950*, p. 396.

million policies had been sold by the time he retired to Independence in early 1953.[8]

So, the results of Harry Truman's skirmishes with organized medicine over public health policy must be judged within the broader half-century historical context. Appreciating the circumscribing dictates of America's legislative system, the economic and intellectual atmosphere in which Truman labored, and both the strengths and weaknesses of the Missourian's leadership capabilities, one must conclude that in the health policy contest the nation's thirty-third president demonstrated conviction as well as self-serving brashness, altruism as well as narrow political partisanship, legislative acumen as well as stubborn rigidity. Above all, Harry Truman, himself a student of evolving presidential prerogative since George Washington, demonstrated an awareness that, even though not immediately accepted, his legislative proposals cast an imprint upon, and influenced, later domestic policymaking. Political scientist Louis Koenig observed correctly in the midfifties that "temporary failure or no, as a political force [Truman's Fair Deal] kept the atmosphere of political and social reform from being dissipated, and heartened the masses of people with solid expectations of better things at hand."[9] Thanks in great measure to Harry S. Truman, those expectations turned into accomplishment for older Americans with the passage of medicare in July 1965.

8. Herman M. Somers and Anne R. Somers, *Doctors, Patients and Health Insurance*, table on p. 548.

9. Louis W. Koenig, ed., *The Truman Administration: Its Principles and Practices*, p. 94.

Bibliography

Primary Sources

National Archives of the United States, Washington, D.C.

Record Group 47, "Records of the Social Security Board"
"Records of the Chairman"
"Records of the Commissioner"
Record Group 51, "Records of the Bureau of the Budget"
Record Group 235, "General Records of the Federal Security Agency"
"General Classified Files"
"Records of the Administrator"
Record Group 250, "Records of the Office of War Mobilization and Reconversion"

Manuscript Collections

Harry S. Truman Library, Independence, Mo.
Democratic National Committee Clippings File; Michael M. Davis Papers, Records of the Committee for the Nation's Health; Frederick J. Lawton Papers; J. Howard McGrath Papers; Charles S. Murphy Papers; Records of the President's Commission on the Health Needs of the Nation; Samuel I. Rosenman Papers; Charles G. Ross Papers; David H. Stowe Papers; Harry S. Truman Papers; James E. Webb Papers.
State Historical Society of Wisconsin, Madison
Arthur J. Altmeyer Papers; American Federation of Labor Papers; Wilbur J. Cohen Papers; Edwin E. Witte Papers.
Dwight D. Eisenhower Library, Abilene, Kans.
Dwight D. Eisenhower Papers.
University of Montana, Missoula
James E. Murray Papers.
Franklin D. Roosevelt Library, Hyde Park, N.Y.
Franklin D. Roosevelt Papers.

Bureau of the Budget, Records Section Depository, Executive Office Building, Washington, D.C.
  Harold D. Smith Papers.
Library of Congress, Washington, D.C.
  Robert A. Taft Papers.
Georgetown University, Washington, D.C.
  Robert F. Wagner Papers.

Private Papers

John D. Dingell Papers. In possession of Rep. John D. Dingell, Jr., Washington, D.C.
Oscar R. Ewing Papers. In possession of Oscar R. Ewing, Chapel Hill, N.C.
Mary W. Lasker Oral History Memoir, Columbia University Oral History Project. In possession of Mary W. Lasker, New York, N.Y.

Interviews

Michael M. Davis, 20 June 1965, Chevy Chase, Md.
Oscar R. Ewing, 6 July 1965, Chapel Hill, N.C.
Isidore S. Falk, 15 July 1965, New Haven, Conn.
Nelle Morgan, 15 July 1964, Independence, Mo.
Harry S. Truman, 29 December 1961, Independence, Mo.

Government Documents

Brewster, Agnes W., ed. *Health Insurance and Related Proposals for Financing Personal Health Services.* Department of Health, Education, and Welfare. Washington: Government Printing Office, 1958.
Ewing, Oscar R. *The Nation's Health—A Ten Year Program.* Washington: Government Printing Office, 1948.
Johnson, Lyndon B. *The Public Papers of the Presidents of the United States, 1965.* Washington: Government Printing Office, 1966.
Truman, Harry S. *The Public Papers of the Presidents of the United States, 1945–1953.* Washington: Government Printing Office, 1961–1966.

Bibliography

U.S., Committee on Economic Security. *Report to the President.* Washington: Government Printing Office, 1935.

U.S., Congress. *Congressional Record.* 75th Cong., 3d sess., 1938–89th Cong., 1st sess., 1965. Washington: Government Printing Office.

———. *House Report 1821.* 80th Cong., 2d sess., 1948.

U.S., Congress, House, Committee on Appropriations. *The Supplemental Federal Security Agency Appropriation Bill for 1949: Hearings before the Subcommittee on Appropriations.* 80th Cong., 2d sess., 1948. Washington: U.S. Government Printing Office, 1948.

U.S., Congress, House, Committee on Expenditures in the Executive Departments. *Investigation of the Participation of Federal Officials in the Formation and Operation of Health Workshops: Hearings before the Subcommittee on Publicity and Propaganda.* 80th Cong., 1st sess., 28 May, 18 June 1947. Washington: U.S. Government Printing Office, 1947.

U.S., Congress, House, Committee on Interstate and Foreign Commerce. *National Health Plan: Hearings before the Subcommittee on Health on H.R. 4312, H.R. 4313, H.R. 4918 and Other Identical Bills.* 81st Cong., 1st sess., 20 May–6 July 1949. Washington: U.S. Government Printing Office, 1949.

———. *Senate Report 1444.* 80th Cong., 2d sess., 1948.

U.S., Congress, Senate, Committee on Appropriations. *Supplemental Federal Security Appropriation Bill for 1949: Hearings before the Subcommittee on Appropriations.* 80th Cong., 2d sess., 1948. Washington: U.S. Government Printing Office, 1948.

U.S., Congress, Senate, Committee on Education and Labor. *Hospital Construction Act: Hearings before the Committee on Education and Labor on S. 191.* 79th Cong., 1st sess., 1945. Washington: U.S. Government Printing Office, 1945.

———. *Interim Report from the Subcommittee on Wartime Health and Education: Subcommittee Report No. 3 Pursuant to S. Res. 74.* 78th Cong., 2d sess., January 1945. Washington: U.S. Government Printing Office, 1945.

———. *National Health Program: Hearings before the Committee on Education and Labor on S. 1606.* 79th Cong., 2d sess., 2 April–10 July 1946. Washington: U.S. Government Printing Office, 1946.

———. *To Establish a National Health Program: Hearings before the Subcommittee on Health on S. 1620.* 76th Cong., 1st sess., 27 April–13 July 1939. Washington: U.S. Government Printing Office, 1939.

———. *Wartime Health and Education: Hearings before the Subcommittee on Wartime Health and Education Pursuant to S. Res. 74.* Part 1. 78th Cong., 1st sess., 30 November–3 December 1943. Washington: U.S. Government Printing Office, 1944.

U.S., Congress, Senate, Committee on Labor and Public Welfare. *Hospital Survey and Construction (Hill-Burton) Act Amendments: Hearings before the Subcommittee on Hospital Construction and Local Public Health Units on S. 205, S. 231, S. 614, Title III of S. 1679, and Title IV of S. 1581.* 81st Cong., 1st sess., 4, 5, 9 May 1949. Washington: U.S. Government Printing Office, 1949.

———. *National Health Program: Hearings before the Subcommittee on Health on S. 545 . . . and S. 1320. . . .* 80th Cong., 1st sess., 1947–1948. Washington: U.S. Government Printing Office, 1948.

———. *National Health Program, 1949: Hearings before the Subcommittee on Health Legislation on S. 1106, S. 1456, S. 1581, and S. 1679.* 81st Cong., 1st sess., 23 May–29 June 1949. Washington: U.S. Government Printing Office, 1949.

U.S., Department of Health, Education, and Welfare. *The Nation and Its Older People.* Washington: Government Printing Office, 1961.

U.S., Interdepartmental Committee to Coordinate Health and Welfare Activities. *Health Security.* Washington: Government Printing Office, 1939.

———. *Proceedings of the National Health Conference.* Washington: Government Printing Office, 1938.

U.S., President's Commission on the Health Needs of the Nation. *Building America's Health: A Report to the President.* Washington: Government Printing Office, 1952.

U.S., Public Health Service. *Public Health Reports.* Vol. 60, reprint no. 2685. Washington: Government Printing Office, 28 December 1945.

Bibliography

U.S., Social Security Board. *Fifth Annual Report, 1944*. Washington: Government Printing Office, 1944.

Publications of Private and Professional Organizations

American Association for Public Opinion Research. *The Public Opinion Quarterly*. Vol. 13. Princeton: Summer 1949.

American Medical Association. *Digest of Official Actions, 1846–1958*. Chicago: American Medical Association, 1959.

———. *Journal of the American Medical Association*. Vols. 122–187. Chicago: 26 June 1943–6 February 1965.

Committee on the Costs of Medical Care. *Medical Care for the American People: The Final Report*. Chicago: University of Chicago Press, 1932.

Committee on Political Parties of the American Political Science Association. *Toward A More Responsible Two-Party System*. New York: Rinehart and Company, 1950.

Congressional Quarterly Service. *Congress and the Nation, 1945–1964*. Vol. 1. Washington: Congressional Quarterly Service, 1965.

———. *Congressional Quarterly Almanac*. Vols. 5–6. Washington: 1949–1950.

National Conference on Social Security. *Social Security in the United States*. Meetings nos. 2, 9, 10. New York: American Association for Social Security, 1929, 1936, 1937.

National Health Assembly. *America's Health: A Report to the Nation*. New York: Harper and Brothers, 1949.

Proceedings of the National Conference of Social Work. Vols. 53, 57, 64, 67, 75. Chicago: University of Chicago Press; New York: Columbia University Press.

Proceedings of the National Conference of Charities and Correction. Vols. 29–41. Boston, Mass., and Fort Wayne, Ind.: Publisher varies.

Newspapers

Independence (Missouri) *Examiner*, 8 December 1927
Kansas City Star, 16 October 1928
New York Daily Mirror, 19 August 1949
New York Herald Tribune, 20 November 1945

New York Sunday News, 22 April 1945
New York Times, 21 July 1938–22 July 1959
Philadelphia Record, 21 November 1945
St. Louis Post Dispatch, 26 April 1946
Washington Times-Herald, 22 April 1945

Secondary Sources

Unpublished Studies

Byrne, Thomas R. "The Social Thought of Robert F. Wagner."
    Ph.D. dissertation, Georgetown University, 1951.

Dalfiume, Richard M. "President Truman's National Health
    Insurance Proposal and the A.M.A." Master's thesis, San
    Jose State College, 1963.

Hand, Samuel P. "Samuel I. Rosenman: His Public Career."
    Ph.D. dissertation, Syracuse University, 1960.

Hinchey, Mary H. "The Frustration of the New Deal Revival."
    Ph.D. dissertation, University of Missouri, 1965.

Poen, Monte M. "The Truman Administration and National
    Health Insurance." Ph.D. dissertation, University of Mis-
    souri, 1967.

Schmidtlein, Eugene F. "Truman the Senator." Ph.D. disserta-
    tion, University of Missouri, 1962.

Books

Ables, Jules. *Out of the Jaws of Victory*. New York: Henry
    Holt and Co., 1959.

Allen, Robert S., and Shannon, William V. *The Truman
    Merry-Go-Round*. New York: Vanguard Press, 1950.

Altmeyer, Arthur J. *The Formative Years of Social Security*.
    Madison: University of Wisconsin Press, 1966.

Bachman, George W., and Meriam, Lewis. *The Issue of Com-
    pulsory Health Insurance*. Washington: Brookings Institu-
    tion, 1948.

Bailey, Stephen K. *Congress Makes a Law: The Story Behind
    the Employment Act of 1946*. New York: Random House,
    Vintage Edition, 1964.

Bibliography

Beveridge, Sir William. *Social Insurance and Allied Services.* New York: Macmillan Co., 1942.

Blum, John. *From the Morgenthau Diaries: Years of War, 1941-1945.* Boston: Houghton Mifflin and Co., 1967.

Bremner, Robert H. *From the Depths: The Discovery of Poverty in the United States.* New York: New York University Press, 1956.

Bruno, Frank J. *Trends in Social Work.* 2d ed. New York: Columbia University Press, 1957.

Bryce, James. *The American Commonwealth.* Vol. 1. New York: Macmillan Co., 1924.

Burns, James MacGregor. *The Deadlock of Democracy: Four Party Politics in America.* Englewood Cliffs, N.J.: Prentice Hall, 1963.

————. *Roosevelt: The Lion and the Fox.* New York: Harcourt, Brace and World, 1956.

————. *Roosevelt: The Soldier of Freedom, 1940-1945.* New York: Harcourt, Brace, Jovanovich, 1970.

Burrow, James G. *AMA, Voice of American Medicine.* Baltimore: Johns Hopkins Press, 1963.

Cannon, Ida. *On the Social Frontier of Medicine.* Cambridge, Mass.: Harvard University Press, 1952.

Cantril, Hadley, ed. *Public Opinion, 1935-1946.* Princeton: Princeton University Press, 1951.

Carter, Richard. *The Doctor Business.* Garden City, N.Y.: Doubleday and Co., 1958.

Chambers, Clarke A. *Seedtime of Reform: American Social Service and Social Action, 1918-1933.* Minneapolis: University of Minnesota Press, 1963.

Cochran, Bert. *Adlai Stevenson: Patrician Among the Politicians.* New York: Funk and Wagnalls, 1969.

Coffin, Tris. *Missouri Compromise.* Boston: Little, Brown and Co., 1947.

Commons, John R. *Myself.* New York: Macmillan Co., 1934.

Cornwell, Elmer E., Jr. *Presidential Leadership of Public Opinion.* Bloomington: Indiana University Press, 1965.

Dalfiume, Richard M. *Desegregation of the U.S. Armed Forces.* Columbia: University of Missouri Press, 1969.

Daniels, Jonathan. *The Man of Independence.* New York: J. B. Lippincott Co., 1950.

Davies, Richard O. *Housing Reform During the Truman Administration.* Columbia: University of Missouri Press, 1966.

Davis, Michael M. *Medical Care for Tomorrow.* New York: Harper and Brothers, 1955.

Fainsod, Merle, and Gordon, Lincoln. *Government and the American Economy.* New York: W. W. Norton and Co., 1941.

Falk, Isidore S. *Security Against Sickness.* New York: Doubleday, Doran, and Co., 1936.

Farrar, Ronald T. *Reluctant Servant: The Story of Charles G. Ross.* Columbia: University of Missouri Press, 1969.

Frankel, Lee K., and Dawson, Miles. *Workingmen's Insurance in Europe.* New York: Russell Sage Foundation, 1910.

Garceau, Oliver. *The Political Life of the American Medical Association.* Cambridge, Mass.: Harvard University Press, 1941.

Glenn, John M.; Brandt, Lilian; and Andrews, F. Emerson. *Russel Sage Foundation, 1907–1946.* New York: Russell Sage Foundation, 1957.

Goldman, Eric F. *The Crucial Decade—And After.* New York: Random House, Vintage Edition, 1960.

Goldmann, Franz. *Voluntary Medical Care Insurance in the United States.* New York: Columbia University Press, 1948.

Gompers, Samuel. *Labor and the Common Welfare.* Compiled by Hayes Robbins. New York: E. P. Dutton and Co., 1919.

Gross, Bertram M. *The Legislative Struggle.* New York: McGraw-Hill, 1953.

Gunther, John. *Taken at the Flood: The Story of Albert D. Lasker.* New York: Harper and Brothers, 1960.

Hamby, Alonzo L. *Beyond the New Deal: Harry S. Truman and American Liberalism.* New York: Columbia University Press, 1973.

Harris, Seymour E. *The Economics of American Medicine.* New York: Macmillan Co., 1964.

Hartmann, Susan M. *Truman and the 80th Congress.* Columbia: University of Missouri Press, 1971.

Herring, E. Pendleton. *The Politics of Democracy.* New York: W. W. Norton and Co., 1940.

Hillman, William. *Mr. President.* New York: Farrar, Straus and Young, 1952.

238

Bibliography

Hirshfield, Daniel S. *The Lost Reform: The Campaign for Compulsory Health Insurance in the United States from 1932 to 1943.* Cambridge, Mass.: Harvard University Press, 1970.

Hoffman, Frederick L. *More Facts and Fallacies of Compulsory Health Insurance.* Newark: Prudential Press, 1920.

Huthmacher, J. Joseph. *Senator Robert F. Wagner.* New York: Atheneum, 1968.

Johnson, Walter. *1600 Pennsylvania Avenue.* Boston: Little, Brown, and Co., 1963.

Kelley, Stanley, Jr. *Professional Public Relations and Political Power.* Baltimore: Johns Hopkins Press, 1966.

Kirkendall, Richard S. *The Truman Period As a Research Field: A Reappraisal, 1972.* Columbia: University of Missouri Press, 1974.

Koenig, Louis W., ed. *The Truman Administration: Its Principles and Practices.* New York: New York University Press, 1956.

Latham, Earl. *The Communist Controversy in Washington: From the New Deal to McCarthy.* New York: Atheneum, 1969.

Lubell, Samuel. *The Future of American Politics.* New York: Harper Brothers, 1952.

Lubove, Roy. *The Struggle for Social Security.* Cambridge, Mass.: Harvard University Press, 1968.

McCleary, George F. *National Health Insurance.* London: H. K. Lewis Co., 1932.

McConnell, Grant. *Private Power and American Democracy.* New York: Alfred A. Knopf, 1967.

McCoy, Donald R., and Ruetten, Richard T. *Quest and Response: Minority Rights and the Truman Administration.* Lawrence: University Press of Kansas, 1973.

Martin, Joe. *My First Fifty Years in Politics.* New York: McGraw-Hill, 1960.

Matusow, Allen J. *Farm Policies and Politics in the Truman Years.* New York: Atheneum, 1970.

Mayer, George H. *The Republican Party, 1854–1966.* New York: Oxford University Press, 1967.

Millis, Walter, ed. *The Forrestal Diaries.* New York: Viking Press, 1951.

239

Mott, Frederick D., and Roemer, Milton I. *Rural Health and Medical Care*. New York: McGraw-Hill Book Co., 1948.

Munts, Raymond. *Bargaining for Health: Labor Unions, Health Insurance, and Medical Care*. Madison: University of Wisconsin Press, 1967.

Patterson, James T. *Congressional Conservatism and the New Deal*. Lexington: University of Kentucky Press, 1967.

———. *Mr. Republican: A Biography of Robert A. Taft*. Boston: Houghton Mifflin Co., 1972.

Paul, Arnold M. *Conservative Crisis and the Rule of Law*. Ithaca, N.Y.: Cornell University Press, 1960.

Perkins, Frances. *The Roosevelt I Knew*. New York: Viking Press, 1947.

Phillips, Cabell. *The Truman Presidency*. New York: Macmillan Co., 1966.

Porter, Kirk H., and Johnson, Donald B., eds. *National Party Platforms, 1840–1956*. Urbana: University of Illinois Press, 1956.

Pumphrey, Ralph E., and Pumphrey, Muriel W., eds. *The Heritage of American Social Work*. New York: Columbia University Press, 1961.

Redding, Jack. *Inside the Democratic Party*. New York: Bobbs-Merrill Co., 1958.

Roosevelt, Elliott, ed. *FDR: His Personal Letters*. New York: Duell, Sloan and Pearce, 1950.

Roosevelt, Franklin D. *The Public Papers and Addresses of Franklin D. Roosevelt*. Vols. 7–13. Compiled by Samuel I. Rosenman. New York: Macmillan Co., 1941–1950.

Rose, Arnold M. *The Power Structure: Political Process in American Society*. New York: Oxford University Press, 1967.

Rosen, George. *A History of Public Health*. New York: M. D. Publications, 1958.

Rosenman, Samuel I. *Working with Roosevelt*. New York: Harper and Brothers, 1952.

Rosenman, Samuel I., and Rosenman, Dorothy R. *Presidential Style: Some Giants and a Pygmy in the White House*. New York: Harper and Row, 1976.

Ross, Irwin. *The Loneliest Campaign: The Truman Victory of 1948*. New York: New American Library, 1969.

Bibliography

Rubinow, Isaac M. *Social Insurance.* New York: Henry Holt and Co., 1913.

Schattschneider, Elmer E. *Party Government.* New York: Farrar and Rinehart, 1942.

Seager, Henry R. *Social Insurance.* New York: Macmillan Co., 1910.

Shearon, Marjorie. *Blueprint for the Nationalization of Medicine.* Pamphlet. 2d printing. Washington: n.p., 1947.

Sherwood, Robert. *Roosevelt and Hopkins.* New York: Harper and Brothers, 1948.

Simons, Algie M., and Sinai, Nathan. *The Way of Health Insurance.* Chicago: University of Chicago Press, 1932.

Sinai, Nathan; Anderson, Odin W.; and Dollar, Melvin L. *Health Insurance in the United States.* New York: Commonwealth Fund, 1946.

Somers, Herman M., and Somers, Anne R. *Doctors, Patients, and Health Insurance.* Washington: Brookings Institution, 1961.

Sundquist, James L. *Politics and Policy: The Eisenhower, Kennedy, and Johnson Years.* Washington: Brookings Institution, 1968.

Taft, Philip. *The AFL in the Time of Gompers.* New York: Harper and Brothers, 1957.

Truman, David B. *The Congressional Party.* New York: John Wiley and Sons, 1949.

————. *The Governmental Process.* New York: Alfred A. Knopf, 1963.

Truman, Harry S. *Memoirs.* Vol. 1, *Year of Decisions.* Vol. 2, *Years of Trial and Hope.* Garden City: Doubleday and Co., 1955, 1956.

————. *Mr. Citizen.* New York: Bernard Geis Associates. Popular Library Edition, 1961.

Truman, Margaret. *Harry S. Truman.* New York: Morrow, 1973.

Tully, Grace. *FDR: My Boss.* New York: Scribner and Sons, 1949.

Wilensky, Harold L., and Lebeaux, Charles N. *Industrial Society and Social Welfare.* New York: Russell Sage Foundation, 1958.

Williams, Pierce. *The Purchase of Medical Care Through*

Fixed Periodic Payment. New York: National Bureau of Economic Research, 1932.

Wilson, Elizabeth W. *Compulsory Health Insurance.* Studies in Individual and Collective Security, no. 3. New York: National Industrial Conference Board, 1947.

Wilson, Woodrow. *Congressional Government.* Boston: Houghton Mifflin and Co., 1885.

Witte, Edwin. *Social Security Perspectives: Essays.* Edited by Robert J. Lampman. Madison: University of Wisconsin Press, 1962.

Young, Roland. *Congressional Politics in the Second World War.* New York: Columbia University Press, 1956.

Articles

Abbott, Edith. "Hospitals Are Not a Health Program." *The Social Service Review* 14 (March 1940): 138–39.

Altmeyer, Arthur J. "The Wisconsin Idea and Social Security." *Wisconsin Magazine of History* 24 (Autumn 1958): 20–25.

"The American Medical Association: Power, Purpose and Politics in Organized Medicine." *Yale Law Journal* 63 (May 1954): 937–1022.

Andrews, John B. "While Millions Suffer." *American Labor Legislation Review* 30 (March 1940): 3–4.

"The Battle for the Nation's Health." *Nation* 162 (20 April 1946): 450.

Becker, Harry. "Organized Labor and the Problem of Medical Care." *Annals of the American Academy of Political and Social Science* 273 (January 1951): 122–30.

Bernstein, Barton J. "America in War and Peace: The Test of Liberalism." In *Twentieth Century America: Recent Interpretations,* edited by Barton J. Bernstein and Allen J. Matusow, pp. 350–75. New York: Harcourt, Brace & World, 1969.

"Canning the Planners." *Commonwealth* 38 (11 June 1943): 192.

"Capitol and Labor on Each Other's Necks." *Survey* 37 (27 January 1917): 494–96.

Chenery, William L. "Good Medicine Doesn't Mean Socialism." *Collier's,* 5 March 1949, p. 78.

"Clarence F. Lee." *Current Biography, 1946,* p. 334.

Committee on Public Administration Cases. "The Transfer of the Children's Bureau." In *Public Administration and Policy Development*, edited by Harold Stein, pp. 17–29. New York: Harcourt, Brace and Co., 1952.

"Comparison of Johnson, GOP, AMA Medical Care Bills." *Congressional Quarterly*, week ending 5 March 1965, pp. 340–41.

"Compulsory Health Insurance." *Survey* 70 (April 1934): 127.

"Constitution of the American Association for Labor Legislation." *American Labor Legislation Review* 1 (January 1911): 121–23.

Cunningham, R. M. "Can Political Means Gain Professional Ends?" *Modern Hospital* 77 (December 1951): 53–55.

Davis, Allen F. "The Social Workers and the Progressive Party." *American Historical Review* 69 (April 1964): 671–88.

Davis, Michael M. "Government Participation in Medical Care." *American Labor Legislation Review* 32 (September 1942): 112–19.

———. "Health–Today and Tomorrow." *Survey Graphic* 34 (February 1945): 40–42.

———. "A Milestone in Health Progress." *Survey Graphic* 34 (December 1945): 485–86.

———. "Organization of Medical Service." *American Labor Legislation Review* 6 (March 1916): 16–20.

———. "Surgeon General Parran . . . An Accounting." *Survey Graphic* 37 (July 1948): 352–53, 359–60.

———. "Who Will Pay the Costs?" *Survey* 134 (June 1948): 191–93.

Devine, Edward T. "The New Health." *Survey* 32 (4 July 1914): 377–78.

Devine, Thomas. "For the Record." *Survey* 83 (October 1947): 274–76.

De Voto, Bernard. "Doctors Along the Boardwalk." *Harper's Magazine* 185 (September 1947): 215–24.

"The Doctor Gets a Bill." *New Republic*, 21 February 1949, pp. 7–8.

Engel, Leonard. "The AMA's Slush Fund." *Nation* 161 (12 February 1949): 181–82.

Ferguson, Homer. "Radio Address." Detroit, 3 May 1947, *Congressional Digest* 26 (June–July 1947): 186.

"Forrest C. Donnell." *Current Biography, 1949*, pp. 164–66.

"For the Nation's Health." *Time*, 29 December 1952, pp. 32–33.

"The Fortune Survey." *Fortune*, July 1942, pp. 8–10, 12, 14, 18.

"Free Health." *Survey* 26 (13 May 1911): 270.

"Free Medicine, How Much?" *U.S. News*, 29 April 1949, pp. 19–20.

"General Discussion." *American Labor Legislation Review* 2 (June 1912): 320.

Griffith, Charles M. "The Veterans Administration." In *Doctors at War*, edited by Morris Fishbein, pp. 321–35. New York: E. P. Dutton and Co., 1945.

Griffith, Robert. "Truman and the Historians: The Reconstruction of Postwar American History." *Wisconsin Magazine of History* 59 (Autumn 1975): 20–50.

Halleck, Charles. "Speech Before the Republican National Committee, April 21, 1947." *Congressional Digest* 26 (June–July 1947): 188–89.

Harness, Forest A. "Our Most Dangerous Lobby–II." *Reader's Digest*, December 1947, pp. 63–66.

Harris, Richard. "Annals of Legislation: Medicare." *New Yorker*, 2 July 1966, pp. 29–62; 9 July 1966, pp. 30–77; 16 July 1966, pp. 35–91; 23 July 1966, pp. 35–63.

"Health and Harmony." *Newsweek*, 17 May 1948, pp. 59–60.

"Health by Compulsion." *Life*, 2 May 1949, pp. 40–41.

Healy, Paul F. "The Senate's Big Itch." *Saturday Evening Post*, 3 December 1949, pp. 36–37, 154–57.

Herter, Christian A. "Our Most Dangerous Lobby." *Reader's Digest*, September 1947, pp. 5–10.

Holly, Hazel. "Reinsurance Has No Magic." *Woman's Home Companion* 82 (May 1955): 13, 15, 64.

"Invisible Congress: Marjorie Shearon." *New Republic*, 17 June 1946, p. 855.

"It's Socialized Medicine, All Right, Says AMA." *Newsweek*, 17 December 1945, p. 84.

Kaplan, Abraham. "American Ethics and Public Policy." In *The American Style*, edited by Elting E. Morison, pp. 3–110. New York: Harper and Row, 1958.

Kellogg, Paul. "New Beacons in Boston." *Survey* 64 (15 July 1930): 341–47, 361, 367.

Kirkpatrick, Evron M. " "Toward A More Responsible Two-

Party System': Political Science, Policy Science, or Pseudo-Science." *The American Political Science Review* 65 (December 1971): 965–90.

La Follette, Robert, Jr. "Turn the Light on Communism." *Collier's* 119 (8 February 1947): 73–74.

Leet, Glen. "Amendment Season for Social Security." *Survey* 74 (December 1938): 375.

Lewis, R. Cragin. "New Power at the Polls: The Doctors." In *Politics in the United States*, edited by Henry A. Turner, pp. 180–85. New York: McGraw Hill Book Co., 1955.

Mayer, Milton. "The Rise and Fall of Doctor Fishbein." *Harper's* 189 (November 1949): 76–85.

"Medical Care for All." *Science News Letter* 46 (16 December 1944): 388.

"Medical Care in a National Health Program." *American Journal of Public Health* 34 (December 1944): 1252–56.

"Medicine and Politics Don't Mix." *Collier's*, 14 May 1947, p. 86.

"Methods of Democratic Chief McGrath." *U.S. News*, 14 November 1947, pp. 56–59.

Mitchell, Stephen A. "Adlai's Amateurs." In *As We Knew Him: The Stevenson Story by Twenty-One Friends*, edited by Edward P. Doyle, pp. 66–92. New York: Harper and Row, 1966.

Neustadt, Richard E. "Congress and the Fair Deal: A Legislative Balance Sheet." *Public Policy* 5 (1954): 349–81.

————. "The Presidency and Legislation: The Growth of Central Clearance." *American Political Science Review* 48 (September 1954): 641–71.

————. "Presidency and Legislation: Planning the President's Program." *American Political Science Review* 49 (December 1955): 980–1021.

"The Next Step in Workingmen's Insurance—The Road to Efficiency." *Survey* 26 (8 April 1911): 91–93.

"Opposition to Welfare Bills Called 'Political Folly.'" *American Labor Legislation Review* 9 (June 1919): 265–74.

"Oscar R. Ewing." *Current Biography, 1948*, p. 194.

Parron, Thomas. "The United States Public Health Service in the War." In *Doctors at War*, edited by Morris Fishbein, pp. 249–73. New York: E. P. Dutton and Co., 1945.

Parsons, Talcott. "Social Change and Medical Organization in the United States: A Sociological Perspective." *Annals of the American Academy of Political and Social Science* 346 (March 1963): 21–33.

Perkins, Frances. "Public Policy in Preparation Now to Meet Postwar Problems." *American Labor Legislation Review* 32 (March 1942): 5–9.

"Platform of Industrial Minimums." *Survey* 28 (6 July 1912): 517–18.

Porter, Amy. "Do We Want National Health Insurance?" *Collier's*, 27 January 1945, pp. 20–21, 66.

"Report of Work." *American Labor Legislation Review* 12 (March 1922): 78.

Rivet, Kathleen. "Lost, A National Health Program." *American Labor Legislation Review* 31 (September 1941): 120–22.

Roemer, Milton. "Changing Patterns of Health Services: Their Dependence on a Changing World." *Annals of the American Academy of Political and Social Science* 346 (March 1963): 44–56.

Rubinow, Isaac. "20,000 Miles Over the Land: A Survey of the Spreading Health Insurance Movement." *Survey* 38 (3 March 1917): 631–65.

Seager, Henry R. "Plan for a Health Insurance Act." *American Labor Legislation Review* 6 (March 1916): 21–25.

"Senator Pepper's Emergence as Champion of Left Wing Groups." *U. S. News*, 7 June 1946, pp. 56–57.

"Should We Adopt a Compulsory National Health Insurance Program?" on "Town Meeting of the Air." ABC Radio Debate, 548th broadcast, 22 February 1949.

"Should We Adopt Compulsory Health Insurance?" on "Round Table." NBC Radio Discussion no. 566, 23 January 1949.

"Sickness Inusrance." *American Labor Legislation Review* 4 (December 1913): 49–101.

Silverman, Milton. "The Post Reports on Health Insurance." *Saturday Evening Post*, 7 June 1958, pp. 25–27, 127–28; 14 June 1958, pp. 36, 124–26; 21 June 1958, pp. 30, 100–102.

"Social Forces." *Survey* 26 (22 April 1911): 117–18.

"Social Insurance and Assistance." *International Labour Review* 43 (January 1941): 105–7.

Spencer, Steven M. "Do You Really Want Socialized Medicine?" *Saturday Evening Post*, 28 May 1949, pp. 29, 133–36.

————. "How Britain Likes Socialized Medicine." *Saturday Evening Post*, 14 May 1949, pp. 22–23, 148–50, 151–53.

————. "How British Doctors Like Socialized Medicine." *Saturday Evening Post*, 21 May 1949, pp. 32–33, 172–74.

"State Medicine Ahead." *U.S. News*, 6 April 1945, pp. 53–54.

"The States are Feeling the Heat." *Saturday Evening Post*, 19 May 1945, p. 108.

"Strong Editorial Support for the Health Insurance Bill." *American Labor Legislation Review* 9 (June 1919): 261.

Taylor, Henry J. "Shouldn't Doctors Have Rights Too?" *Reader's Digest*, April 1949, pp. 101–2.

"Truman and Labor." *New Republic*, 10 June 1946, p. 820.

"U.S. Medicine in Transition." *Fortune*, December 1944, pp. 156–63.

Wade, Alan D. "Social Work and Political Action." *Social Work* 8 (October 1963): 3–10.

Walker, Forrest A. "Compulsory Health Insurance: 'The Next Great Step in Social Legislation.'" *Journal of American History* 56 (September 1969): 290–304.

Warren, Earl. "My Plan for Health Insurance." *Look*, 22 June 1948, pp. 58, 60, 63–64.

"Welfare, Eisenhower Style." *Business Week*, 23 January 1954, p. 27.

"What Price the Welfare State?" *Newsweek*, 2 May 1949, p. 17.

"White House Conference." *Hospitals* 20 (October 1948): 104.

Wright, Wade. "Insure for Health," *Survey* 63 (1 January 1930): 424.

Index

A

Adams, Sherman, 213
Addams, Jane, 6, 221
AFL. *See* American Federation of Labor
Aiken, George, 165
Altmeyer, Arthur J.: as Wisconsin progressive, 15; as Social Security Board chairman, 20, 30, 34, 49; conference with Roosevelt, 35; as health security advocate, 80; and medicare idea, 190; on social security, 224; mentioned, 221
AMA. *See* American Medical Association
American Association for Labor Legislation (AALL): as social insurance lobby, 5–6; standard health bill of, 6–8; abandons effort, 14, 21; demise of, 42
American Association for Social Security (AASS): as sponsor of health bill, 21; opposes Social Security Act, 24; demise of, 42
American Bar Association, 89
American Dental Association, 89, 194–95
American Farm Bureau Federation, 26, 90
American Federation of Labor (AFL): opposes health security, 11–12; shift in position of, 12, 19–20, 24; promotes health security, 34–35, 152; and the Committee for the Nation's Health, 177–78, 207. *See also* Gompers, Samuel; Green, William
American Hospital Association (AHA): opposes health security, 26, 27, 89, 167–68; conference with Truman, 137; favors Hill-Aiken bill, 165, 166; and medicare, 215
American Medical Association (AMA): advocates state-financed health plan, 12; shifts attitude toward social insurance, 12–13; opposes group medical practice, 13; organization of, 13, 15; and National Health Conference, 20; and Social Security Act, 25; opposes W-M-D bills of 1943–1944, 45–46; and Morris Fishbein, 46, 55, 151; and National Physician's Committee, 47, 142–43; conference with Truman, 54–55; opposes W-M-D bills of 1945–1946, 55–56, 86–87; and Hill-Burton Act, 87; promotion of voluntary insurance, 87, 121, 151, 159, 170; allies of, 89–90, 161–62, 180, 187; and GOP Eightieth Congress, 93–94, 96, 103; and Raymond Rich Associates, 116; and National Health Assembly, 121; and Taft bill, 121–22; Truman's letter to, 132–33; dissent within ranks of, 143, 151; opposes Murray-Dingell omnibus bill, 144, 145–51; and Whitaker and Baxter, 144, 151; national education campaign of, 145–51; justice department's investigation into, 170; and 1950 elections, 180–82, 187–88; on Truman, 184–85, 192, 213–14, 223; opposes social security disability

mittee: and 1948 Democratic party platform, 124; promotion of Truman program,
172, 178–79; and the Com-
mittee for the Nation's
Health, 178; and medicare,
218
Department of Health, Education, and Welfare (HEW),
57, 214
De Voto, Bernard, 101
Dewey, Thomas E.: as health
security opponent, 131, 171;
and 1948 campaign, 131,
228; mentioned, 48–49
Dingell, John: cosponsors
W-M-D bill, 31; objects to
Paul Douglas's compromise,
169; and AMA, 182; seeks
Truman's help, 182–83, 185,
186; cosponsors prototype
medicare bill, 199; men-
tioned, 221. *See also* Murray-Dingell omnibus health
bill; Wagner-Murray-Din-
gell bills
Dix, Dorothea, 9
Devine, Edward, 6
Donnell, Forrest, 106–7,
108n46
Doughton, Robert, 201
Douglas, Helen Gahagan, 49
Douglas, Paul, 168–69
Dulles, John Foster, 171

E

Economic bill of rights, 41–42
Education and Labor, Com-
mittee on. *See* Senate, U.S.:
Committee on Education
and Labor
Edwards, India, 172, 179
Eightieth Congress. *See* Legis-
lative process
Eisenhower, Dwight D.: Tru-
man's opinion of, 205–6;

and AMA, 210–14, 216; re-
insurance plan of, 210–12;
pooling plan of, 212; "medicare" program of, 213; ap-
points Federal Council on
Aging, 216; health messages
of, 216; views of on health
security, 216–17; mentioned,
207
Eldercare: as alternative to
medicare, 220
Eliot, Martha, 25
Ely, Richard, 5
Employment Act (1946), 226
Epstein, Abraham: promotes
Capper bill, 21, 24; opposes
Social Security Act, 24;
death of, 42; mentioned, 221
Ewing, Oscar R.: liberalism
of, 114, 115; as administrator of the Federal Security
Agency, 114, 142; and Truman's reelection strategy,
114, 119, 126; and National
Health Assembly, 119–21;
and *The Nation's Health—
A Ten Year Program*, 122,
128–29, 160; and hospital
associations, 137–38, 167–
68; and Fulton Lewis, Jr.,
141; as health security promoter, 153, 154, 157, 159–
60, 173, 175–76, 178; and
"socialized medicine" label,
163, 164; and effort to elevate the Federal Security
Agency, 163–64, 176–77;
British tour of, 169; as medicare promoter, 192; men-
tioned, 221. *See also* Federal
Security Agency

F

Falk, Isidore S.: on need for
medical-care reforms, 15–17;
and New Deal health pro-